W9-ADM-112

EXPERIENCE USA

There are as many ways to define the United States as there are Americans. To a farmer in Amish Country, America might be one small town in Indiana filled with generations of the same families he's known all his life. To a new immigrant in Brooklyn, America is where she can finally start her own small business and send her children to college. Or, to members of the Navajo or Hopi tribe, this land is the sacred birthplace of their ancestral home.

This book is not your typical guidebook. Rather than describe hotels or restaurants, we want to introduce you to the personality and, dare we say, the very soul of American culture. You will find out what makes us tick, and – this being America – that we would love nothing more than to invite you right in to experience that for yourself.

Which means this book is broken up not into regions or sights, but into five chapters divided by the calling-card personality traits that make up the behind-the-scenes workings of US culture:

→ **Big & Bold** Majestic Nature, Epic Journeys & Cultural Powerhouses

→ **Americanarama** Cars, Bourbon, Barbecue & the American Spirit

→ **Melting Pot** A Multicultural Blend of Irresistible Cuisine, Music & Customs

→ **Innovation & Creation** World-Famous Arts, Music & Culture

→ **Surprising Experiences** The Underrated, Unexpected & Downright Mysterious

This book will lead you on a page-by-page scavenger hunt for the one-of-a-kind historical figures, festivals and experiences that create this kaleidoscope of culture. We'll weave in a true taste of the American experience: from small-town diners and urban markets, through hot-rod car shows and grand train journeys, on to the smallest and quirkiest museums, as well as to the most explosive Fourth of July celebrations and the tragically cool live music capital of the world.

When Americans talk about freedom, this is it. Life in modern America is hard and not always fair, but there is always hope, potential and opportunity. You could, say, be a near-7ft-tall-in-heels drag performer in San Francisco named Peaches Christ, a professional storm chaser in the Midwest, or a cattle herder in the Wild West. Or, seeing as this is America, you could be all three.

We want to show you in this book how, when all 325 million of us come together – bringing the best of our cultures and traditions and combining them with American ingenuity and generosity – we create something bigger than any of us could on our own. We are still a work in progress, not sure where we'll end up (it could, quite literally, be Mars someday soon) but dammit, we are seriously going to enjoy this ride.

...and with that,
welcome to the **USA**

Contents

Landscapes, Wildlife & Journeys

Tropics, glaciers and everything in between

To the early settlers, nature was an untamed wild beast, savagely encroaching upon proper civilization. By the mid-1800s, luminary environmental writers like Ralph Waldo Emerson and his protégé Henry David Thoreau started writing about the pleasures of our wilderness, but it wasn't until the early 20th century when two of the USA's greatest contributions to society – the National Park System and the highway road trip – were born.

By the late 1910s, the call of the wild – especially in the brand-new states out west – lured adventurous drivers now looking to get away from the savage beasts that were US cities. What is now our current 417-strong state and national park system became the jewel in the USA's landscape crown. Some of the first federal highway projects took visitors from park to park, and volcanoes to caves.

The five-day cross-country drive is a rite of passage for any self-respecting US road-tripper, as is the John Muir Trail for hardy through-hikers. The self-same John Muir was instrumental in creating not only Yosemite (where, ironically, there are now calls to ban cars due to overcrowding), but exploring Alaska and the rest of the West. Want to venture to Alaska in swashbuckling style? Skip a flight or cruise and camp on deck on board the Alaska Marine Highway ferry.

Rural USA favors a slower pace, from the buffaloes in the Badlands to the hills and hollers of the Appalachians. For a classic road trip, we highly suggest you rent a convertible (surfboards optional), throw on the Beach Boys and cruise California's Pacific Coast Highway. Or, trip back in time and tour the iconic small towns and new galleries on the Southwest's Route 66.

Experiences

Food & Drink

Any cuisine, from any culture, any time, day or night

You want a double-decker bacon burger with processed cheese slices at an all-American diner? How 'bout an organic gluten-free quinoa bowl? Pad Thai? Belgian waffles? Ethiopian injera bread?

The best part about not having a traditional cuisine is that Americans can eat everything, any time. We do love our burgers and fast food, but more and more, it's considered just as American to chow down mu shu pork, carne asada or kimchi tacos at a local farmers market.

But what *is* distinctly American is the way we innovate eating, sometimes with a reverent nod to our agrarian past, other times with a sheepish shoulder shrug to our cardiologists. For instance, we might install urban chicken coops in our front yards or combine farms with high-end dining, but we're also not afraid to try deep-fried butter at the state fair or a doughnut burger. Oh, yes. Doughnut burgers.

America's drinking culture is surprisingly tame (after college, at least) and is now better known for artisanal innovation rather than bingeing. The Pacific Northwest is currently a hotbed for fancy-pants coffee, beer and wine, and in the rolling hills of Kentucky horse country, you can sip small-batch bourbon along the Mississippi, where aged barrels used to float down to New Orleans to be sold up to 300 years ago.

While meatloaf, mac 'n' cheese and apple pie are classically American dishes that you can try in any good diner worth its weight in a Philly cheesesteak, the US has dozens of distinctly regional cuisines. The most notable is the jambalaya, beignets and fried alligator of New Orleans, but regional dining is gaining traction all over the country, including spam musubi in Hawaii, barbecue in Texas and the South, and the summery goodness of Maine lobster shacks. In Maine, even McDonalds sells lobster rolls.

Experiences

People, Culture & History

Just do it

Above **Mardi Gras,** New Orleans

In Italy, to preserve the sanctity of Italian culture and history, they say *'Non si fa'*: One does not do that. In the USA, we say 'Just do it.'

That US culture is well described by an advertising slogan is no accident. We have always been a nation focused on betterment, be it financial, physical or sociological. We give more money to charities and volunteer more than almost any other nation on Earth. We might not be anywhere close to perfect, but that freedom to stretch our boundaries gives us the opportunity to strive to be better, bigger, bolder.

One day, a kid from Chicago who liked to draw wanted to build a park. So he created Disneyland, and later Disney World, and then the entire Walt Disney empire. Because a few enterprising railroad workers and government officials wanted to do a little gambling in the Wild West desert at the end of Prohibition, we ended up with the neon lights and flashy hotels of Las Vegas. If you and your hippie anarchist pirate friends want to build an off-the-grid floating-home community in the San Francisco Bay, you can. Well, technically, you can't, but this is America, so people did it anyways.

The American motto is *E Pluribus Unum:* out of many, one. While we haven't figured out quite how to do this yet – Are we a melting pot of cultures becoming one? Or are we a mosaic? Or a tossed salad? – we do know that the richness of the American experiment comes together best when our cultures weave together and create something even stronger, like in the blended African, Cajun and French traditions of New Orleans or the cultural explosion that is New York City.

After a shameful history, the United States is finally celebrating the very first Americans' artistically and culturally rich traditions, including the Navajo of the Grand Canyon and the Tlingit and Haida tribes of Alaska.

Experiences

Art & Music

A kaleidoscope of creativity

Above **Burning Man festival,** Nevada

In the USA, no one ever has to do anything just because 'that's how it's always been.' Americans can try new things. No, Americans *must* try new things. And nowhere can you find this quest for pushing the boundaries more than in the arts and music scene.

We have our fine arts masters, of course, and a thriving classical music scene. But where the USA really lights up is when we combine innovation with playfulness, with an eye toward the unknown future and what could be. In the 1960s, pop art icons like Andy Warhol or Robert Rauschenberg produced groundbreaking works that changed not only the art world, but society in general. In the music world, festivals like Woodstock and South by Southwest have often helped usher in a generation.

Nothing demonstrates that better than Burning Man, an annual money-less festival in the Nevada desert driven by creativity, invention and generosity. Show up each August wearing your best tutu, self-invented LED-light boots, or driving your favorite steampunk snail.

Burning Man too much, too soon? Start small. Dress up as a superhero for a day at Comic-Con, or two-step your way through Texas. To see where the soul of American music began, drive down the Mississippi Blues Highway, wind in your hair, foot

Above **Blues legend John Lee Hooker (1917–2001)**

tapping to the sounds of Robert Johnson. In fact, it would be impossible to overstate the overwhelming influence of the African American community on the majority of US music and culture. Not just boogie-woogie, ragtime and blues, but gospel, jazz, rock, Motown and hip-hop.

Sometimes the US arts scene is more quietly bold. At the age of 12, the folk artist who became known as Grandma Moses was a maid. At 78, she started painting. Her work has since appeared on postage stamps, and one painting even hangs at the White House.

Even in Hollywood, think about it: this is a city filled with people who practice an artistic craft for a living. Yes, there are celebrities, but there are also more than 100,000 set designers, writers and make-up artists making Southern California a surprising hotbed of culture.

Experiences

Impressions

To understand the United States, it helps to get to know the nation's characters and personality, as well as its struggles and triumphs, and the American spirit that makes its culture so fascinating.

Above **Michelle Obama,** Democratic National Convention, 2016

'It is so important to remember that our diversity has been and will always be our greatest source of strength and pride here in the United States.'
Michelle Obama, Former First Lady

'The greatness of America lies not in being more enlightened than any other nation, but rather in her ability to repair her faults.'
Alexis de Tocqueville, French Historian

'The essence of America – what really unites us – is not nationality, or ethnicity, or religion – it is an idea. And what an idea it is: that you can come from humble circumstances and you can do great things.'
Condoleezza Rice, Former Secretary of State

'Americans will put up with anything provided it doesn't block traffic.'
Dan Rather, Journalist

'I think the most un-American thing you can say is, "You can't say that."'
Garrison Keillor, Author

'In our every deliberation, we must consider the impact of our decisions on the next seven generations.'
Iroquois Saying

'I love America more than any other country in the world, and, exactly for this reason, I insist on the right to criticize her perpetually.'
James Baldwin, Writer & Social Critic

'America did not invent human rights. In a very real sense, it is the other way round. Human rights invented America.'
Jimmy Carter, 39th US President

'It's Fourth of July weekend, or, as I call it, Exploding Christmas.'
Stephen Colbert, Comedian

'I've always felt, in all my books, that there's a deep decency in the American people and a native intelligence – providing they have the facts, providing they have the information.'
Studs Terkel, Author *(interview on PBS website, December 19, 2003)*

Movies

12 Years a Slave (2013)

Citizen Kane (1941)

Dazed and Confused (1993)

Do the Right Thing (1989)

GoodFellas (1990)

The Good, the Bad and the Ugly (1966)

It's a Wonderful Life (1946)

Rocky (1976)

Thelma & Louise (1991)

Vertigo (1958)

Groundhog Day (1993)

Books

The Absolutely True Diary of a Part-Time Indian (2007) Sherman Alexie

Alexander Hamilton (2004) Ron Chernow

The Brief Wondrous Life of Oscar Wao (2007) Junot Diaz

The Color Purple (1982) Alice Walker

The Electric Kool-Aid Acid Test (1968) Tom Wolfe

The Essential Calvin and Hobbes (1988) Bill Watterson

Gone with the Wind (1936) Margaret Mitchell

Adventures of Huckleberry Finn (1884) Mark Twain

Travels with Charley (1962) John Steinbeck

Walden (1854) Henry David Thoreau

A Day in the USA

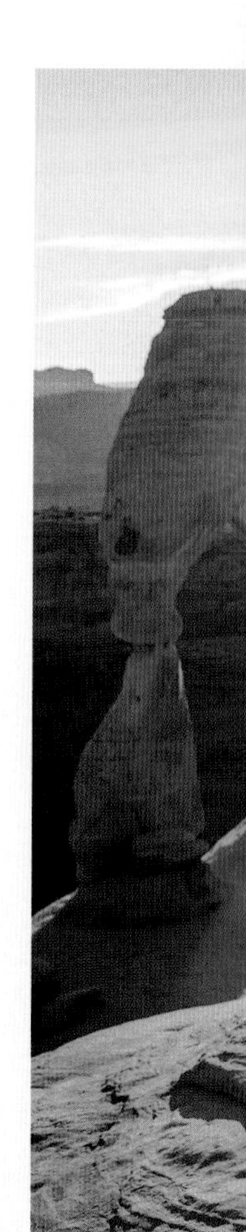

Bacon and eggs might be the 'typical' American breakfast, but in any given week, an American is welcome to grab cereal or granola (stores regularly carry 50 to 100 versions), a kale smoothie, a drive-through coffee or doughnut, the college-student choice of cold pizza, or nothing at all.

After breakfast, we jump in our most favorite symbol of freedom: the car. Americans work more than almost any other nation, but our jobs are often an enormous source of pride. The first thing Americans ask when they meet each other is, 'What do you do?' Part of the new American dream – especially for the many immigrants and children of immigrants – is to become an innovator, outlier or inventor of the Next Big Thing, like so many before.

Throughout the day, we engage in one of our most cherished pastimes: small talk. Try out this friendly, community-building chitchat by remarking on the weather at a diner in the South, commiserating about the ref's bad call around the company watercooler in the Midwest, or even during a customer-service phone call to Arizona.

Some Silicon Valley start-ups have recently combined all of the above in truly American innovative fashion: a few company founders are driving (their beloved Porsches or BMWs, of course) for ride-sharing apps, simply to use the abundant small-talk networking opportunities.

After braving rush-hour traffic home, we love to get comfy. We watch more television than any other nation, but we are getting outside more and more. One-quarter of adults have played an organized sport and one-third of us have tried yoga.

After a demanding workweek, we become a nation of Weekend Warriors. We watch sports in boisterous groups (nachos or hot dogs de rigueur), we rock climb the Appalachians in the East or the Sierra Nevada in the West, we take the Harley out for our *Easy Rider* moment. The United States literally invented summer camp, and the pinnacle of vacationing is maximizing our precious few days off, often with an annual tradition: girls' weekends, fishing trips, family or school reunions.

Above **Zion National Park,** Utah
Right **Chicago**

Experiences by Region

CANADA
UNITED STATES OF AMERICA
ROCKY MOUNTAINS
GREAT PLAINS
APPALACHIAN MOUNTAINS
NORTH PACIFIC OCEAN
NORTH ATLANTIC OCEAN
MEXICO
Gulf of Mexico
BAHAMAS
CUBA
Lake Superior
Lake Michigan
Lake Huron
Lake Ontario
Lake Erie
Great Salt Lake
Washington
Oregon
California
Nevada
Idaho
Montana
Wyoming
Utah
Colorado
Arizona
New Mexico
North Dakota
South Dakota
Nebraska
Kansas
Oklahoma
Texas
Minnesota
Iowa
Missouri
Arkansas
Louisiana
Wisconsin
Illinois
Michigan
Indiana
Ohio
Kentucky
Tennessee
Mississippi
Alabama
Georgia
Florida
South Carolina
North Carolina
Virginia
West Virginia
Maryland
Delaware
Pennsylvania
New Jersey
New York
Connecticut
Rhode Island
Massachusetts
Vermont
New Hampshire
Maine
SAN FRANCISCO
LOS ANGELES
AUSTIN
DETROIT
NEW YORK CITY
1
2
3
4
5
6
7
8
9
10
11
12
13
14
15
16
17
18
19
20
21
22
23
24
25
26
27
28
29
30
31
32
33
34
35
36
37
38
39
40
41
42
43
44
45
RUSSIA
Chukchi Sea
CANADA
Alaska
Bering Sea
NORTH PACIFIC OCEAN
Hawaii
NORTH PACIFIC OCEAN
N
S
E
W

The West

Above **Yosemite National Park,** California

200 years and still pioneering

Nothing encapsulates the spirit of the American West quite like the pioneer. Back in the day, that might have meant an immigrant family riding a covered wagon across the Rocky Mountains to their new homestead in Utah, a 49er panning for a new life in the California Gold Rush, or the black-and-white-film directors who founded Hollywood. Pioneers – a good number of them immigrants – can still be found, in Seattle's aerospace and technology industries, in Silicon Valley's start-ups, or raising organic chickens in Portland's backyards.

The patron saint of the West's pioneer spirit was the 19th-century Scottish-born conservationist John Muir, who helped turn Yosemite into one of the USA's first national parks. Hikers on the John Muir Trail can traverse no less than three national parks in just a small region of California's grand Sierra Nevada mountains. In fact, the West is home to 34 of the USA's 58 national parks.

From the top of 20,310ft (6190m) Denali in Alaska to the black lava beaches of Hawaii, even the landscape of the West is rugged. Seven of the top 10 fittest US cities are in the West, and that's no accident. Rain in Oregon? Snow in Colorado? No worries. Throw on some hiking boots or jump on your snowboard and it's all good, man.

'Rugged individualist' is a thread you'll see throughout your journey in this region. Westerners revel in the freedom to be themselves, whether that's building a steampunk art car at Burning Man, sculpting a giant troll under a bridge in Seattle, or ranching 1000 acres in Montana.

For visitors, this is very good news. While in Las Vegas, you can thank the innovators who turned the Nevada desert into a haven of neon lights, craps tables and high-end restaurants. In Southern California, Walt Disney created a magic kingdom from a cartoon mouse. The summer of love has left San Francisco and the dot-com boom has moved in (bringing with it the highest rents in the world), but there's still nothing as romantic as a cable-car ride past hills of Victorian flats.

The Southwest

Above **Starlight Theater,** Terlingua, Texas

America's desert flower

Above **Coronado National Forest,** Arizona

Before Washington, DC, New York or even Philadelphia, the pueblo of Santa Fe, New Mexico, was the first capital city in the US, way back in 1610. This region of New Spain eventually became Mexico, but the vestiges of foreignness remain in not only the historic adobes, but also the New Age towns and extraterrestrial highways. The Republic of Texas was also its own country, from 1836 to 1846, and it's still not quite ready to completely let that go.

The Southwest feels ancient. No wonder, as it is older than even the oldest buildings in New England. The Taos and Acoma Pueblos date back to as early as AD 800, and you can feel the history of the ancestral Native American tribes in and around the cliff houses at Mesa Verde or when looking at the artwork of the Pueblo tribes.

This region is where the legends of the Wild West came from, and visitors can still see honest-to-goodness cowboys (or at least cowboy hats and boots) or stay in dude ranches. The expansive desert landscape, with its saguaro cacti and painted dusty pink and red hills, is what enticed both artist Georgia O'Keeffe and architect Frank Lloyd Wright to leave their Midwestern roots and East Coast careers to set up shop here.

Tumbleweeds start in the dry plains and fields of the Southwest, rolling across the desert, often into people's homes and pools. In Chandler, Arizona, the town's annual Christmas 'tree' is a collection of up to 1000 tumbleweeds, collected by local residents.

Compare that to Austin, the live music capital of the USA. Its South by Southwest festival attracts digital, musical and artistic creatives, who meet every spring to usher in the nation's Next Big Thing.

There's no better American experience than driving Route 66 from California through Arizona, New Mexico, Oklahoma and Texas. Stop in small towns for classic Americana: dusty barbecue joints, neon signs, cowboy kitsch and even some modern art galleries.

The South

Above **New Orleans,** Louisiana

Southern hospitality is the real deal

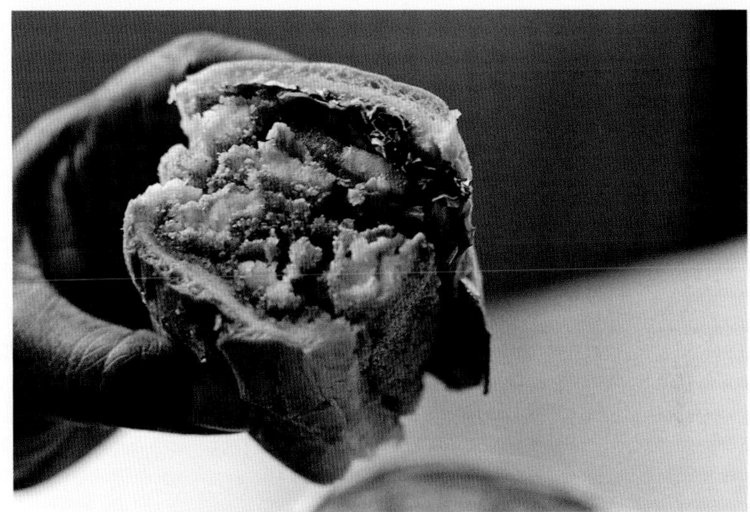

Above **Fried catfish po'boy,** New Orleans, Louisiana

Y'all might could pull up a front porch rocking chair, grab a fiddle or plate of barbecue, and slow right on down. Beyond the infamous history and stereotypes of the South is a region filled with diverse cities, paradisiacal scenery and sacred traditions like college football tailgate picnics, fried chicken and hand-written thank-you notes.

You're not imagining it; people here really are friendlier. Want to get your car's oil changed in Alabama? Prepare to spend ten minutes chatting about last night's big game. Invited to a dinner party in Savannah? Be sure to bring your well-thought-out hostess gift.

To understand the South, you must understand the weight of its traditions. More than any other region in the United States, the ongoing day-to-day life in the South is rooted in its past and its heritage. Almost half of Southerners live in rural areas; far more than other regions. Debutantes are still presented to society at balls, families have been supporting the same college football team for generations, and the WPAQ radio station in North Carolina plays old-time music in-between notices for lost pigs. And there ain't nothin' like the traditions of New Orleans, steeped in hundreds of years of Catholic, Cajun and African American history: Mardi Gras krewe floats, brass band jazz funerals, or the jambalayas, po'boys and fried alligator that make New Orleans the most distinct culinary city in the United States.

When you're in the South, listen for the accents. You've got your Alabama twang, your low-country Georgia or South Carolina sing-song, each very different from a Texas drawl or a North Carolina lilt. Although it's geographically part of the South, there is a line in the pink sands of South Florida where Waffle Houses end and Cuban sandwiches and sultry salsa nightclubs begin.

And if you're not yet convinced you need to visit the South, we have one word for you: barbecue.

The Midwest

Above **St Charles Air Line Bridge,** Chicago, Illinois

Dependable, reliable and sturdy

Above **Round Island Lighthouse,** Mackinac Island, Michigan

The Midwest is content to leave all that fancy city-slicker nonsense to the Northeast, most of the flashy landscape to the West, and all that time-consuming genteelness to the South. In the plains states, they work, they farm, they make things (*real* things!) and they take care of their neighbors. The flat accent is as broad as the cornfields that go on seemingly forever.

As the economic and cultural cornerstone of the Midwest, 'Second City' Chicago would point out that it's far more liveable than New York, if not for its famous Midwestern modesty. In the late 19th and early 20th centuries, the city welcomed Eastern European and Scandinavian immigrants, and African Americans from the post–Civil War South, who all arrived ready to work hard and make a better life for their families. The Midwest is still where you'll find the backbone of American manufacturing in states like Ohio, Michigan and Indiana.

Despite the bitterly cold winters, several Midwest states now receive distinctions for being among the happiest and friendliest, and it's here that you'll still find a great many of the American diners, beloved car and hot rod shows, or quirky small museums that help shape good ol' Americana.

But it's not all church picnics and pond hockey games; tourism is having a renaissance in the Midwest. Michigan has the second-most coastline of any state (behind Alaska), with hundreds of islands, beaches and cliffs swirling around the Great Lakes. Sailing, sunsets and bear-spotting are all an art form in and around the isolated Upper Peninsula. If it's a 600lb cow sculpted out of butter you're after, that'll be at the Iowa State Fair.

America loves an underdog, which is why we're all rooting for Detroit. With a proud history steeped in the automotive industry and Motown, the Motor City is now a hotbed for urban gardening and a thriving new music scene. Are you a writer? If you promise to take good care of it and volunteer in the community, Detroit will give you your own house for free.

The Northeast

Above Manhattan, New York City

Fast-paced cities with a side of bucolic

Above **Woodstock,** Vermont

Yes, the Northeast is temperamental, gruff and fast-paced; you gotta problem with that?

New York towers over the rest of the United States like a steel skyscraper amid amber waves of grain. From Boston through the Big Apple, Hartford, Providence, Philadelphia and surrounds, the hustle and bustle of the Northeast megalopolis is anything but sterile. These are Cities with a capital C, where people live in dense neighborhoods, take subways and are too busy to worry about niceties.

Pilgrims arrived in Massachusetts on the *Mayflower* in 1620, and the region quickly became the agricultural, cultural, educational and financial capital of the United States. Long before the car suburbanized the rest of the USA, the Northeast developed its signature styles: tightly packed brick row houses and brownstones, stately neoclassical buildings and picturesque small towns. British immigrants established Harvard in 1636 as America's first college, and not long after, the Baw-stin accent took root. Eastern European immigrants arrived by way of New York's Ellis Island in the 19th century, and Asian, Latin American and African immigrants soon thereafter, enlivening the famously staid region with an international mix of arts, cuisine and culture.

The residents of the Northeast are fiercely loyal to their unique blend of cultural diversity and history, no matter what that might look like. Hot dogs at Yankee Stadium is exactly as authentic as ordering Japanese-Spanish seafood fusion delivery at 3am.

Step outside the urban corridor and life slows down in proportion to how much the scenic beauty ramps up. From the bucolic Hudson River Valley to the organic farms of Vermont and the rugged coastline of Maine (and even the surprisingly beautiful rural landscape of New Jersey), the scenery of New England and the Northeast is some of the United States' most surprisingly peaceful. And once fall foliage season starts? Oy vey. Fuhgeddabout it.

Big & Bold

Majestic Nature, Epic Journeys & Cultural Powerhouses

Think Big. It's not written on the nation's currency or anything, but it is the unofficial motto. The very size of the USA has inspired its citizens from the beginning. What's on the other side of those mountains? What's down that river? People needed ingenuity, ambition and confidence to find out.

In modern times, this means when a mobster points to the Nevada desert and vows, 'I'm going to bring neon, gambling, showgirls and glitz to that sand patch,' it happens, as in Las Vegas. Or when a developer says, 'I'm going to build a mega shopping center with room for roller coasters, ziplines, shark tanks and a wedding chapel,' it gets done, à la the Mall of America. Or even when a Connecticut shop owner thinks, 'I'm going to build the world's largest jack-in-the-box, with a 600lb head that springs from a grain silo,' voilà, it pops up.

So big ideas are at work, and then we add the mighty landscape. Covering some 3.8 million sq miles (9.8 million sq km; an area that trails only Russia and Canada), the USA provides a lot of ground that's eye-popping and jaw-dropping. The kaleidoscopic chasm of the Grand Canyon and fiery spews of Hawai'i's volcanoes fit the bill, along with heaps more national parks.

Monumental journeys also abound that put you in the thick of it. For trekkers, the John Muir Trail blazes through the sky-high Sierra Nevada wilderness. By train, Amtrak chugs up and over the snow-hammered Rocky Mountains. By boat, ferries ply the whale-laden Alaska Marine Highway. And by car, the Great River Road unfurls a 2000-mile (3219km), north–south ramble past eagles' nests and juke joints, pine forests and plantations.

That's just for starters. There's a lot to see in this vast country, but you're up for a challenge, right?

Native Americans of the Grand Canyon

ARIZONA / CULTURE & LANDSCAPES

We all know about the canyon's distinct and unparalleled beauty, its awesome geologic canvas and its draw for lovers of the great outdoors. Less recognized, perhaps, is the Grand Canyon's compelling human history, the drama that lies in the stories and cultures of those who have lived in and around the canyon for millennia.

Right **Mather Point,** South Rim

Above **Desert View Watchtower,** South Rim

Much like the past geological eras revealed in the cliff walls, there are distinct layers of human culture here too. Maybe you'll spot petroglyphs on the walls beneath the South Rim, or explore the ruins of a 12th-century Ancestral Puebloan community who lived in the canyon. Perhaps you'll visit a cliff dwelling outside Flagstaff, or hear the echoes of some of the earliest legends told about this place.

Stories about the Grand Canyon range from estranged lovers and lightning-bolt-hurling brothers to timeless sagas about the creation of humankind. The Hopi have a particularly special relationship with the Grand Canyon – this is the site of their emergence on Earth. In the Southwest, certain Pueblo tribes believe that the universe consists of several worlds stacked one upon the other. In order to pass from one world to the next, Spider Grandmother gave her people a reed, which they used to climb up through the old dying world's ceiling, emerging through the floor of the new world. For many Hopi clans, this birthplace is not just a myth – it is an actual location known as the *sipapuni*, a domed mineral spring located on the floor of the Grand Canyon. Although the Hopi eventually settled on the mesas to the east, over the centuries they have continued to make return pilgrimages to their sacred *sipapuni*.

All together, there are eight contemporary tribes that have ties with the land in and around the Grand Canyon. Which part of the canyon you visit will determine which cultures you will have the opportunity to learn about.

Rafting the Colorado River

Considered the trip of a lifetime by many river enthusiasts, rafting the Colorado offers an all-access pass to the Grand Canyon, in all its wildness, peace and ancient, mighty glory. There's the rush of running rapids beneath spectacular canyon walls and the serenity of floating down calmer sections, listening to the musicality of ripples and birdsong. Rafters have the exclusive privilege of hiking to secret side canyons, hidden waterfalls, petroglyphs and ruins. As you fall asleep on a sandy beach beneath the stars, you'll feel an undeniable connection to the people who have lived here throughout the centuries.

South Rim

The three rims of the Grand Canyon – South, North and West – offer quite different experiences. Over 90% of visitors only visit the South Rim, which is easily accessible and has historic buildings and particularly dramatic viewpoints. If you're visiting the South Rim, look out for the following sights.

Desert View Watchtower

The marvelously worn winding staircase of Mary Colter's 70ft (21m) stone tower, built in 1932, leads to the highest spot on the South Rim (7522ft/2293m). From here, unparalleled views take in not only the

Left **Antelope Canyon,** North Rim

canyon and the Colorado River, but also the San Francisco Peaks, the Navajo Reservation and the Painted Desert. The tower was designed in the style of Ancestral Puebloan structures found in Mesa Verde, Hovenweep and Chaco Canyon; murals by Hopi artist Fred Kabotie, depicting the snake legend, a Hopi wedding and other scenes, grace the interior walls. The Kiva Room, which mimics the underground ceremonial rooms found in all Pueblo villages, is a lovely place for a rest.

Tusayan Ruins & Museum

Just west of Desert View and 22 miles (35km) east of Grand Canyon Village, these small ruins and museum examine the culture and lives of the Ancestral Puebloan people who lived here 800 years ago. Pottery, jewelry and split-twig animal figurines on display date back 2000 to 4000 years. The ruins are only partially excavated, and the best way to visit is to join a ranger-led tour. All told, there are some 4300 ruins within the national park, though Tusayan is the only one officially open to the public.

Hopi House

A beautiful Mary Colter–designed stone building, the stepped-roof Hopi House was inspired by the structures of Old Oraibi, the oldest continually inhabited village in the United States. The structure was built by the Hopi from native stone and wood, and some of them originally lived on the upper floors. Be sure to walk upstairs to visit the Native American Art Gallery. This is an excellent place to find high-quality American Indian jewelry, basketwork, pottery and other crafts.

Above **Hopi traditional dress,** Arizona

Walnut Canyon

East of Flagstaff, the Sinagua cliff dwellings are set in the nearly vertical walls of a small limestone butte amid this stunning forested canyon. The mile-long Island Trail steeply descends 185ft (56m; more than 200 stairs), passing 25 rooms built under the natural overhangs of the curvaceous butte. The site was abandoned about 700 years ago – learn more at Flagstaff's excellent Museum of Northern Arizona, which spotlights local Native American archaeology, history and culture.

North Rim

Solitude reigns supreme on the North Rim. There are no shuttles, bus tours, museums or shopping centers – if you're after pristine overlooks and quiet trails, this is your spot. Often accessed from Las Vegas, a trip to the North Rim can be combined with a visit to the Navajo Reservation.

Antelope Canyon

Unearthly in its beauty, Antelope Canyon is certainly in the running for the world's most famous slot canyon. While the Southwest is home to hundreds of impossibly narrow slot canyons carved like wrinkles into the face of the earth, Antelope is particularly prized for its accessibility (no ropes needed) and magical lighting, a symphony of shapes and textures that are a photographer's dream. Antelope Canyon is 130 miles (209km) northeast of the North Rim, on the Navajo Reservation near Page and the epic Horseshoe Bend overlook. You must reserve a tour far in advance in order to visit.

Ribbon Falls

The Zuni of New Mexico also consider the Grand Canyon sacred. Like the Hopi, the Zuni are considered to be descendants of the Ancestral Puebloans: the enigmatic civilization, sometimes erroneously referred to as the Anasazi, who dominated the Four Corners region from roughly 700 to 1300 AD and are particularly famous for their cliff dwellings and black-on-white pottery. The Zuni also tell a story of progressively climbing through four stacked worlds, and believe that they emerged in the current world at Chimik'yana'kya dey'a – the place now known as Ribbon Falls on the North Kaibab Trail, which descends from the North Rim to Phantom Ranch.

West Rim

West of the national park boundaries are the Havasupai Reservation and the Hualapai Reservation. Both tribes have been living in the area for centuries, and the reservations offer a unique glimpse of the Grand Canyon's vast western region, before the Colorado River reaches the Hoover Dam.

Havasu Canyon

The people of the blue-green waters, as the Havasupai call themselves, take their name from the otherworldly turquoise-colored waterfalls and creek that run through this canyon. Due to limestone deposits on the creekbed, the water appears sky-blue, a gorgeous contrast to the deep red of the canyon walls. The only ways into and out of Havasu Canyon are by foot, horse or helicopter, but those who make the 10-mile (16km) trek are richly rewarded by the magic of this place, epitomized by spectacular Havasu Falls. Most visitors spend the night at Havasupai Lodge in Supai, the only village located within the Grand Canyon. It's a three- to four-hour drive from most major access points.

Sleep in a Navajo Hogan

At Shash Diné EcoRetreat, Baya invites visitors to stay in a simple wooden hogan on her family's ranch. Baya herself grew up in her grandmother's hogan, a permanent structure which still stands and was, improbably, built with pieces of the set left over from the making of the 1965 epic *The Greatest Story Ever Told,* after her grandfather appeared in the film as an extra. Baya's land is in the west of the Navajo Nation, not far from Antelope Canyon. Bring your own food to enjoy around the campfire, while watching for stars shooting across the night sky.

Skywalk

The main attraction within the million-acre Hualapai Reservation, this horseshoe-shaped glass bridge is cantilevered 4000ft (1219m) above the canyon floor and juts out almost 70ft (21m) over the canyon, allowing visitors to see the canyon through the glass walkway. The only way to visit is to purchase a packaged bus tour; there is no hiking on the reservation. However, driving to the reservation from the South Rim is a four-hour delight through some of the most eerily beautiful desert landscape in the region.

To read about:
The USA's Volcanic Wonders see page 74
Alaska Native Celebration see page 114

Las Vegas Lights Up the Desert

NEVADA / ENTERTAINMENT

An oasis of indulgence dazzling in the desert, Vegas' seduction is unrivaled. The Strip shimmers hypnotically, promising excitement, entertainment, fortune and fame. That sensory overload of blindingly bright neon lights means you've finally landed on Las Vegas Blvd. Seeing is believing.

To read about:
Hollywood Stars in LA see page 86
Nevada's Extraterrestrial Highway see page 250

© ISAAC BREKKEN FOR NEON MUSEUM

Road-Tripping the Pacific Coast Highway

WASHINGTON, OREGON & CALIFORNIA / ROAD TRIPS

Follow the West Coast route from Seattle to San Francisco to find free-spirited cities, Pacific vistas and forests of epic proportions.

Start: Seattle, Washington
Finish: San Francisco, California
Distance: 1050 miles (1690km)

Above **Golden Gate Bridge,** San Francisco

Right **Humboldt Redwoods State Park,** California

Above **Interstate freeways,** Seattle

Opened in 1926, US Hwy 101 is laid along 1540 miles (2478km) of ancient wood and wild water, linking the Pacific Coast from Washington state to California. It's a route and a region that has always attracted adventurers and rebels and, somehow, for all the RVs (recreational vehicles) and visitor centers, the 101 still retains that sense of wilderness and opportunity.

Seattle seems a fitting point of departure: the Northwest's dominant metropolis is also the USA's youngest, fastest-growing city. A city of geeks and freaks that gave us Jimi Hendrix, Kurt Cobain, Microsoft and Amazon, Seattle is switched-on, radical and proud of it (and a great place to sample a microbrewed beer or three).

Leaving Seattle means a car ferry across Elliott Bay, sufficient enough to blow away any happy-hour cobwebs. At once the traffic thins and the trees close in, and after an hour or so at the rigorously enforced speed limit, you're into deepest, darkest Washington state: the Olympic Peninsula, a virgin enormity of forests and mountains that wasn't fully mapped until last century.

With a couple of hundred miles under your wheels, you will have grasped why licence plates hail Washington as the Evergreen State. After *Twilight*-heavy Forks, and an optional side trip to the Hoh Rainforest's Hall of Mosses – where every bough is eerily draped in cobwebby beards of hanging vegetation – Hwy 101 swings southwest and soon hits the super-sized coastal scenery that will grace it for the bulk of its progress: a thousand-mile parade of lighthouse-topped bluffs and surf-sculpted sea stacks.

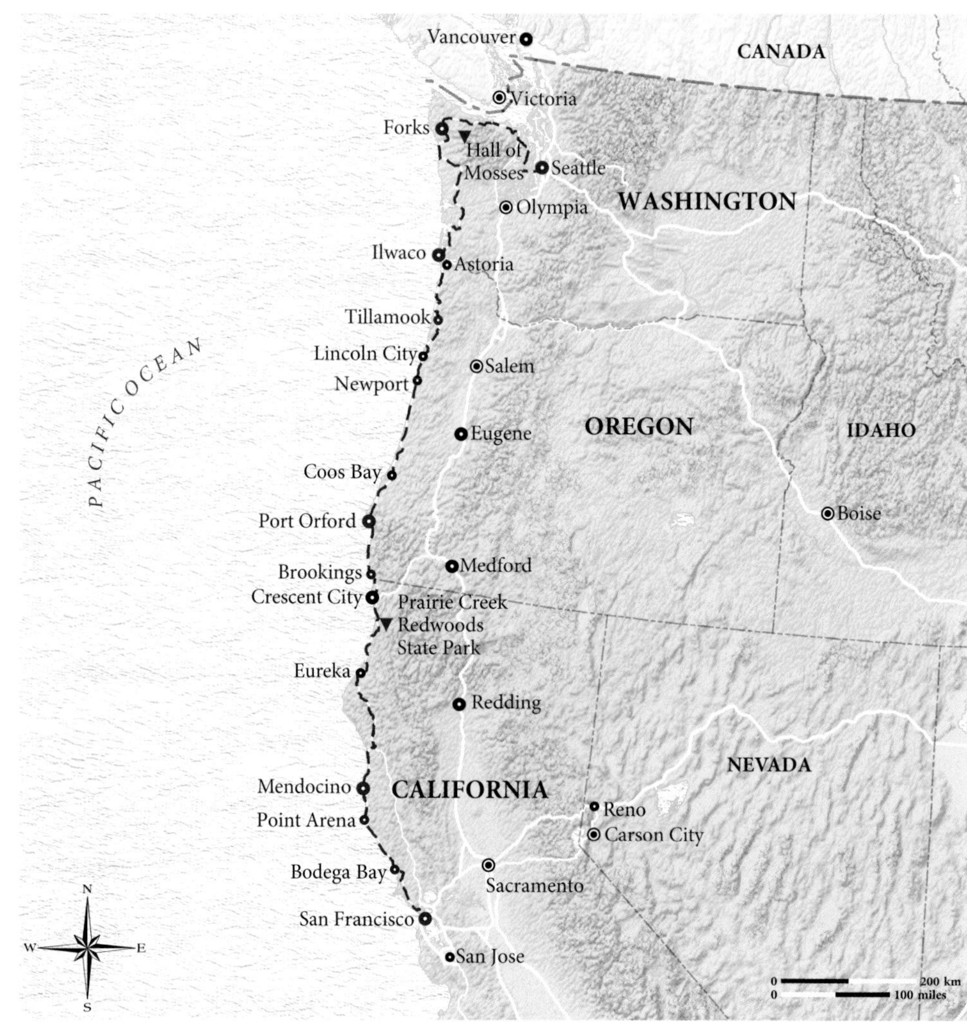

The mighty weather that carved this coast makes its presence thrillingly felt at Waikiki Beach, just outside Ilwaco. Heave the car door open against the roaring wind, clamber atop the bleached heaps of driftwood logs and behold an ocean that is Pacific in name only. Waikiki Beach is named in honor of a Hawaiian sailor whose body was beached on its sands after an 1811 shipwreck – one of the countless victims of what still ranks among the world's most perilous maritime passages.

Drive onwards into Oregon and the road is no longer yours alone, with RVs and long-distance cyclists joining the shiny lumber trucks whose payload leaves the roadside lined with drifts of red bark. Fish-canning ports give way to beach resorts, and the wildlife becomes ever-less retiring. A lively pod of gray whales may snort puffs of water into the clearing sky, and down in the surf, below a viewpoint car park, some plump, sleek sea lions bark and loll recklessly in a spume-churned cove. Their well-fed presence pays tribute to a fecund ocean. Fish and chips is a regional institution, with even high-end salmon and halibut given the low-brow treatment.

Perched on a grassy headland and wedged between two magnificent state parks, Port Orford is a small working fishing port and the most westerly town in the lower 48 states. Boasting an artistic community, the ageless main street is home to glass-blowers and art galleries, and there's a restaurant where braised kale and butter lettuce have elbowed the coast's normally ubiquitous chowder clean off the menu.

The miles come easy now, and the 101 comes into its own as it approaches California – broad, smooth and majestically engineered, a sinuous two-lane blacktop almost casually thrown along the jagged, rearing coast. Under a big blue sky, the open road has never seemed so open – until it's quite abruptly closed, hemmed in by colossal ochre trunks.

This is the redwood empire, the Prairie Creek Redwoods State Park, which was established in 1923 when the first stirrings of environmental panic kicked in. Fewer than 5% of old-growth redwoods survived the logging onslaught, most of them felled in the age before chainsaws, when cutting one down might take a team of loggers a month.

The world's tallest tree – a 379-footer (115m) – and the oldest redwood, predating the Roman Empire by half a millennium, both stand in this forest, their locations kept secret for their own good. There is no such thing as a small old-growth redwood, of course, and strolling among them feels like a tour of some overbearing art installation. A sepulchral quiet reigns; most of the animal life is way up in the distant canopy. At ground level, nothing survives without the redwoods' blessing: the odd spindly hemlock clinging gratefully to one for support, sword ferns suckling on the mulch of a fallen 'nest log' that will take several centuries to rot away.

The road flails about like a dying snake as it heads southwest back to the sea, twisting up through a farewell army of redwoods and the tourist trappings of a less-enlightened age: drive-through trees, chainsaw-carved representations of Bigfoot and $5 take-away redwood seedlings.

Then the trees part and a very different California emerges, one that is drier, browner and balder, where the thin coastal vegetation is decorated with garish tufts of pampas grass. Seaside settlements soon begin to multiply, their names a reminder that this was Spanish-Mexican territory until the middle of the 19th century. Named by early Hispanic navigators, the small town of Mendocino became one of California's first outposts. One of the state's oldest churches is here, looking down a handsome main street that actually recalls New England, complete with grand wooden houses and fancy old water towers.

A couple of hours south, the traffic builds and quickens; the 101 morphs from homely traveling companion to faceless freeway. The Golden Gate Bridge makes a grand finale to an epic drive, the giant leap for humankind that ushered in America's automobile age. And perhaps, after 1000 glorious miles, it's time for another local brew, or two.

Hot Tips

→ Winter can be dreary, but may appeal to storm watchers; gray whales migrate north from March to June or south from November to February. July to September is dry and sunny, but be prepared for a busier drive.

→ For a neon-and-jukebox roadhouse experience, stop by San Francisco's It's Tops (www.itstopscoffeeshop.com).

To read about:

Driving the Great River Road see page 52
Hiring a Classic Car see page 98

Museums for Everything Big & Small

Mega-museums – the kind that span city blocks and let you stand goggle-eyed in front of Amelia Earhart's plane or Picasso's paintings or mastodon skeletons – loom around the country. Then there are the museums that are tucked into side-yard sheds, which stash collections of cat art or Bigfoot memorabilia. These inspire equal awe.

USA-WIDE / ART & HISTORY

Smithsonian Institution

If the USA was a quirky grandfather, the Smithsonian would be his attic. Rockets, dinosaurs, Dorothy's ruby slippers, George Washington's sword, even the 45-carat Hope Diamond shows up in the nation's premier trove. There's room for the whole caboodle, since the Smithsonian is actually a collection of 19 museums.

Most are in Washington, DC, and all of them are free. The National Air and Space Museum (Amelia Earhart's plane! Skylab!) and Natural History Museum (mummified cat! giant squid!) are the group's rock stars, while the Freer-Sackler Galleries (Asian art) and Hirshhorn Museum (modern works) provide quieter spaces for contemplation.

World's Smallest Museum

So what if the Smithsonian Institution has 156 million artifacts in its arsenal? The World's Smallest Museum isn't afraid to compete. The teeny shed in Superior, Arizona, has an aisle through the center and glass cases on each side where you can ogle a smattering of rocks, typewriters, buttons, a photo of Clint Eastwood at a local gas station, and one very large piece of chalk. The museum is dedicated to 'artifacts of ordinary life,' as the front sign says. Afterward, plates of chicken fried steak await at the diner next door.

Rock & Roll Hall of Fame & Museum

The Rock Hall in Cleveland bursts with groovy finds: Jimi Hendrix' Stratocaster, Keith Moon's platform shoes, John Lennon's Sgt Pepper suit and a 1966 piece of hate mail to the Rolling Stones from a cursive-writing Fijian. Music fans go gaga – just look at that guy trying to touch Neil Peart's drum set.

How did such a world-renowned site end up in rust-belt Ohio? Because Cleveland is the hometown of Alan Freed, the disk jockey who popularized the term 'rock and roll' in the early 1950s. This place is pop culture at its best.

Metropolitan Museum of Art

You want big? How about 17 acres of galleries? The Met is mighty, holding the USA's vastest art collection. Here's what fills a smidge of the first floor in the New York City whopper: a full-on stone temple to the goddess Isis, 4300-year-old Egyptian tombs, a hall of pointy medieval weapons and a famed nude statue of Hercules wearing a lion's skin. Caravaggio paintings, Van Gogh landscapes, Picasso portraits, Da Vinci drawings, Persian carpets and vintage instruments stuff the four floors beyond. You could spend days meandering the marbled halls.

Bigfoot Discovery Museum

Some museums enshrine Old Masters artworks, others preserve Bigfoot action dolls. The Bigfoot Discovery Museum in Felton, California, falls into the latter category. Locals say the hulking apeman roams the surrounding Santa Cruz Mountains, and they've stocked their little red museum with castings of Sasquatch footprints, videos and voluminous news clippings ('I Had Bigfoot's Baby') to prove it. Don't forget to pick up your Bigfoot coloring book and Yeti lapel pin while on-site.

Right **Metropolitan Museum of Art,** New York City

ASIA 100
THE MET ASIAN ART CENTENNIAL 2015
The Roof Garden Commission
Pierre Huyghe
Through November 1, 2015

American Museum of the House Cat

When cat videos aren't enough, the house cat museum fills the need for cute images of fluffy critters. Opened in 2017 by a kitty-obsessed gentleman with a staggering collection of cat artifacts, the venue displays antique cat toys, cat paintings, cat beer steins, a cat carousel and – the pièce de résistance – a petrified cat that was rescued from a chimney in 16th-century England. Meow! Proceeds fund the owner's nearby no-kill shelter for felines, so you'll be doing a good deed by stopping by the Sylva, North Carolina, marvel.

National Civil Rights Museum

Built around the Lorraine Motel in Memphis, Tennessee, where Martin Luther King Jr was assassinated in 1968, the Civil Rights Museum documents the African American struggle for freedom and equality. Powerful interactive exhibits let you sit at a segregated lunch counter and on a vintage bus next to Rosa Parks (well, a statue of her).

The finale comes when you arrive at Room 306, preserved with shabby beds and butt-filled ashtray as it was the day MLK stepped out on the balcony and was shot to death. It's like time-traveling into the anguished moment of American history.

Above American Museum of Natural History, New York City

Lunchbox Museum

People of a certain age will remember the days of toting lunch to school in a metal box, usually with a matching thermos tucked inside. If you want to see your old lunchtime pal again, chances are you'll find it at the world's largest lunchbox collection in Columbus, Georgia. Located in the back room of an antiques shop, this isn't a museum in any usual sense of the word, but rather a haphazard hoard of lunchboxes featuring pop culture icons from *Star Trek* to *Peanuts* to Wonder Woman to Pac-Man.

American Museum of Natural History

Kids go wild at this New York City wonderland. They know dinosaurs are where it's at, and the museum's collection of menacing skeletons – including a badass *Tyrannosaurus rex* with 6in teeth – is one of the world's largest. Hulking meteorites from Greenland, stuffed Alaskan brown bears, a 94ft (29m) model of a blue whale, a groovy planetarium...necks will ache from looking up so much. The museum always ranks near the top of the USA's most-visited list.

International Banana Museum

It's no surprise that the bright yellow stuffed banana sitting outside the bright yellow building in North Shore, California, heralds the International Banana Museum. *Guinness World Records* crowned it the

Food Fetish

The Banana Museum is just an appetizer when it comes to the nation's one-of-a-kind food galleries. A smorgasbord awaits across the land, from the kooky condiments at the National Mustard Museum (Middletown, Wisconsin) to the earthy spuds at the Idaho Potato Museum (Blackfoot, Idaho) to the sweet pork magic at the SPAM Museum (Austin, Minnesota). The Jell-O Gallery (Le Roy, New York) and Pez Museum (Burlingame, California) satisfy cravings for those with a sweet tooth.

world's largest collection devoted to one fruit, and who's to argue. Banana cookie jars, banana pepper shakers, banana clocks, a banana turntable and 20,000 other banana-themed trinkets pack the whimsical room, all born of one man's passion. And it doesn't stop at bananabilia: the on-site bar sells banana splits, banana sodas and banana milkshakes.

To read about:

Pop Art see page 202
Seattle's Peculiar Sculptures see page 210

Left National Air and Space Museum, Washington, DC

Colossal Shopping Experiences

USA-WIDE / SHOPPING

Neighborhood boutiques and local markets? Those are for amateurs. If you really want to give your wallet a workout, it's time to go big. Flex your spending power with these outré shopping experiences, from ritzy shopping districts to mega-malls and big-box stores. Each one offers a wildly different experience — and each one is a destination in itself.

To read about:
Las Vegas see page 40
Los Angeles see page 84

Rodeo Drive

Pricey, glamorous and unapologetically pretentious, Rodeo Drive is exactly the kind of tony shopping experience you would expect in Beverly Hills, California. It may only be three blocks long, but its fame has spread far and wide, attracting sample-size shoppers in search of Chanel, Armani and Dior along the cobblestone streets. Fashion retailer Fred Hayman opened the strip's first luxury boutique – Giorgio Beverly Hills – back in 1961. The store allowed its well-heeled clients to sip cocktails while shopping and have their purchases home-delivered in a Rolls-Royce.

Mall of America

The phrase 'staggeringly enormous' doesn't even begin to describe the Mall of America in Bloomington, Minnesota. There are hundreds upon hundreds of stores and restaurants, of course, and obviously it has a skating rink and movie theater. But why stop there? Add in a zipline, an amusement park, and the state's largest aquarium. There's even a wedding chapel, because – well, we're not actually sure why. To navigate this jumbo-size mall-city, you'll need a map, a plan and a really sturdy pair of shoes. Luckily, the mall also has a tourism office that will help you plan your visit.

Vegas Shops

Whether you win or lose, Vegas is determined to keep your money. Winners have a second chance to part with their cash at the high-end casinos' elaborate themed shopping 'experiences.' The Forum Shops in Caesars Palace boast a Caligula-like excess, set among fountains, statues, people who dress like statues – there's even an over-the-top animatronic show. At the Venetian, singing gondoliers ferry you through the Grand Canal Shoppes, and shoppers can watch street performers in a faithful re-creation of St Mark's Square under a painted-on Venetian sky.

Walmart Museum

How did Walton's, a typical 1950s five-and-dime store from tiny Bentonville in Arkansas, become the ubiquitous behemoth known as Walmart? Visit the place where the empire began at the Walmart Museum, housed in the original building on Main St in Bentonville. Details such as the preserved ceiling and floor tiles give visitors a glimpse into Walton's world as he pioneered the deep-discount no-frills business model. The meticulously curated museum provides a comprehensive look at how Sam Walton forever changed the retail landscape in the USA. The museum is free and open daily.

Unclaimed Baggage Center

What happens to those lonely suitcases that are left circling the airport's baggage carousel? If the airlines can't identify their owners, off they go to the Unclaimed Baggage Center in Scottsboro, Alabama. Covering more than a city block, it's like the world's best thrift store, stocked with items that their owners never intended to part with: brand new clothes, up-to-date tech and, of course, lots of luggage. You might also find treasures like moose antlers, a Scottish kilt or an engraved headstone.

Left **Rodeo Drive,** Los Angeles

Driving the Great River Road

MIDWEST & SOUTH / ROAD TRIPS

The Mississippi is the USA's most important river. It gave birth to the blues, Huckleberry Finn, Budweiser and much more. It witnessed the Civil War and the end of slavery. Take a few days or a week and follow it all the way down to New Orleans, bidding it farewell as it seeps into the Gulf of Mexico.

Start: St Louis, Missouri
Finish: New Orleans, Louisiana
Distance: 750 miles (1207km)

The USA is indeed a country renowned for classic road trips. Yet even among that plethora of riches, one of the most iconic is traveling down the Great River Road, a 750-mile (1207km) journey from the Mississippi's headwaters in the northern lakes of Minnesota all the way to where the river empties into the Gulf of Mexico. In total, the Mississippi runs some 2350 miles (3782km), with a drainage basin that extends from the Rockies to the Alleghenies, covering an astonishing 40% of continental USA. It drains more water than the Nile – only the Amazon and the Congo carry a greater volume of water to the sea. Fittingly, the river's name is a corruption of the old Ojibwe word *misi-ziibi*, meaning 'great river.'

A journey all the way along its banks is a trip redolent with good ol' US history, glam and color. You'll be awed by the sweeping scenery as you meander alongside North America's second-longest river, from the rolling plains of Iowa down past the cotton fields of the Mississippi Delta. And you'll never be far from a riverboat casino.

The Journey

Follow the Big Muddy into St Louis and stop to marvel at the Gateway Arch. At 630ft (192m) it is a massive statement against the clear blue sky. On a tour through the Anheuser-Busch Brewery's Victorian-era building (complete with free beers at the end), you'll learn that beer was once made from Mississippi water and stored in barrels in dugouts on the riverbanks.

Back in the car, it's time to hit the trail of Elvis. Pull out of St Louis, following the I-55S to Memphis, another classic Mississippi town. Graceland is there, of course,

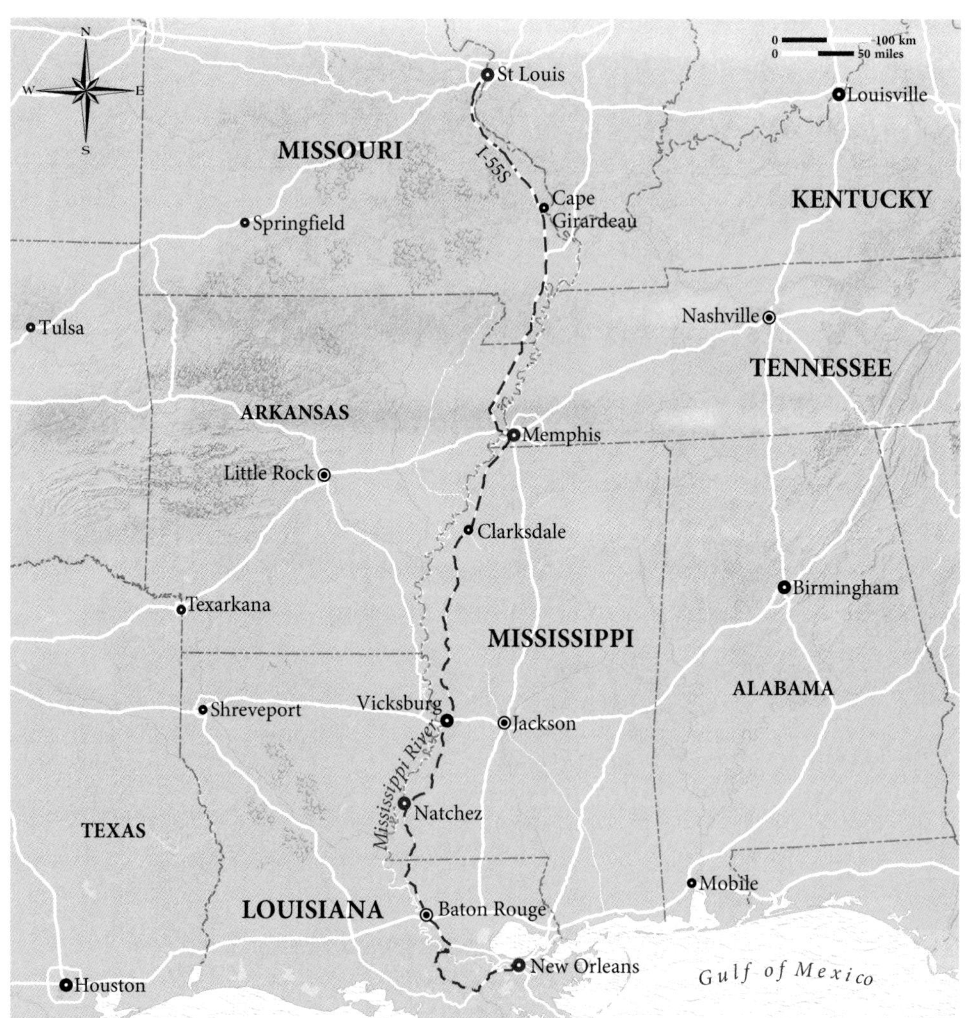

as are Sun Studio and Stax Records: it's Music City. Steep yourself in modern lore at the Smithsonian's Memphis Rock 'n' Soul Museum, which devotes itself to the history of blues music in the Mississippi Delta – the blues being the fuel that propelled Elvis' legendary Sun Studio sessions. Then take the monorail to the Mississippi River Museum, part of Mud Island River Park. Satiated with the rich history of the river, head to the Peabody Hotel to ponder a strange ritual: every day at 11am and 5pm, a flock of ducks is marched from the penthouse to the marble lobby fountain. Weird, sure, but all part of the way they do things differently along the Mississippi. And if it was good enough for Elvis, who was known to be delighted by the Peabody ducks, then it's good enough for us.

Finally, it's on to New Orleans. Many words have been written about the Cajun and Creole cuisine of southern Louisiana. You could spend weeks searching the alleys of New Orleans for the best samples, but even a few days will give you a taste for the marvelous cooking to be found. It's generally agreed that Cajun food is more rustic while Creole food is more refined, but the differences blur into one meta-cuisine more often than not. Try boiled crawfish (crayfish) in crawfish étouffée, a classic Cajun dish of seafood in a spicy reddish sauce served over rice.

The Mississippi River defines New Orleans, not just geographically but emotionally, culturally, probably even metaphysically. Through New Orleans, the river's depth averages around 200ft (61m), and the city's location commands the entrance to the river, with the most important trade, conquest and exploration of the continent tied to the Mississippi and its variegated moods.

Detour: Natchez Trace Parkway

It began as a trail for bison and giant sloth, and still has a low speed limit at 50mph (80km/h). The parkway, 444 miles (715km) from Natchez, Mississippi, to Nashville, Tennessee, is exactly what its name suggests – a long, narrow park. Like most parks it has restrictions, regulating food, fuel, lodgings, advertising and even trucks.

A beautifully surfaced road stretching from the banks of the Mississippi to the home of Country Music USA, the winding parkway runs through forest that changes color with the seasons, while roadside information tablets track its history. There are services at regular intervals, as well as historic monuments, such as the eerie ruins of the antebellum Windsor mansions near Port Gibson.

To read about:

Hiring a Classic Car see page 98
The Mother Road: Route 66 see page 104

Essential Experiences

- → Exploring Memphis' Slave Haven Underground Railroad Museum, learning about the transportation of slaves down the river to freedom.
- → Making a pilgrimage in Memphis to Elvis Presley's Graceland, and getting a dose of the blues in Clarksdale.
- → Enjoying the French Market on the riverbanks in New Orleans.
- → Savoring river cuisine: slow-burning tamales and melt-off-the-bone ribs in Clarksdale; chili tamales and steaks in Greenville; and the full gamut of Cajun and Creole cuisine in New Orleans.
- → Armchair Mississippi read: *As I Lay Dying* (William Faulkner). The Mississippi is a feature of Faulkner's brilliant and slightly off-kilter novels about the South. This 1930 stream-of-consciousness novel is set in Yoknapatawpha County, Mississippi, a fictionalized version of his home county of Lafayette.
- → Armchair Mississippi watch: *O Brother, Where Art Thou?* (2000). The Coen Brothers are attracted to the river, and their version of Homer's *Odyssey* uses the Mississippi to striking effect.

Candy Crush: Iconic Sweet Treats

USA-WIDE / FOOD

Sweet, rich, iconic, occasionally sickening, never good for your teeth, always impossible to resist, and in many cases with a long and fascinating history...these are the USA's favorite sweet treats. Dig in.

Right **Snickers** Frank Mars invented the Snickers bar in 1930 and named it after his favorite horse. Each bar contains about 16 peanuts, and some 100 tons of peanuts go into making the 15 million Snickers bars that are produced every day.

Right **Hershey's Kiss** More than 70 million Kisses are produced every day. The name supposedly comes from the sound the early machines made when depositing the chocolate onto the conveyor belt, which sounded like a smooch.

To read about:
American Diners see page 130
Comic-Con International see page 224

Left **Reese's Peanut Butter Cup**
A genius combination of peanut butter and chocolate has made these one of the top-selling candies in the USA. Former Hershey employee HB Reese started his own company and invented the peanut butter cup in 1928: they were originally called 'penny cups' for their price. Elvis once had his own limited-edition flavor (peanut butter and banana cream cup).

Left **Skittles**
Invented in 1974, Skittles are chewy fruit candies and social media stars. With more than 25 million followers, Skittles is one of the most 'liked' brand pages on Facebook. More than 200 million Skittles are produced each day.

Left **KitKat**
Nestlé's KitKat, which has a unique square-ish shape, came about because the manufacturer wanted to make a bar that workers could stuff inside their lunch sacks. They're known for their bright red wrapper and distinctive 'snap' when broken apart. And they're big in Japan!

Big & Bizarre Attractions

Ah, the supersize: America's reverence of all things gigantic was around long before a certain fast-food company co-opted the word. Biggest bee, largest working chainsaw, tallest beer cans – you never know what you'll run into out there. Glorious things arise when folks with passion, imagination and maybe a little too much time on their hands go big.

USA-WIDE / WEIRD & WONDERFUL

Largest Jack-in-the-Box
So you're driving along the road in Middletown, Connecticut, and all of a sudden a maniacally smiling, 600lb (272kg) clown head pops up from atop a grain silo. It bobs back down, then a minute later – AAH! – it's up again, staring at you. The world's largest jack-in-the-box fronts an offbeat collectibles store, and yes it is every bit as creepy as you imagine.

Largest Chainsaw
The enormous tool in Ishpeming, Michigan, isn't just for show. Big Gus, as it's called, really *works*. Staff at Da Yoopers Tourist Trap, the shop where Gus guards the grounds, can rev up the truck-size saw so you can hear its mighty rumble. Bonus: Big Ernie, the world's largest working rifle, also shoots on-site.

Largest Six-Pack
La Crosse, Wisconsin, knows how to quench a thirst (and provide a prime photo op). The 'cans' looming over 3rd St S are actually storage tanks for City Brewery. As the sign in front says: they hold enough beer to fill 7.3 million cans, or enough to provide one lucky person with a six-pack a day for 3351 years.

Largest Killer Bee
In 1990 the first killer bees flew into the USA at Hidalgo, Texas. This was not the buzz the town wanted. So it decided to own its infamous image, and how better to do so than by building a two-ton, 20ft-long, anatomically correct statue of the deadly bug, complete with beady eyes and pointy proboscis? Get the camera ready.

Largest Maze
The world's largest maze sprawls at the Dole Pineapple Plantation a short distance from Waikiki, Hawaii. Enter the spooky labyrinth hewn from hedges of croton, hibiscus and other local plants. You'll likely get lost, but no need to unfurl a trail of string to find your way out: most people emerge within 45 minutes, raring for their Dole Whip frozen treat.

Tallest Uncle Sam
The two-ton, fiberglass patriot lords over the parking lot of an amusement park in Lake George, New York. And he means business, all 38 regal feet of him, from the tip of his star-spangled top hat to his blue tailcoat to his red-and-white striped trousers.

To read about:
Nevada's Extraterrestrial Hwy see page 250
Spooky Houses & Multiverses see page 296

Right **Killer Bee Statue,** Hidalgo, Texas

Where to Spy a Bear (and a Moose)

USA-WIDE / WILDLIFE

The sight of a bear is a heart-stopping event, even for seen-it-all rangers, and for many people it is the ultimate wilderness experience. The world's largest land-based predators, bears generally live a sedentary life and will typically avoid contact with humans, which makes encounters with them all the more special.

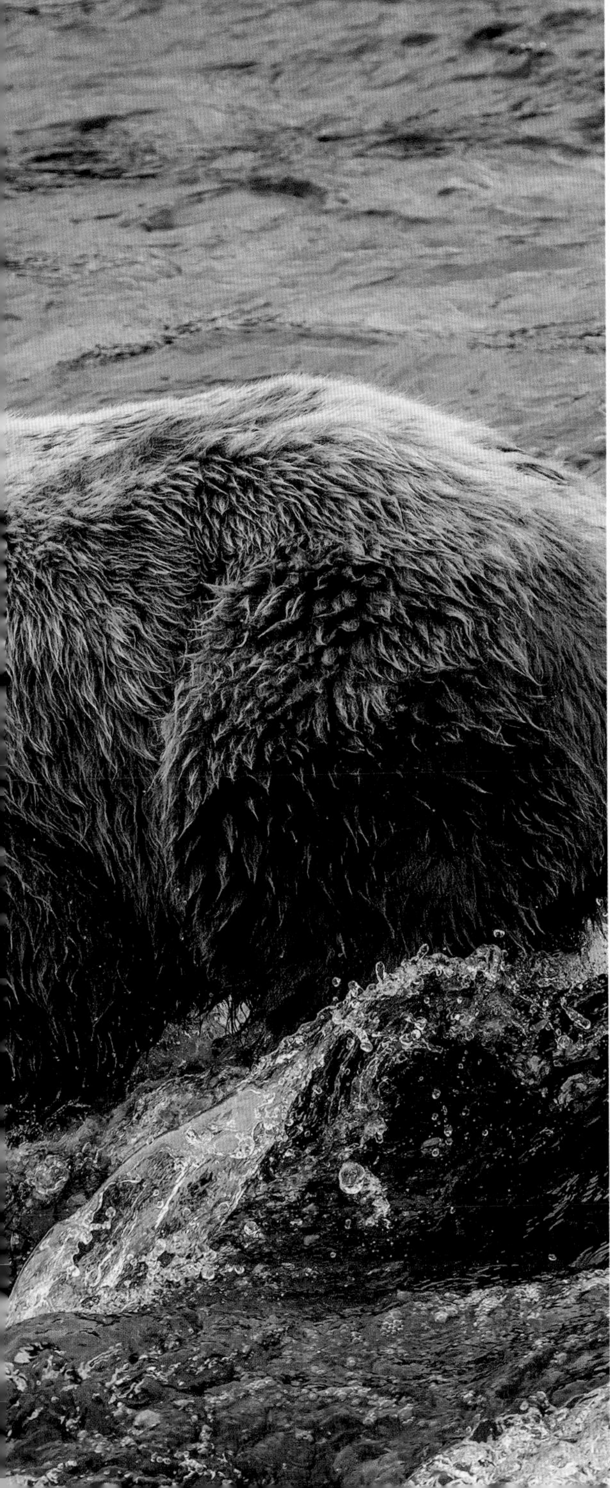

Bears are primarily vegetarian foragers who would just as soon gobble a pawful of grubs or acorns as a delicious groundhog or deer. After emerging from hibernation between early March and late May, they feed mostly on roots and winter-killed carrion, before turning to fresh meat and spawning fish in late June where available. When fruits and berries come into season they can pack on 3lb to 5lb (1kg to 2kg) a day in weight as they eat up to 100,000 berries daily in preparation for the winter hibernation.

Black bears *(Ursus americanus)* are the most common bear in the United States, with numbers estimated between 340,000 and 465,000; their population is stable and in some cases increasing. While formidable fighters, they are less aggressive than their larger cousin, the grizzly. Despite their name only about half are black in color; others are brown or cinnamon.

They are found in their largest numbers throughout the northeast of mainland USA – the Appalachian Mountains, northern Midwest, the Rockies and West Coast, as well as Alaska, in areas of relatively inaccessible terrain, particularly heavily vegetated montane and subalpine forests. Black bears are also the only species of bear that live in California, where they're active throughout the Sierra Nevada, particularly around Yellowstone National Park.

Maine has a 30,000-strong population – the largest in the US, while the densest population of 1500 to 2000 black bears can be found in the Great Smoky Mountains National Park, and a further 300 to 500 roam Shenandoah National Park. Black bears have become so widespread and common in the Smoky Mountains – at a crowded two bears per square mile – that chances of seeing one are high.

Where to Spy a Moose

The largest of the world's deer species, moose typically stand 5ft to 7ft (1.5m to 2.1m) at the shoulder, can reach 10ft (3m) in length and weigh as much as 1000lb (450kg). They have a brownish-black coat and a thick, black horselike muzzle. The male (bull) has massive, cupped antlers, each weighing up to 50lb (23kg), which are shed after the fall rut. Moose populations are facing decline, possibly due to a lack of food sources, and fires in the summer ranges of migrating moose.

An estimated 200 moose are found in Yellowstone National Park, favoring marshy meadows such as Willow Valley, just south of Mammoth Springs, or on the east side of Lamar Valley. They are also found throughout the lower elevations of the Tetons, especially in summer, and they migrate to subalpine and forests of Douglas fir during the winter. Moose eat mainly aspen and willows, but also feed on aquatic plants. Superb swimmers, they can dive to depths of 20ft (6m).

It doesn't pay to get close to a moose: they can become aggressive if cornered or if defending calves, and may strike out with powerful blows from their front hooves.

The more solitary grizzly bear *(Ursus arctos horribilis)* once ranged across western USA, but in 2009 it returned to the endangered species list across the contiguous USA. Grizzlies can reach up to 8ft

(2.4m) in length (from nose to tail), stand 3.5ft (1m) high at the shoulder (when on all fours) and can weigh more than 1000lb (450kg) at maturity at the end of a summer. They can live up to 30 years and each requires more than 800 sq miles of territory – they roam a more open, higher-elevation forest habitat than the black bear.

Today the grizzly population in the lower 48 has been reduced to fewer than 1500, with 600 grizzlies inhabiting Wyoming in the Greater Yellowstone region, 800 in Montana and an estimated 70 to 100 in northern and eastern Idaho. In recent years, the population of grizzly bears has increased in Grand Teton National Park, where they were previously rare, while the 30,000-odd grizzly population in Alaska is densest along the coast where food supplies, such as salmon, are more abundant.

What Bear Is That?

Grizzly Blonde to black in color; are larger with a distinctive shoulder hump; have a dish-shaped face with short, rounded ears; can't climb trees well; and have tracks with long, straight front claws (2–4in).

Black Blonde to black in color; have no shoulder hump; have a straight profile from nose to tail, with pointed ears; climb trees; and have tracks with short, curved front claws (1–2in).

Brown Have the same characteristics as grizzlies (they are the same species), except they live along the coastline instead of in the interior.

Being Bear Aware

Bears often flee at the sight, sound or smell of people, but are obsessed with food and rarely 'unlearn' knowledge acquired in finding it.

→ Never leave food unattended. Use bear boxes or lock it in a car. Hanging food in a tree no longer works, as bears have figured out that trick.

→ Never store food or eat in a tent.

→ Don't sleep in clothes worn while fishing or cooking.

→ Don't camp downwind of a food stash.

The main causes of human-bear conflict include the presence of food, the animal's instinctual protection of its young and surprise encounters with people. We suggest keeping a distance of 300ft (100m) from any bears.

When hiking stay alert and make plenty of noise on the trail, and never hike after dusk. While bears have a highly acute sense of smell and can smell food miles away, they may not catch human scent if approached from downwind. Some hikers wear 'bear bells,' but bears hear deeper sounds better, such as shouting or clapping.

If a bear is encountered at close range:

→ Do not run – bears can easily outrun humans and will instinctively pursue a fleeing animal.

→ Do not drop your pack as a decoy – this may teach the bear that threatening humans procures food.

→ Back away slowly, talking soothingly to the bear while avoiding direct eye contact.

→ Bears very often 'bluff charge' an intruder, veering away at the last instant.

→ Using a pepper spray may deter a charging bear: use it when the bear is charging to within 30ft to 60ft (10m to 20m). And, no, it doesn't work like mosquito repellent, so don't spray it all over your tent or body!

To read about:

Sierra Nevada Wildlife see page 67
Bison on the Tallgrass Prairie see page 112

Hiking California's John Muir Trail

CALIFORNIA / HIKING

Step out into a wilderness that inspired over a century of conservation, following a historic trail through the lofty ranges, peaceful meadows, bear-grazed forests and fresh-air splendor of California's Sierra Nevada.

Start: Yosemite
Finish: Mt Whitney
Distance: 213 miles (344km)

Above **Pacific Crest Trail**

Right **Thousand Island Lake,** John Muir Trail

Above **Yosemite National Park,** John Muir Trail

John Muir: inventor, conservationist, writer, tramp – and one of the most important people of the past millennium. Yet most people outside the US have never heard of him, and might wonder what his claim is on one of that country's best-known hikes. The answer's simple: without Muir there'd likely be no trail, and no wilderness here worth walking through. This eccentric Scot, who immigrated to the States at the age of 11, was at the forefront of the national parks movement. He spent years walking across backwoods America, living off the land, living for the land, getting 'as near to the heart of the world' as he could. His passions stoked, he focused them on persuading presidents to safe-keep the country's wildest places. We owe him much.

Fitting, then, that this 213-mile (344km) hike across Muir's beloved Sierra Nevada, from the great granite valley of Yosemite to 14,505ft (4421m) Mt Whitney, bears his name. The trail was advocated by the Sierra Club, the environmental organization Muir founded; construction began in 1914, the year he died. It was 1938 before the route was finished, having forded rivers, negotiated forests and surmounted high-altitude passes.

There's lots of up and down: walk the entire route, north to south, and the total ascent is 42,000ft (12,802m); walk south–north and it's 46,700ft (14,234m). But, despite this, the trail seldom feels tough – gradients are mostly gentle, the way largely sheltered. The toughest part is being self-sufficient. There are no real towns or shops en route, and hikers must carry much of what they need, meaning weeks of dried food and watery porridge.

But the trail compensates for this culinary fatigue with sheer wow factor. This

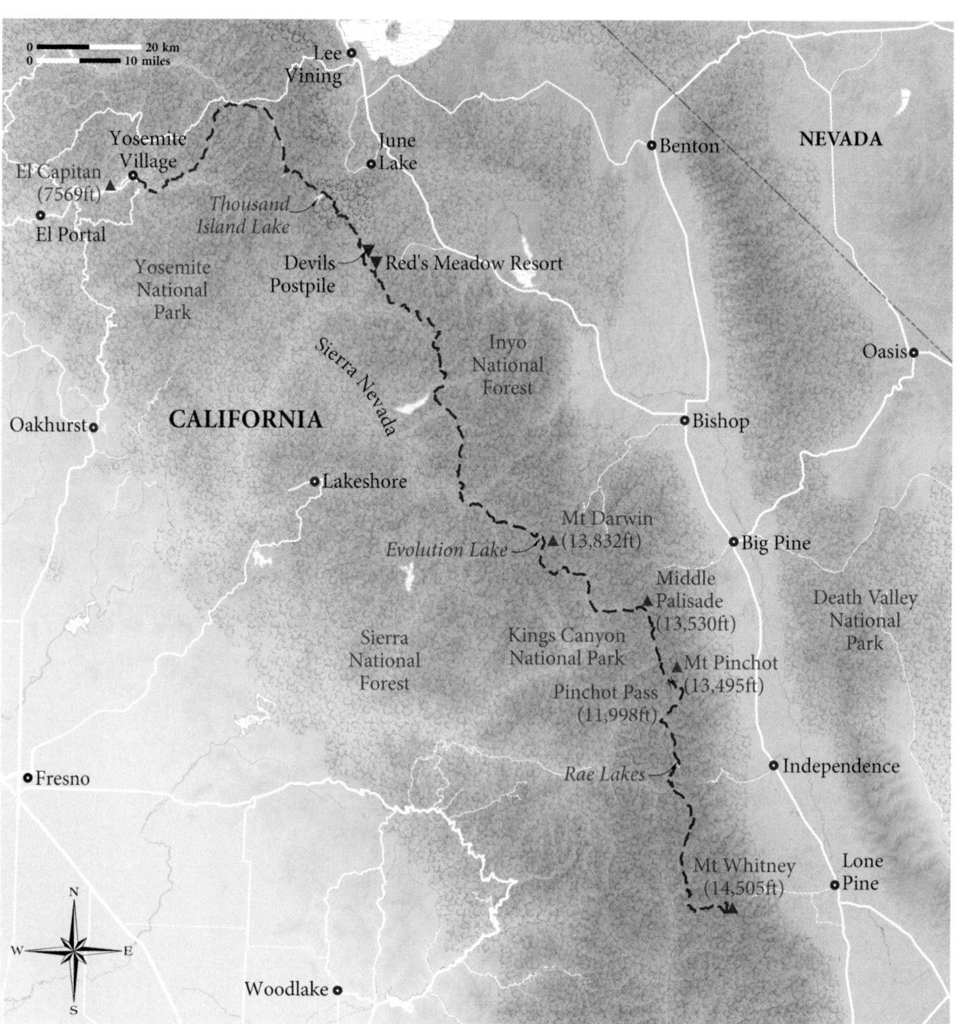

is magnificent countryside, where every step seems to reward with yet another deer-nibbled valley or lake-reflected mountain range; where every night's camp, even if busy with other hikers, makes you feel a bit like a pioneer.

At your night's camp, you can lie back and feel the last of the earth's warmth seep into your tired but contented bones. Later, as myriad stars sprinkle the sky like fairy dust, despite the residual burn in your legs and back, you'll never feel more alive.

Making It Happen

Most hikers tackle the John Muir Trail (JMT) north–south (Yosemite to Mt Whitney). You can take a bus from San Francisco to Yosemite, via Merced. You need a Wilderness Permit from the reservation station nearest to your starting point, which you can apply for online or by post, up to 24 weeks in advance. You must be self-sufficient, carrying everything you need including camp kit and filtering water. Pack plenty of food and prearrange resupplies at points en route; and make sure to keep food in bear barrels. Local companies run organized full and shorter JMT hikes if you don't feel like going it alone.

Sierra Nevada Wildlife

There's a wealth of wildlife in the Sierra Nevadas. More than 1500 types of flower fleck the region: blooms such as mountain violet, azaleas and red columbine color lower elevations, while orchids, mariposa lilies and alpine monkey flowers grow on the higher slopes. For birdspotters, there are many species easily found including red-tailed hawks, turkey vultures and bold Steller's jays. If you listen closely after dark, the night's soundtrack will reveal owl-calls. Small mammals like ground squirrels, racoons and marmots are most commonly seen, and mule deer thrive, as hunting is not permitted in protected areas. You might spot black bears, and they often raid camping grounds at night, so follow advice and keep your wits about you.

Pacific Crest Trail

The John Muir Trail not enough for you? The Pacific Crest Trail follows the JMT through southern Yosemite – though this is merely one small step on its 2635-mile (4240km) journey from the Mexican border (near the small town of Campo) to the Canadian border at Manning Park. This truly epic hike across California, Oregon and Washington traverses old-growth rainforests, high deserts, low deserts and all the major western mountain ranges. Every year around 300 'thru-hikers' attempt it in one go; tramping an average of 20 miles (32km) a day, and allowing for plenty of rest days, it generally takes five or six months.

Essential Experiences

- → Watching the sun set and rise over Thousand Island Lake.
- → Marveling at the basalt columns of the Devil's Postpile, then warming your bones under a hot-spring-powered shower at Red's Meadow Resort.
- → Camping beside the remote mountain-hugged Evolution Lake.
- → Casting a line (if you have a fishing permit) into the five serene pools of Rae Lakes.
- → Standing atop Mt Whitney, gazing over the rugged wilderness you've just traversed.

Armchair Reading

John Muir Trail (Cicerone; 2015) Dedicated trekking guide that breaks the route into 21 stages and includes planning and preparation info.

On the Trail of John Muir (Cherry Good; 2000) An investigation of the man behind the hike; looks at Muir's life and work, as well as his legacy.

Sierra Nevada: The John Muir Trail (Ansel Adams; 1938) Iconic black-and-white images by the famed American photographer.

John Muir Trail: The Essential Guide (Elizabeth Wenk and Kathy Morey; 2014) The latest edition of this US hiking guide contains GPS coordinates for landmarks and topographical maps.

The Eight Wilderness Discovery Books (John Muir; 1992) A compendium of Muir's nature and conservation writing, including 'My First Summer in the Sierra' and 'The Yosemite.'

Wild (Cheryl Strayed; 2012) True account of a young woman's solo thousand-mile trek along the Pacific Crest Trail.

To read about hiking in:
LA County see page 90
The Appalachians see page 284

Big Weather: Tornado Alley

SOUTHWEST & MIDWEST / NATURE

The sky turns green and the air gets eerily still. Then comes the wind, carrying swirling dust and debris. A hulking mass of a cloud starts spiraling at its base, forming a funnel. To most people, that's a sign to take cover. But for storm chasers, the fun is just beginning.

They call it Tornado Alley – that swath of the Great Plains from Texas up through Oklahoma, Kansas and Nebraska. While tornadoes are not unique to the area, the conditions there are just right for forming swirling funnel clouds accompanied by high winds, rain, lightning and hail that comes in sizes ranging from 'golf ball' to 'grapefruit.'

When a major tornado touches down, it doesn't transport you to the magical land of Oz like in the Judy Garland movie. It destroys everything in its path, chewing through the landscape and tossing aside everything that's not firmly attached to the ground. They range in intensity from 'There goes my roof,' to 'There goes a mobile home,' to 'What happened to that building that used to be here?'

Destruction aside, one of the things that makes tornadoes particularly terrifying is their unpredictability. Tornadoes can go wherever they darn well please, and they seem to take pride in their ability to change direction at a moment's notice.

So why would anyone choose to put themselves anywhere near a funnel cloud? Scientists chase storms to track data including wind speeds and barometric pressure. Photographers try to get close enough to score that once-in-a-lifetime shot. But a growing number of people are doing it out of the sheer thrill/insanity of seeing a tornado in real life.

Half a mile away is generally considered a 'safe' distance – provided you can jump in your car and take off if the tornado decides to head your way. But with the surge in the popularity of storm-chasing, you might find yourself facing a road full of other curious onlookers who are blocking your egress.

If you absolutely insist on experiencing an atmospheric adventure firsthand, don't go it alone. Join a tornado safari with experienced storm trackers who have the equipment, experience and common sense (hopefully) to know where to go and, more importantly, when to leave.

Of course, you can always have a zero-risk mini adventure. In Chicago, you can control a 40ft (12m) tornado made of vapor at the Museum of Science and Industry. You'll miss the part where debris flies at your head, but you will get an appreciation for how they work.

Or you could visit the tiny town of Wakita, Oklahoma, which was chosen as a film location for the movie *Twister* after a real-life twister demolished its downtown in 1993. The studio helped them rebuild, partly by taking away all the debris to use as movie props. The film also turned Wakita into an unlikely tourist destination, complete with its own Twister Movie Museum – one of the nicer things a tornado has ever left behind.

To read about:
Volcanoes see page 74
Caves see page 290

Great Train Journeys: California Zephyr

The California Zephyr shows how the West was won. Ride this route, which straddles North America's mightiest mountain ranges, to appreciate engineering mastery, natural splendor, the company of new friends and the adventurous spirit of pioneers past.

WEST & MIDWEST / CLASSIC JOURNEYS

Zephyrus was the ancient Greek god of the west wind, blower of the gentlest spring breezes. Trains on his namesake rail route, which puff across the USA in the same direction, from Chicago to the Pacific Coast, are rather less demure.

The California Zephyr doesn't do gentle. The scenery outside the windows of the 'Silver Lady' is massive and majestic, domineering and elemental. For sections of the trip the mountains, soaring to over 13,000ft (3962m), are tipped with snow, even in summer; raw gorges are gouged by white water; hostile desert extends seemingly forever; and tunnels and switchbacks do battle with the Continental Divide. This is wild country, which the human race has, just about, sneaked through.

It was in 1869 that Abraham Lincoln's dream was realized: railroaders hammered in the final spike at Promontory, Utah, and the Atlantic and Pacific sides of the United States were finally connected by train. This paved the way for convoys of cowboys, gold prospectors, oil workers and outlaws to expand into the western frontier. A journey that would previously have taken months to complete on horse and foot could now be done, for a few dollars, in just a week.

Today that original line, the Overland Route, transports freight only (unless snowfall forces Zephyr trains to divert onto its historic tracks). But the California Zephyr, which has run under various guises since 1949, follows some of the same line, and showcases similarly impressive feats of engineering along the way: the 6.2-mile (10km) Moffat Tunnel, which burrows through the Continental Divide to save a 162-mile (260km) detour around it; and the stretch of track atop 7087ft (2160m) Donner Pass, which allowed the first rail passage over the Sierra Nevadas, and just happens to be one of the country's most scenic stretches of track.

Like the breeze, travel west. Starting from Chicago you should still pass the mountains in daylight, even if the train departs late. You'll also be channeling the spirit of those original pioneers and traveling into dazzling desert sunsets.

Right **California Zephyr,** c 1950

WP
CALIFORNIA ZEPHYR

The Journey Today

You've swapped blackjack tips with a croupier from Reno, and discussed politics with a Sacramento-bound student. Meanwhile, out the window, the most remarkable mountain scenes are streaming by – white-whip tops and river-rumbled gorges. And you haven't even had to move a muscle yet.

The Sightseer Lounge Car is the place to be. In these panoramic carriages, walls have been swapped for windows, offering uninterrupted views of whatever you're passing: the marshy Mississippi, the bright lights of Denver, the drama of the Rocky Mountains. This is also the place to chat, to meet fellow travelers who've swapped airplanes and automobiles in favor of the train.

They're a growing breed, from a low base. In 1970, usage was so low that the Zephyr ceased operation until 1983. But in 2010 it carried almost 378,000 passengers, a 9% increase on 2009. Air travel is increasingly laden with security rigmarole, and fuel prices are rising; there have been promises of investment in Amtrak, the company running the railways. Put simply, US trains are on the up.

And it's about time too – this is travel at its most civilized. Seats are comfy, even in Coach class. A reasonably priced dining car offers sit-down meals – though if you want to bring your own supplies that's fine. You'll even get commentary, with experts from the California State Railroad Museum pointing out the sights between Sacramento and Reno. This iconic journey is steeped in cultural history and landscapes

as old as the hills. Ridden nonstop, trains on the Zephyr route take 51 hours and 20 minutes to connect Chicago with San Francisco. But with so many stops with so much potential, it's a journey you can mold into your own glimpse of rail-side USA.

Alternative Train Journeys

In 1870 America's railway-building pioneers ploughed south from Denver, their goal being to reach El Paso, Texas. The Denver & Rio Grande Western Railroad (D&RGW) aimed to conquer the Rockies, cutting through the ranges rather than detouring around them. The tracks never made it to Texas, terminating instead at Santa Fe, New Mexico. But the D&RGW was still impressive. Its 10,236ft (3120m) Tennessee Pass was the highest mainline track in the USA. The Durango & Silverton Narrow Gauge section, which serviced gold mines in the San Juan Mountains, is now a 45-mile (72km) heritage track plied by steam locos, and one of the best rides in the country.

Take a different route from Chicago to the Pacific Ocean on Amtrak's Southwest Chief. Ploughing a more southerly trail than the Zephyr, the Southwest Chief takes 40 hours to get from Chicago to LA via the red-rock badlands of the American West. Stop off at Albuquerque, for forays into New Mexico, and Flagstaff, Arizona, for access to the Grand Canyon. Alternatively, trains on the Empire Builder route head north from Chicago, meeting the West Coast at Seattle, having trundled for 46 hours via the sweeping plains of North Dakota and Montana's big-sky country.

Essential Experiences

→ Hitting the Obama trail on a tour of Chicago's rejuvenated South Side.

→ Disembarking at Colorado's Winter Park for high-altitude pistes and miles of cross-country ski trails.

→ Rafting, mountain biking and hiking around Glenwood Springs, or simply enjoying the views of the Colorado River scouring 12-mile-long Glenwood Canyon.

→ Winning big at the casinos of fluoro-kitsch Reno.

→ Finding a prime Sightseer Lounge Car seat to take in the peaks, canyons and cascades of the Sierra Nevada.

→ Complementing your train travel with a visit to the California State Railroad Museum in Sacramento.

→ Raising your binoculars at Northern California's Suisun Marsh, a vast brackish wetland teeming with birds.

→ Playing train driver for a day, renting a vintage diesel engine from the Western Pacific Railroad Museum in Portola, California.

To read about:
Ferrying Down the AMHS see page 80
A Tour of Mark Twain's USA see page 232

Armchair Experiences

Stranger on a Train (Jenny Diski; 2002) The British author travels America by rail, documenting the fleeting landscapes and quirky characters she meets, quite reluctantly, en route.

Nothing Like It in the World: The Men Who Built the Railway That United America (Stephen Ambrose; 2000) The story of the hardy souls who constructed the transcontinental railroad.

Riding the Rails in the USA (Martin Sandler; 2003) From opening up the Wild West to shifting modern-day commuters, a look at the impact of trains in US life.

'California Zephyr' (Hank Williams; 1955) Classic country-music crooner's paean to the eponymous train.

Denver & Rio Grande (1952) High-drama Hollywood version of the construction of the railroad over the Rocky Mountains, filmed on location near Durango, southern Colorado.

National Park Volcanic Wonders

Catch a fascinating glimpse into the earth's fiery core at the USA's volcanic national parks. Witness the magical glow and hiss of molten lava at Kīlauea, the earth's youngest and most active shield volcano; traverse the untrammeled wilderness of Lassen National Park; and walk over the remains of Yellowstone's supervolcano, which gives rise to 180ft (55m) geysers and pools of bubbling mud.

WYOMING, CALIFORNIA & HAWAI'I / VOLCANOES

Yellowstone National Park

With half the world's geysers, the country's largest high-altitude lake and a plethora of blue-ribbon rivers and waterfalls, all sitting pretty atop a giant supervolcano, Yellowstone might be one of nature's most fabulous creations.

This isn't all scenic mountains and wildflower meadows. This is fields of burbling mud like something out of *Curse of the Swamp Creature*. This is cracks in the earth that belch steam and howl like the mouth of hell. This is pastel-blue hot springs that will boil an adult alive in three seconds flat. This is geysers that erupt without warning, sending sulfurous water hundreds of feet in the air.

Yellowstone sits atop an active caldera, the remnants of a supervolcano that last erupted 650,000 years ago. Volcanic activity beneath the caldera has resulted in more than 10,000 geothermal features within the park, including geysers, fumeroles (cracks in the ground that release steam) and hot springs.

Wandering through Geyser Country, the area of the park with the most impressive geothermal features, is like visiting another planet. Time things right, and you can see half a dozen geysers erupt within a few hours.

Yellowstone was inhabited by Native Americans for some 11,000 years before trapper John Colter, the first European-American to see it, reported it in 1807 as a place of 'fire and brimstone.'

Today, more than three million visitors hit the park each year. To visit Yellowstone is to cross a major item off many people's bucket list.

Lassen Volcanic National Park

Off the beaten path in Northern California, Lassen is a secret almost too wonderful to reveal.

Nearly three-quarters of the park is pure wilderness, threaded by hiking trails, chains of lakes and the remnants of ancient lava beds and cinder cones. Fewer than half a million people visit this volcanic zone each year. At night, the only sounds you're likely to hear outside your tent are the spine-tingling howls of wild coyotes.

At the northern edge of the Sierra Nevada range, Lassen Peak is the southernmost active volcano in the Cascade Range, which extends throughout the Pacific Northwest. Astoundingly, all of the world's different volcano types – shield, plug dome, cinder cone and composite – are found here, along with boiling mud pots, steaming vents and sulfurous hot springs.

At the boundary of three distinct ecological regions, Lassen has long been a meeting point for Native American tribes. The Maidu, Yahi, Yana and Atsugewi peoples traditionally came here during the summer to hunt and to gather plants for food, medicine and weaving coiled baskets with geometric patterns.

Geologically speaking, the hubbub began 825,000 years ago – and it's still

Right **Grand Prismatic Spring,** Yellowstone National Park

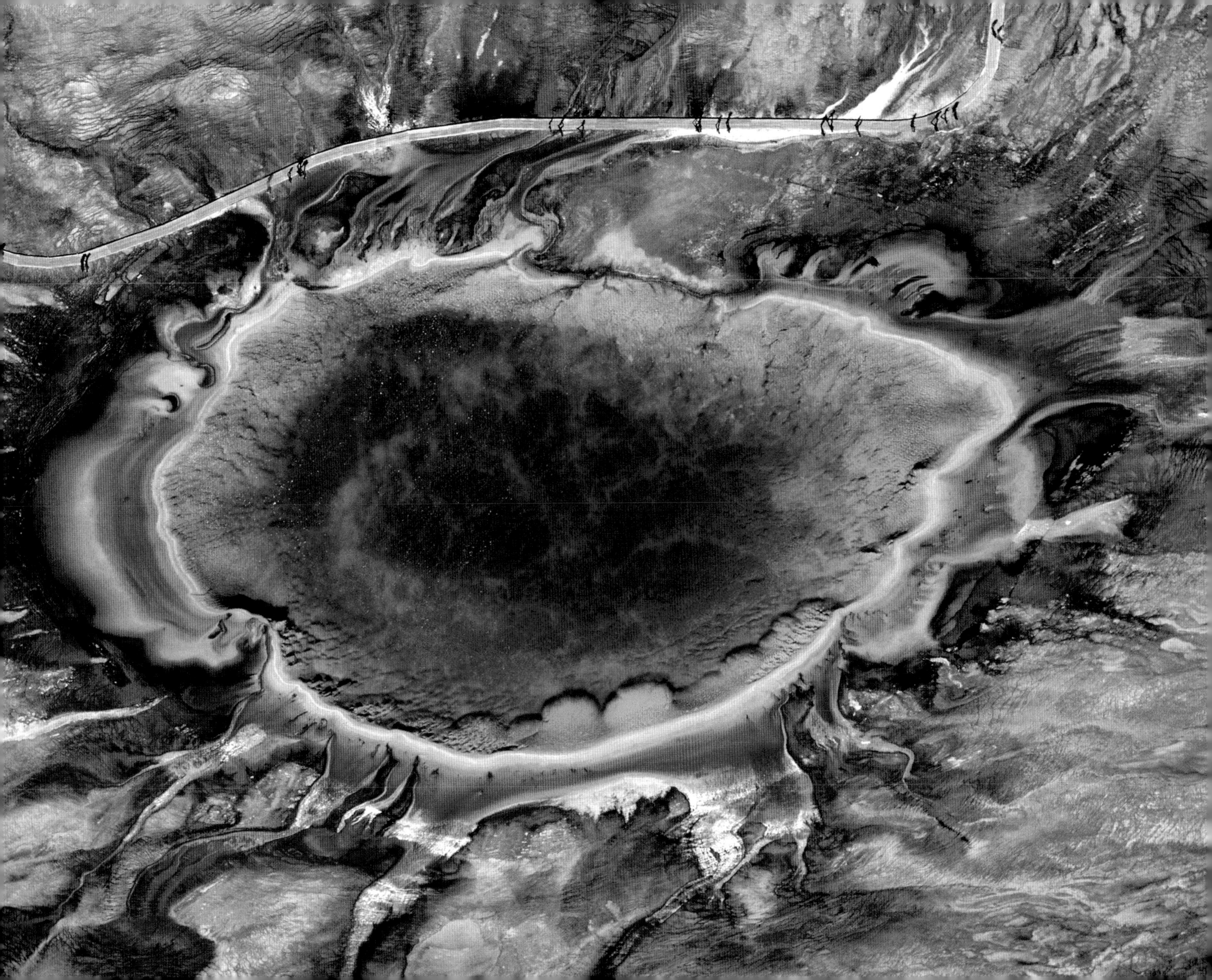

Above **Cinder cones,** Lassen Volcanic National Park

going on. Lassen Peak last erupted in 1915, just one year before it became a national park. Witness the chaos of a morphing landscape in the park's unique hydrothermal areas, which still hiss and bubble dramatically today.

Hawai'i Volcanoes National Park

Newly born earth churns and fiery lava glows in the chaotic realm of Pele, the Hawaiian goddess of volcanoes.

For more than 70 million years, volcanoes in the deep have been giving birth to the Hawaiian Islands. After emerging as bare rocks from under the sea, the islands later become oases for unique plant and animal life, then eventually tumble into flat coral atolls flung over thousands of miles of open ocean.

Today Hawai'i, also known as the Big Island, sits directly atop a 'hot spot' deep beneath the earth's crust, making it the only Hawaiian island that's still volcanically active. Don't be alarmed, though: Hawaiian volcanoes rarely explode – instead, they usually just ooze streams of molten lava. And when that red-hot lava hits the ocean, you'll witness apocalyptic plumes of steam billowing upward.

Life and the landscape here are never static. Kīlauea Volcano has been erupting continuously since 1983, when lava fountains dramatically spewed into the sky. In 2008 Halema'uma'u Crater, home of the hot-tempered Hawaiian trickster god Pele, was transformed into a lava lake, just as it was when famous 19th-century travelers Isabella Bird and Mark Twain ventured here on horseback.

Whether you come for a startling geology lesson or to get in touch with living Hawaiian traditions, this park doesn't disappoint.

Above Kīlauea Volcano, Hawai'i Volcanoes National Park

National Parks in Numbers

Lassen Volcanic National Park
Area: 166 sq miles (431 sq km)
Tallest mountain: Lassen Peak, 10,463ft (3189m)
Last volcanic eruption: May 22, 1915

Hawai'i Volcanoes National Park
Area: 505.4 sq miles
Years that Kīlauea Volcano has been erupting: 33
Acres of new land created since eruption began: 500

Yellowstone National Park
Area: 3468 sq miles (8982 sq km)
Highest geyser: Steamboat, 300ft (91m)
Number of grizzly bears: 674–839

Native Hawaiians first walked this land, etching petroglyphs and burying the *piko* (umbilical cord) of newborns in lava rocks. They left behind footprints fossilized in the volcanic ash and performed sacred hula dances on the crater rim. They also summited Mauna Loa, at 13,680ft (4170m) the world's most massive shield volcano – that's higher than Mt Everest when measured from the ocean floor.

To read about:
Caves see page 290
Wildlife in Yellowstone National Park see page 61

Burning Man: Build It Up, Burn It Down

The utopia of Burning Man is all about building a community, expressing yourself freely and, above all, leaving no trace. Iconoclasts, rebels, artists, soul-seekers and the irrepressibly curious celebrate and create in the shimmering heat of the Black Rock Desert.

NEVADA / FESTIVALS

About two hours' drive north of Reno and 60 miles (97km) north of the southern shore of Pyramid Lake, Nevada, the dusty, former railway town of Gerlach hovers for most of the year in a state of limbo on the edge of the Black Rock Desert. Although this vast wilderness is primed for outdoor adventures year-round, most will only visit over one week in August, when Burning Man explodes onto the surrounding sun-baked desert playas, drawing up to 70,000 'Burners' from around the world.

Begun as a small gathering on a San Francisco beach in 1986, Burning Man has evolved into much more than a festival, and for many is an alternative universe; a whirlwind of outlandish theme camps, a community of sharing and bartering, costume-enhanced nudity and a general relinquishment of inhibitions that climaxes in the ritual and symbolic immolation of a towering effigy (the 'Burning Man').

The temporary installation of Black Rock City is governed by its 10 founding principles of radical inclusion, gifting, decommodification, radical self-reliance, radical self-expression, communal effort, civic responsibility, leaving no trace, participation and immediacy. In-between, everything and anything goes, including peace, love, music, art, nakedness, drugs, sex and frivolity. For many, Burning Man's unique culture and way of life offers an alternative vision for the future, and its founding principles have been taken up by countless other organizations around the globe.

To read about:
Music Festivals see page 212
Summer of Love see page 246

Ferrying Down the Alaska Marine Highway

The thrum of the engines crescendos into an enveloping, metallic roar. As the ship moves away from port, an adventure begins – a journey unlike any other in the US. Serving 3500 miles (5633km) of coastline and islands that are without roads, the Alaska Marine Highway System is both an integral part of the communities it serves and an experience unlike any other.

ALASKA / CLASSIC JOURNEYS

A network of braided waterways, mountain-embraced inlets and volcanic islands stretching into the Pacific make up Alaska's southern coast. In most cases there are no roads linking these communities to each other or the outside world – including Juneau, the state's isolated capital. For these communities, the Alaska Marine Highway System (AMHS) is a lifeblood, transporting everything from hospital equipment to construction materials. In a few remote villages, the only restaurant in town is the on-board cafeteria when an AMHS ship is in port.

For travelers, these ferries offer a chance to experience an Alaskan cruise on a budget. Camping on deck is often half the price of a typical 'big ship' cruise, and the AMHS allows more flexibility. Want to spend more time in Sitka? Simply catch the next ferry.

History

The system began in 1948 with three men: Steve Homer and brothers Ray and Gustav Gelotte, residents of Haines, Alaska, who wanted to provide dependable transportation that served the remote communities of Alaska's southeast coast. The service began with one ship called the MV *Chilkoot,* a 100ft-long former navy vessel that could carry 14 cars and 20 passengers. The endeavor proved difficult and after just a few years of service, the trio faced bankruptcy. The territorial government of the time stepped in to buy the company in 1951.

In the decades that followed, an expansion of service saw the total number of ferries rise and the reach of the service extend to Southcentral and Southwest Alaska. Although air travel to these remote regions was increasing, the new ferry service eased the feeling of isolation among these communities.

Today, funding shortages and equipment repairs threaten the system. In 2017 the MV *Tustumena* which runs the popular southwest route from Homer to Dutch Harbor, was discovered to be in need of serious repairs. The ship's sailings were canceled for most of the summer season. That same year, the AMHS tried to auction off a retired ship called the MV *Taku* for $1.5 million. When the ship didn't sell, the state lowered the price to $700,000; it still didn't sell.

Still, the service's necessity is the single element that will protect its longevity. Communities along the coast rely on the AMHS's continued service, using it for trips to the grocery store in the nearest town or to bring a new baby home from the hospital.

Aiding in an Emergency

On March 24, 1989, the *Exxon Valdez* struck a reef in Prince William Sound, spilling an estimated 11 million gallons of oil. The MV *Bartlett* and later the MV *Aurora*, two AMHS ferries that served the area, were pressed into service as the state's emergency response vessels. The ferries were loaded with suction trucks to aid in the clean-up.

Main Routes

Southeast Alaska

Beginning in Bellingham, Washington, and stretching north toward Juneau, the Southeast Route is the service's most popular itinerary. The service takes travelers up the Inside Passage, the famed cruise passage that weaves through the islands of the Pacific Coast of British Columbia and Alaska. Studded with glacial fjords and opportunities for wildlife viewing, the region is also home to fascinating Alaska Native and First Nation communities.

Southcentral Alaska

A wide, oceanic cul-de-sac of spectacular coastal scenery, calving glaciers and calm waters, Prince William Sound will keep your eyes on the horizon. Everywhere the land rises sharply from the shoreline, rising into snow-capped mountains or yielding deep fjords. The protective sound is also home to a vast array of wildlife, including sea lions, sea otters, porpoises and whales. Plus, as the ship crisscrosses the sound, you're never far from your next port.

Southwest Alaska

Jutting out of the landmass of Alaska like an alligator tail, the Alaska Peninsula and Aleutian Islands offer an island-hopping itinerary where a few dots of raw land split the Bering Sea to the north and the Gulf of Alaska to the south. These smoking volcanic islands feature some of the world's best birding, unique communities that fuse the region's Alaska Native and Russian heritage, and the surprising story of the islands' WWII history.

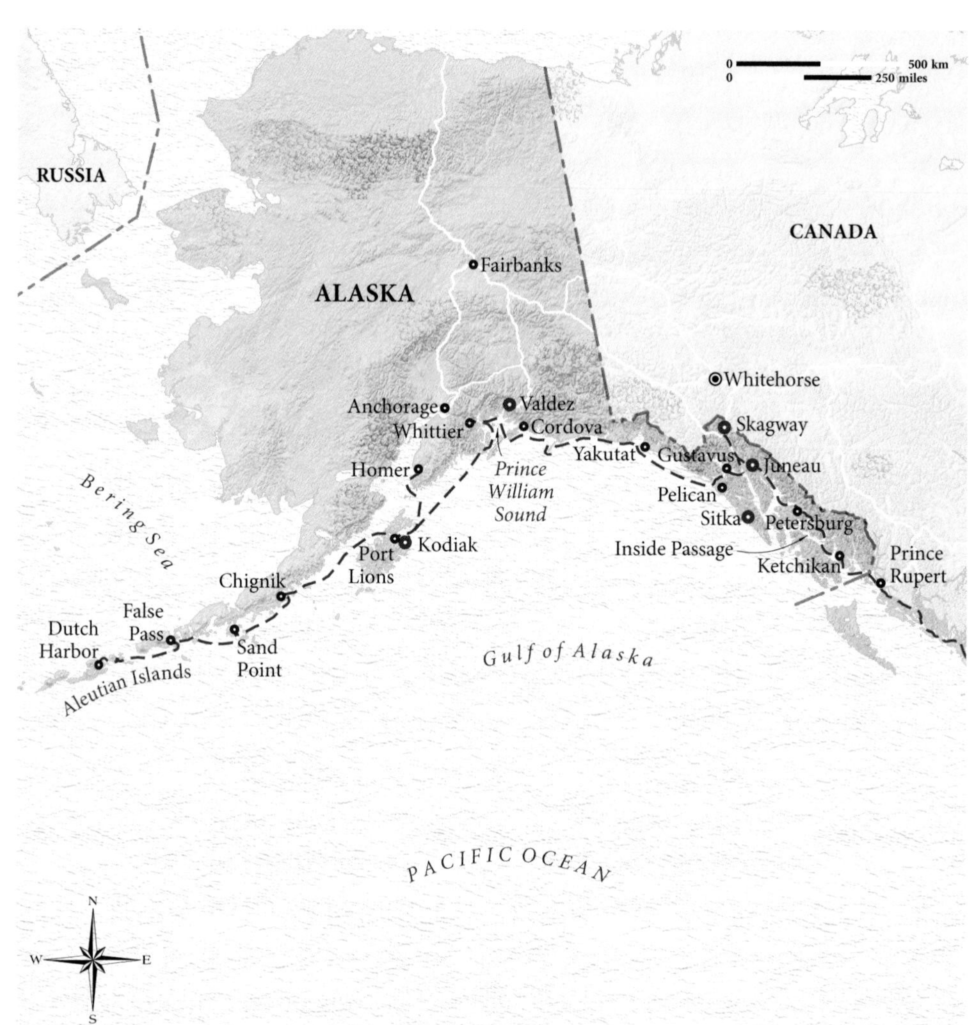

Amenities

A typical cruise this is not – you will find no swimming pools, organized shore excursions or entertainment save for the occasional whales breaching on the horizon (although three AMHS ships have movie theaters on board). There is no wi-fi, and cellular data can be spotty while you're out at sea. Most rely on entertainment of the ancient sort: savoring the misty fjords and tumbling glaciers of the coast or chatting with fellow passengers.

The spartan-but-comfortable ferries are equipped with food services, lounge areas, observation decks and covered solariums with deck chairs. Accommodations range from two-person sleeper berths without windows to four-person cabins with a window and a private restroom. But many choose to sleep on any available surface: unfurling sleeping bags on lounge chairs, popping up tents on the open-air deck or snoozing on an empty carpet.

From the Gold Rush town of Skagway to the sawtooth horizon of Valdez, from Kodiak bear country to the culturally rich Aleutian Islands, the AMHS is Alaska at its best. The network is so spectacular that it's been designated a National Scenic Byway and All-American Road by the US Department of Transportation, the only marine route to have such a designation.

To read about:
Driving the Great River Road see page 52
A Tour of Mark Twain's USA see page 232

LOS ANGELES

City of Angels

LA doesn't really do subtlety, or understatement, or – let's be honest – angelic. In this bold, imaginative, eternally optimistic city that brashly markets itself to the world in capital letters, dreams are a serious business and fantastical thoughts are actively encouraged. The result is an electrifying whirlpool of creativity: edgy art spaces, cult-status rock venues, acclaimed concert halls and thought-provoking stages, all fueling a city addicted to the weird, the wonderful and the downright scandalous.

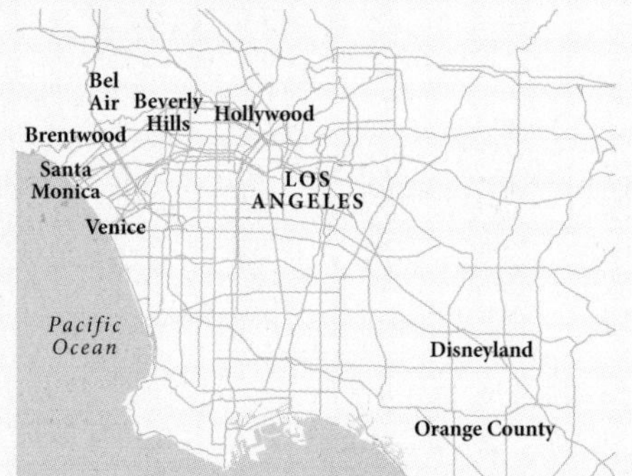

Andy Warhol once described LA as plastic; Jack Kerouac claimed it was lonely; Woody Allen has regularly poked fun at its supposed lack of authenticity. But more often than not, charges of LA's superficiality are, in themselves, superficial. The City of Angels remains one of the world's great cultural metropolises, home to exceptional art collections (including Warhols), world-shaking architecture and an extraordinary melting pot of cultures. The boldness isn't just reflected in its confidence. Despite a heaving head count, LA is a city closely tied to mighty Mother Nature. Here, dense, vibrant neighborhoods back onto golden beaches, city streets lead up to flower-carpeted hillsides, and huge, deep-blue skies are an IMAX screen for lingering sunsets made to pierce your heart.

LA's identity is indelibly linked to Hollywood, the la-la-land of movie legend where small-town dreamers can make it big, and the hand and footprints of entertainment deities are immortalized in concrete. Beyond Hollywood lie Beverly Hills, Bel Air and Brentwood, a triptych of mega-mansions, luxury wheels and tweaked cheekbones that encapsulate the LA of international fantasies.

Those in need of some karmic counterbalance head to the beaches. Santa Monica is LA's cute, alluring, hippie-chic little sister and, to many, its salvation. Venice is a boho beach town and long-time haven for artists, new-agers, road-weary tramps, freaks and free spirits. But LA wouldn't be LA without its extremes. Poised self-assuredly to the south is Orange County, the Los Angeles of cars, freeways and shopping malls. If LA is SoCal's seat of liberal thinking, the OC's heritage is of mega-churches and ultra-conservative firebrands. If LA is Hollywood glam, the OC is *Real Housewives*.

To anyone who has ever been a kid, all roads in la-la-land lead to Disneyland, the self-proclaimed 'Happiest Place on Earth,' an 'imagineered' hyper-reality where the streets are always clean, 'cast members' are always upbeat and there are parades every day. As syrupy as it may seem, Disney remains a magical experience, an exaggerated extension of LA's gregarious personality – sunny, good-looking and highly irresistible.

HOLLYWOOD
EL CAPITAN
EXHIBITION & 3D FILM
JOURNEY TO SPACE
TCL CHINESE THEATRES
Highland Av
PED XING
Dolby Theatre
DO NOT BLOCK INTERSECTION
ON RED
RIGHT LANE MUST TURN RIGHT
Starline
Citysightseeing

MAKING IT BIG IN THE MOVIES

LOS ANGELES / ENTERTAINMENT

The world's entertainment capital, LA is a beacon for countless small-town dreamers yearning to share their tales on screen or in song and reap the attendant fame and fortune. And each year, countless others descend on the City of Angels hoping to catch a glimpse of those dreamers living the dream.

Right Walk of Fame, Hollywood Boulevard

First things first: there's a big difference between Hollywood the neighborhood and Hollywood the international fame and fortune factory. Unless you've got a ticket to the Oscars, about the only stars you're likely to spot around Hollywood Boulevard are the brass ones on the Walk of Fame. Picking up a map of the stars' homes probably won't help much either – you think they're awaiting you with a welcoming lemonade?

Don't despair, though, there are plenty of other places to see stars in the flesh; just go to their natural habitats.

Start with a studio tour. Universal Studios Hollywood may be the most famous, but there are better places for star-spotting – the visitor experience here is much more theme park than working studio, though it's still tons of fun. Instead, try Warner Bros, Paramount Pictures and Sony Pictures for behind-the-scenes visits. Even the most jaded star-hater may thrill to walking these storied grounds on small group tours through working costume shops, soundstages and backlots (Hollywood-speak for the outdoor sets that look like streets and public buildings).

Hey, wait! Isn't that...? Ooh, it's on the tip of my tongue...

Another option: get tickets for a live TV taping of your favorite sitcom, talk show or game show. Free tickets are often available online through outfits such as Audiences Unlimited.

And then there's shops and restaurants. Hint: if you've spotted a paparazzi pack outside (they're relentless), you've probably hit the right place. For starters, keep your eyes peeled at the Brentwood Country Mart and Malibu Country Mart, and the Grove and Westfield Century City shopping centers. Hotel hangouts include the quietly secluded Hotel Bel-Air, classic and central Chateau Marmont and the Waldorf Astoria Beverly Hills with its multi-million-dollar views across the city. Restaurants such as Nobu Malibu, the Ivy, Nate 'n Al's deli, the Grill on the Alley, Catch LA, Craig's and Beauty & Essex are all places to make the scene and be seen. And hiking trails like Runyon Canyon help stars – and the rest of us – keep that perfect shape without the personal trainer.

If all else fails, the celebrity gossip site TMZ runs fun, popular tours of stars' homes and the places the best scandals happened; because it's their business, they know all the ins and outs. Sure it's a guilty pleasure, but one you know you want...

To read about:
Drive-In Theaters see page 110
Comic-Con International see page 224

Stars Above, Stars Below

Fame is fleeting, but some stars endure forever, and LA cemeteries welcome visitors to their eternal homes.

Hollywood Forever Cemetery lives up to its name as the final resting place of legends Rudolph Valentino, Judy Garland, Cecil B DeMille and Mickey Rooney. Across town, pay your respects to Marilyn Monroe, Dean Martin, Natalie Wood, Roy Orbison and, most recently, Florence Henderson (TV's Mrs Brady) at Westwood Village Memorial Park. Forest Lawn Memorial Park is no less welcoming of visitors to its two locations in the San Fernando Valley, where James Stewart, Lucille Ball and Bette Davis are *very* long-term residents and Humphrey Bogart is forever 'lookin' at you' (though not literally; that would be creepy).

Hollywood Forever celebrates its stars like nowhere else; on summer weekend nights, a new generation of fans picnic on the lawn as classic movies are projected on the wall of a mausoleum. DJs spin before and after the flicks – entirely fitting considering that punk rockers Johnny and Dee Dee Ramone are also buried here.

WORLD ON A PLATE

LOS ANGELES / FOOD & DRINK

Many of LA's immigrant communities are the largest outside their native countries, including Mexican, Chinese, Korean and Thai. The depth of these communities means that Angelenos of many ethnicities cook for an eater-ship that really understands their food and is proud to share it with other enthusiastic foodies. With more than 180 nationalities, whatever your taste, LA's got a way to slake it.

To read about:

Chinatowns of the USA see page 176
Jewish Cuisine in NYC see page 190

Though you'll find good Mexican restaurants all over Southern California, some of the best are in the Boyle Heights barrio of East LA, across the LA River from Downtown. At Mariachi Plaza, musicians dressed in traditional *charro* suits troll for work as diners flock to tiny shops like First Street Taqueria. A couple of miles away, no-frills Mariscos 4 Vientos serves what might be the greatest shrimp taco of your life from a truck or, if you're in less of a hurry, inside the bustling dining room.

Just west of Downtown, LA's expansive Koreatown is home to the USA's largest (and best) selection of Korean eateries. The quintessential experience is Korean barbecue – such as the one served at Chosun Galbi – where beef, pork and other meats marinated in soy, sesame oil, green onion and garlic are grilled fresh at your table. Thrill your taste buds with spicy *soon* tofu (bubbling tofu stew) at shops like BCD Tofu House. Don't forget your vegetables: meals come with copious small dishes of refillable sides of marinated veggies and *kimchi* (spicy pickled cabbage). Now you're energized for browsing giant Korean malls such as the Koreatown Galleria.

LA has not one, not two but three-and-a-half Japantowns: Downtown's Little Tokyo; Sawtelle Japantown in West LA; in the South Bay around Torrance; and the 'half' is at Sushi Row, a stretch of Ventura Blvd in the San Fernando Valley, where a couple of dozen sushi shops are interspersed with strip malls and auto-care shops. Splurge on sumptuous sushi and dive into heaping bowls of ramen, by all means, then branch out to lesser-known dishes such as *shabu-shabu* (cook-it-yourself hot pots), *okonomiyaki* (savory pancakes) and *izakaya* cuisine (Japanese pub food, including small plates of grilled meats and vegetables on skewers). Perennial favorites include Sushi Nozawa and Daichan on Sushi Row and ramen shops Daikokuya (in Little Tokyo) and Tsujita (in Sawtelle Japantown).

Downtown LA's Chinatown is fun for an aimless wander. Restaurants beckon with dim sum and crispy duck, while shops overflow with curios, ancient herbal remedies and lucky bamboo. Serious Chinese food fans head about 10 miles (16km) east to the San Gabriel Valley, where amid suburban sprawl are branches of the world-famous Taiwanese dumpling house Din Tai Fung, and dim sum restaurants including NBC that seat hundreds and still have lines out the door. Even the Westfield Santa Anita mega-mall has an Asian food court that's simply amazing.

Thai Town in LA is so big it's been called Thailand's 77th province. Jitlada is a transporting taste of southern Thailand, with walls providing evidence of its famous fans. After dinner, drop by sweet shops like Bhan Kanom Thai. And outside of Thai Town, the award-winning Night + Market restaurants have given hipster cred to Thai street food.

LA's got classic deli's covered too. A fixture in the traditionally Jewish Fairfax district since 1931, Canter's serves up the requisite pastrami, corned beef and matzo ball soup with a side of sass by seen-it-all waitresses. And across town at retro Langer's, they've been hand-carving meat since 1947.

Worth a Trip: Little Saigon

In neighboring Orange County, Little Saigon is the USA's largest expat Vietnamese community (population around 190,000). Multi-lane streets and shopping centers lead to places to gorge on pho noodle soups, *banh mi* sandwiches (try the Lee's Sandwiches chain), exotic tea drinks and fabulous fusion cuisine.

SCENIC TRAILS OF LA COUNTY

LOS ANGELES / HIKING

LA County is larger than some US states, and not all of its 4000 sq miles (10,360 sq km) are urban. Angelenos put their parks and national forests to good use – they're voracious hikers. Here's our selection of the top five trails around LA: from quick escapes for inspirational views across the city, out to the Pacific, and among seasonal wildflowers.

Right **Griffith Observatory,** Griffith Park

Runyon Canyon

You don't even need to leave the urban center to escape into nature. This 130-acre (53-hectare) city park sits just above Hollywood for incredibly easy access, even by subway. That makes it also something of a Hollywood scene; the hot bods and exercising celebrities provide just as much eye candy as the panoramic views across the LA Basin. Morning yoga classes complete the posh pedigree.

Griffith Park

One of the USA's largest urban green spaces and five times the size of New York's Central Park, Griffith Park harbors 53 miles (85km) of hiking trails and plenty of other amusements. The most popular trail, Bronson Canyon, has links to the Hollywood sign, and scenes from the *Batman* and *Lone Ranger* TV series were shot in its caves. The landmark 1935 Griffith Observatory lets you look at the stars above or, below, take in earthbound views of the LA Basin and out to the Pacific Ocean.

Huntington Library

Adjacent to Pasadena, the Huntington's neither a traditional hiking course nor a conventional library, but it is one of the most delightful, inspirational spots in LA. Ramble through the stately grounds and over 120 acres (49 hectares) of themed gardens (we're particularly fond of the Chinese, Japanese and desert gardens). Culture vultures can descend on priceless historic books – a Gutenberg Bible, a *Canterbury Tales* manuscript by Geoffrey Chaucer, titles by Marco Polo and Christopher Columbus – as well as galleries of European and US classic and contemporary paintings and decorative art.

Catalina Island

A pretty ferry ride from Long Beach, Catalina is one of LA's most unexpected treasures. Of its 75 sq miles, 88% is nature preserve, and with an easily obtained permit you can hike to your heart's content or make an overnight of it by camping. About your only company will be a herd of bison – we said unexpected – who were brought here for a 1920s movie shoot and have flourished. If backcountry hiking isn't your jam, frequent nature tours by vehicle depart from the port of Avalon.

Flower Viewing Out of Town

After winter rains have saturated Southern California, spring brings torrents of wildflowers. In March and April, the 8 miles (13km) of trails of the Antelope Valley California Poppy Preserve practically glow orange with fields of the state flower, along with yellow and purple from lupine, goldfields and lacy phacelia. It's about an hour north of central LA. A few hours southeast of LA is the Mac Daddy of spring wildflower viewing: Anza-Borrego State Park, California's largest at 1000 sq miles (2590 sq km). The rest of the year it's a festival of cactus and desert shrubs. Overnight in the town of Borrego Springs, and take plenty of water as temperatures can soar.

To read about hiking in:
The Tallgrass Prairie see page 112
The Appalachians see page 284

WORKING OUT ON THE BEACH

LOS ANGELES / ACTIVE

Quick: what image comes to mind when you think of LA? OK, the Hollywood sign. But after that, it's probably the beach, brimming with buff bods. Along Santa Monica Bay the beach runs for dozens of miles, offering fitness opportunities galore – pumping iron, cycling, skate-boarding and beach volleyball – and the weather to enjoy them.

Right Venice Skatepark

Muscle Beach

There are actually two official muscle beaches. Muscle Beach in Venice is an open-air pen where the bodybuilders become as much of the Boardwalk's human carnival as hula-hoop magicians, graffiti artists, old-timey jazz combos, distorted garage rockers, artists (good and bad) and honky-tonk stalls selling T-shirts, cheap sunglasses, 'medical' marijuana and new age, um, we're not quite sure. Purchase a day Muscle Beach pass and you can become part of the scenery.

A quick couple of miles north, Santa Monica claims the Original Muscle Beach, birthplace of SoCal's fitness craze in the 1930s. Steps from the famed pier, this Muscle Beach is free and open to anyone looking to swing on rings, climb ropes, mount parallel bars or walk a tightrope. There's even a Chess Park to exercise brain cells. What better way to work off (or earn) that corn dog and lemonade from the vintage 1940s Hot Dog on a Stick stand nearby?

Venice Skatepark

Extreme sports in SoCal go back to the 1970s, when skateboarders on the Santa Monica–Venice border honed their craft by breaking into dry swimming pools in the backyards of mansions. This beachside trove sets the standard for today's skate punks with 17,000 sq ft (1579 sq meters) of vert, tranny and street terrain, plus a world-class pool and old-school skate run. Get airborne – or take pictures of skaters getting airborne – with the ocean in the background.

South Bay Bicycle Trail

A paved path of 22 miles (35km) connects Will Rogers State Beach in Santa Monica to Torrance County Beach in the south. En route, the trail squiggles inland around the sailboat and yacht harbor of Marina del Rey, heads back beachward at the Ballona Wetlands, streams under roaring planes taking off from LAX at Dockweiler State Beach and gives up-close-and-personal views of the preppy, moneyed sunners, volleyballers and ice-cream lovers in Manhattan Beach. Plenty of rental shops in Santa Monica or on the beach will be happy to outfit you with bikes and helmets.

Pro tip: avoid the Santa Monica and Venice portions on weekend afternoons when they're most crowded, and you may have to swerve to avoid pedestrians, lollygaggers, surfers and stray volleyballs in the 'bike only' lanes.

Beach Volleyball

Beach volleyball originated in Santa Monica during the 1920s, and nowadays thousands of bad-ass volleyballers take to the sand during summer's AVP – the world's oldest and most prestigious volleyball tournament (played since 1960), in Manhattan Beach. Year-round, mere mortals can watch the players practice, or hit the beach courts up and down the coast. Now an Olympic sport, beach volleyball is due to return to its birthplace of Santa Monica when LA hosts the 2028 Summer Olympics.

To read about:

Cycling in Manhattan see page 186
Salsa in South Florida see page 170

Gold's Gym

There are gyms, then there's the Gold's Gym chain, and *then* there's the original 1965 Gold's, the self-titled 'Mecca of Bodybuilding,' a couple of blocks off Venice Beach. This is where the fitness craze arguably started – no less than Arnold Schwarzenegger trained here for the iconic 1977 muscle-mania film *Pumping Iron*. Anyone can buy passes so…no excuses.

Americanarama

Cars, Bourbon, Barbecue & the American Spirit

When the founding fathers made their list and checked off boxes for democracy, liberty and the pursuit of happiness, they set the mold for the American character. Individualism reigns supreme, along with its tenets of independence and freedom, and many things that are quintessentially American play off these traits. Add a bit of nostalgia to the mix, and you have Americana: local culture in its most evocative form.

The nation's love affair with cars is a good example. From the early 1900s, having a car meant liberation. It was a passport to the open road, to see what was beyond the next town. Route 66 became the avenue that took you there. One of the first highways, the 'Mother Road' snaked past pie-filled diners, drive-in movie theaters and oddball roadside attractions. Much of it still exists, and today the time-warped journey rewards with more Americana than you can shake a corn dog at, from neon-lit motels to teepee-shaped curio shops.

What else gives off that American vibe, both unfettered and a tinge wistful? Riding horses and rounding up cattle on a ranch out West. Watching bison roam the wide-open plains. Driving Hwy 61 past blues joints and Elvis' house. Celebrating traditional food and dance at a Native American festival.

Bourbon tells a classic homegrown story. The nation's only indigenous spirit, it was invented by a Kentucky local in his backyard still. Barbecue is another backyard creation, served at tailgate parties and Fourth of July shindigs nationwide. Slather on the right spice or sauce, fire up the right wood, and glory can come to any pit master. Even George Washington was in on the action. The USA's first president enjoyed both a smokehouse and a distillery at his estate in Mt Vernon. And it doesn't get more American than that.

Fourth of July Fireworks

USA-WIDE / CELEBRATIONS

There are no damp squibs in the US on July 4th when, all across the country, extravagant spirals of fire illuminate the night sky to round off a day of parties, parades, baseball, barbecues and copious hot dogs. The spark was first lit in 1777, when 13 rockets flew up over Philadelphia, and has been growing in explosiveness ever since.

To read about:
Rituals in New Orleans see page 178
Music Festivals see page 212

Right **New York City**
Trust the Big Apple to put on the largest fireworks display in the nation. The big bang is sponsored by Macy's, with a colorful array of more than 40,000 shells getting shot 1000ft (305m) in the air over the East River.

Right **Philadelphia**
The USA's oldest July 4th fireworks take place in the city where the Declaration of Independence was signed, rounding off a weeklong festival with a free concert.

Right **San Francisco**
One of the West Coast's best watery firework displays is launched from barges off Fisherman's Wharf that ignite 25 minutes of fiery magic and illuminate many of the city's iconic monuments.

Left **Washington, DC** For some patriotic fervor, head to the National Mall in the US capital where sparkling lights mix with cannon fire, a US Army presidential salute, and a burst of Tchaikovsky's *1812 Overture.*

Independence Day Around the Nation

Lake Tahoe Around 250,000 people, some of them on cruise boats, crowd in and around North America's largest alpine lake (in the Sierra Nevada) to view a highly theatrical fireworks display reflected in the water.

Addison This small Texas town of 15,000 is famous for its unusually large fireworks display called Kaboom Town, which is attended by half a million people every July 3rd.

Detroit On the banks of the Detroit River, the US and Canada celebrate their independence together on the last Monday in June with a joint orgy of fireworks shared between Detroit, Michigan, and Windsor, Ontario.

Boston Since 1973, bookish Boston has celebrated the glittering Pops Festival, kicked off by a military flyover and followed by fireworks synched with music from the Boston Pops Orchestra over the Charles River.

San Diego In 2012, San Diego's fireworks all went off in one go, accidentally. These days, the bangers last the prescribed 18 minutes, but it's still the biggest display on the West Coast.

Nashville Music City's Independence Day celebrations round off a full day of free music with fireworks choreographed by the Grammy Award–winning Nashville Symphony Orchestra.

Hiring a Classic Car

It doesn't get much cooler than road-tripping in a lemon-yellow Mustang convertible, engine revved as you head out on the highway. Unless, of course, you're road tripping in a cherry-red Cadillac Eldorado, top down and chrome-plated wheel covers flashing in the sunlight.

USA-WIDE / CARS

Choosing Your Car

The USA's classic drives beg for a classic car. Whether you're twisting along the Pacific Coast Highway on its viewtastic, cliffside route through central California, or moseying on Route 66 between neon-lit diners and time-warped towns, a sweet vehicle adds to the experience. Even if it's just for a few hours – say, to zip around Memphis à la Elvis or cruise the Las Vegas Strip like a high roller – a groovy car provides a rush. It elicits thumbs-up signs at stoplights and sparks conversations at gas stations.

So what'll it be? The Ford Mustang and Cadillac are the most popular icons. In general, the Mustang is sleeker and racier, while the Cadillac is larger and more luxe. The Chevy Corvette and Chevy Camaro likewise thrill motorheads. All four models are steeped in road-tripping tradition, so you'll look the part no matter which you choose.

A convertible is the next consideration. Hitting the road in a top-popped car is the pinnacle of cool. You know: wind in your hair, unfettered blue skies and the romance of it all. But in reality you may find that you'll put the roof up more often than you think. Rain, sunburn and temperature-dropping pockets of fog all conspire against alfresco drivers. Not to mention the irritations of wind and noise for those who are used to the bubble of modern cars. Still, you can't deny the awesomeness of unimpeded motoring.

Costs & Other Details

Now for the nitty-gritty. To rent a true vintage car, such as a 1960s Mustang or Caddy, expect to pay around $450 per day, with limited mileage included. You'll also have to do some searching. Companies that rent cars from past eras are hard to come by, as insurance and maintenance costs for keeping such fleets are mega high. Glitzy hot spots Los Angeles and Las Vegas offer the most options and are best for longer-term rentals. In other big cities you'll often find companies that rent for the day (usually for weddings or photo shoots). Classic Car Rentals (www.classiccarrentalusa.com) provides listings by state.

Right **1961 Buick Invicta convertible**

ey To
AWN
OP
Coke adds
Life to
Everything NICE
Cola

A couple of things to remember if renting an older vehicle: the car may not have an automatic transmission or power steering, so prepare to put a bit of muscle into it.

If a vintage car isn't doable, you can always rent a modern version of a classic brand. Budget, Hertz and other major companies have updated Ford Mustang and Chevy Camaro convertibles among their stash, and the cost is less than half that of a vintage rental. Enterprise kicks it up a notch with its exotic car collection available in more than 20 cities across the country, prime for hiring a snazzy, open-top Corvette. Models do vary from location to location, but chances are good you'll find something to meet your classic-style desire. Plus you'll have satellite radio, a navigation system and other modern conveniences at hand.

Go ahead, live a little. Rev that V8 engine and take off. The nation's byways and highways await your audacious wheels.

To read about:
The Mother Road: Route 66 see page 104
Highway 61 see page 134

Top right **1959 Cadillac Eldorado**
Bottom right **Ford Mustang**

Quirky Car Sights

Carhenge No one knows who built Stonehenge, or why. But we do know who built Carhenge (American artist Jim Reinders) and why (as a tribute to his father, and because it's funky). The sculpture consists of 39 classic US automobiles, painted gray and assembled in exactly the same formation as Stonehenge. The automotive monoliths have become a kooky cult destination. The site is located 3 miles (5km) north of Alliance, Nebraska.

Cadillac Ranch In 1974 the late, local eccentric millionaire Stanley Marsh planted 10 Cadillacs, hood first, in a wheat field outside Amarillo, Texas. He did it as a salute to Route 66 and the spirit of the American road. The multihued cars under the big, open sky still draw a crowd, and visitors are encouraged to spray paint their own designs on the metal.

Old Car City This sight in White, Georgia (an hour's drive from Atlanta), is a fascinating mash-up of open-air classic car museum and nature preserve. Spend an afternoon walking the 6 miles (10km) of nature trails as they wind through one of the most beautiful junkyards in the world, filled with more than 4000 cars from before 1972. The forest has reclaimed many of the vehicles, creating an eerie, post-apocalyptic atmosphere.

Vintage Cars: Hot Rod Power Tour

Is there anything more American than a road trip? For true classic car lovers, the Hot Rod Power Tour is the ultimate pilgrimage. Each summer for the past couple of decades, a caravan of vintage cars has set out on a seven-day cross-country trip, stopping each afternoon to stage a sprawling free car show.

MIDWEST / CARS

The first Power Tour, in 1995, started out small: the editorial staff of *Hot Rod* magazine decided to take a group road trip in their 'project cars' (aka the vehicle they're always tinkering with). They plotted a path from Los Angeles, California, to Norwalk, Ohio, and invited a few friends to join them. The entourage of vintage cars soon attracted attention – and a few new faces, as friends-of-friends and fellow aficionados dropped in and out along the route. Clearly the team was onto something.

In the years since, the Power Tour has become one of the largest and longest automotive tours in the world. It attracts some 10,000 vehicles, all driven by die-hards eager to show off their treasured cars and trucks to like-minded people around the country. The route changes every summer, to spread the love, and includes as many highways as possible to make the trip a little easier on older engines and to give drivers the chance to see small-town USA unwind outside the windshield.

Each day, the tour stops and sets up a free car show for the community. Some drivers join for just one or two shows, but there's glory in being a 'long hauler' and showing up for all seven. A big level of commitment is required, too, as many of the classic cars lack amenities that most modern drivers wouldn't consider going across town without: power steering, automatic transmissions, air-con and even cup holders. Then again, pilgrimages aren't guaranteed to be comfortable.

The thousands of spectators along the Power Tour route – more than 100,000 in 2017 – have the chance to ooh and ahh over anything from a 1964 all-original Mustang to a low-rider 2005 Ram with a custom paint job. The only requirement is that a vehicle be 'built for performance.'

From another country or don't have a project car of your own? Jump right in by renting a modern performance vehicle. But you might want to check your rental agreement before participating in one of the faster activities on offer, such as hot laps at the local speedway or drag-strip racing.

Despite the variety in what they drive, and even where they come from – including South Africa, Australia and England – participants are united by their passion. There's a spirit of camaraderie, with shared meals and beers common along the route. Walking around the car shows, you'll usually find the owner in a lawn chair alongside his or her car, ready to give a vehicle tour and point out what's a mod and what's original. Food trucks gather, beer is on tap and gearhead jargon is tossed around with no explanations necessary. It's a friendly, festival-like atmosphere, where almost everyone is wearing a car-themed T-shirt or ball cap.

In the age of the electric vehicle, the idea of a traveling car show might sound like a cultural artifact. But for many of the Power Tour's loyal participants, it's an annual event and a celebration of a way of life. For true automobile lovers, it's an 'only in the USA' experience that's not to be missed.

To read about:

Hiring a Classic Car see page 98
Nevada's Extraterrestrial Highway see page 250

POWER TOUR 2014

SKYDIVE LAS VEGAS.com

POWER TOUR 2014

01

The Mother Road: Route 66

WEST, SOUTHWEST & MIDWEST / ROAD TRIPS

The Mother Road knows America best: Route 66 covers more than 2400 miles, eight states and nearly a century of red, white and blue moments.

Start: Chicago, Illinois
Finish: Los Angeles, California
Distance: 2448 miles (3940km)

Above **Santa Monica,** California

Right **Toroweap,**
Grand Canyon National Park

Above **Abandoned gas station,** Holbrook, Arizona

Above **Roy's,** Amboy, California

The Story of 66

Route 66 snakes across the very heart of America. It first connected Chicago with Los Angeles in 1926, and in-between gave rise to a flurry of small towns that provided all the comforts of home to those perpetually on the move: drive-ins, motor courts, the whole transient, garish bit. With so many attractions – monumental and kitschy, natural and plastic – along the route, it's not uncommon to fall woefully behind schedule.

Everything around here has to have a nickname, and the Oklahoma entrepreneur Cyrus Avery was no exception. Known as the 'Father of Route 66,' he came up with the idea for a new national highway linking the Great Lakes with the greater Pacific Ocean, and formed an association to promote and build it. The new highway, itself earning the handle the 'Main Street of America,' was to link existing roads, many of them through rural areas.

Over the decades, the road has attracted American dreamers. In the early 20th century they piled into jalopies to escape the Dust Bowl and find work during the Great Depression. In WWII, soldiers followed the road in the name of duty. In the mid-20th century, liberated motorists embraced car culture and, later, counterculture. Now, nostalgia-seekers board Route 66 to travel back in time on the wide, open road, which runs through Illinois, Missouri, Kansas, Oklahoma, Texas, New Mexico, Arizona and California. This is where the well-worn cliché 'get your kicks on Route 66' kicked in.

But an ambitious new interstate system spelt the end, paving over much of Route 66 while bypassing the rest of it and its

collection of kinky roadside artifacts. Entire towns began to disappear, and Route 66 was officially decommissioned in 1984 and replaced with five interstates.

Today, what remains of the gravel frontage roads and blue-line highways connects you to places where the 1950s never ended – and that's the journey's enduring appeal. But even if retro Americana doesn't start your motor, it's still an awesome trip, with big horizons and superb natural beauty: the Grand Canyon, the Mississippi River, Arizona's Painted Desert and Petrified Forest National Park, and the Pacific beaches of Santa Monica.

On the Road

The car top's down, 'Route 66' is pumping on the radio, and your mind is free, easy and wild. You've only been on the road a short while but already the 'Main Street of America' has delivered the goods. Let's see, now: join an automobile club – check; make sure the car has a spare tire and tool kit – check; good map in the glovebox – check; tank full of gas – check; jettison preconceptions of small-town American life – check!

If you're in a hurry, take the interstate through most of southern Illinois, Missouri and Texas, and concentrate on New Mexico and Arizona. Otherwise, take your sweet time getting to Adrian, Texas, the midway point of Route 66, and home to a sign informing travelers that Chicago and LA are an equidistant 1139 miles (1833km) away. One of the most exhilarating sections is the 159 miles (256km) of uninterrupted road in western Arizona. Be sure to brake for wild ferrets in these parts.

This is the home turf of Angel Delgadillo. Angel's reputation precedes him by more than 1700 miles (2736km) – when your nickname is 'the Godfather of Route 66,' you amass a vast fan base. The barber, who was born in 1927, grew up with his Mexican parents and eight siblings in a modest home on Route 66 in Seligman, Arizona. The date that makes Angel shudder is September 22, 1978, when the interstate south of town opened, killing the town's livelihood. In February 1987, Angel organized a meeting seeking historic designation for the 89 miles (143km) of road from Seligman to Kingman. The group urged lawmakers to post historic signs, which would help preserve the road. Angel's perseverance paid off, and his victory inspired other communities to embrace the cause as well. 'Seligman has the distinction of being the town where Route 66 got its rebirth,' he says. 'We helped save a little bit of America.'

The highway is 90 years old and many people want to ensure the 'great road west' is there to enjoy for at least another 90 more. In 1999, the US government introduced the National Route 66 Preservation Program which allocated money to fund restoration projects throughout the highway, but this program is due to expire. Campaigns are underway to either save the program or have the entire route designated as a National Historic Trail, which would protect its funding.

Arizona outpost Williams was the final town to be bypassed by the interstate, but it didn't die. Instead, it rebounded as the Gateway to the Grand Canyon, arguably the USA's most famous natural attraction. An incredible spectacle of colored rock strata

and the many buttes and peaks within the canyon itself, the meandering South Rim gives you access to amazing views. It can be visited as a day trip from Williams or Flagstaff, another town on Route 66.

The End of the Trail

Route 66 can be an eye-opener. You can drink Jack Daniels with country-and-western stars in Missouri. Visit Native American tribal nations and contemporary pueblos across the Southwest. Follow the trails of miners and desperados deep into the Old West. And swing past Cadillac Ranch, a surreal art installation where old-school Caddys are buried nose-down in the dirt, and the subject of many a rock song.

It won't be all plain sailing though. Despite your map you might go and get yourself lost trying to find one more roadside curio town. You'll suffer through realignments of the route, dead-ends in farm fields and tumbleweed-filled desert patches, and rough driving conditions. But getting lost is what makes it all so interesting. And besides, ending up in an unplanned stop at a small town is really what it's all about: the taste of the Mother Road is often most piquant in such places, where the vintage neon signs flicker after sunset and there's only one bar to mix with the locals. And then the next morning, you can cure your hangover with a greasy, full breakfast at one of those old-time diners you've seen so often on TV. What's not to love?

Route 66 originally terminated on Broadway and Seventh St in Downtown LA. It's at this intersection that you'll find a small blue sign: 'Original terminus of Route 66 (1926–1939).' On Santa Monica Pier, the last of the three finales, end your classic Americana experience by snapping a picture of the 'End of the Trail' sign, flashing a knowing smile that you've done Route 66 right.

Roadside Kitsch

If you're a lover of kitsch, Route 66 is most definitely your kind of trip. Two of the best-loved examples can be found on the Illinois section of the route: Gemini Giant, a fiberglass astronaut with a rocket in his hand, and the Black Madonna Shrine in Eureka, built by a Polish émigré Franciscan monk. The shrine features a series of folk-art grottoes hand-decorated with shells, glass and statuary surrounding an open-air chapel. Inside hangs a copy of the *Black Madonna* painting, associated with miracles in the Old World. Other oddities include Holbrook's WigWam Motel in Arizona, where you can stay in concrete tipis filled with cozy 1950s furniture.

To read about:
Highway 61 see page 134
Extraterrestrial Highway see page 250

Essential Experiences

- → Enjoying that essential Route 66 small-town flavor in McLean (Texas), Tucumcari (New Mexico), Santa Rosa (New Mexico) and Needles (California).
- → Counting off the unique parade of Mother Road icons including the Gemini Giant in Illinois; Black Madonna Shrine, Meramec Caverns and Red Oak II in Missouri; Arcadia's Round Barn in Oklahoma; Cadillac Ranch and Big Texan Steak Ranch in Texas; Rainbow Rock Shop, Wig-Wam Motel and Jackrabbit Trading Post in Arizona; and Elmer's Place and Bob's Big Boy in California.
- → Stopping off to enjoy some of the USA's best national parks, natural monuments and vast outdoor recreation areas, all close to the road, including the Chain of Rocks Bridge and Wilson's Creek in Missouri; Sandia Tramway, Sky City, El Morro and El Malpais in Texas; Petrified Forest, Painted Desert, Grand Canyon and Wupatki Monument in Arizona; and Mojave Desert and Santa Monica State Beach in California.
- → Getting yourself into a road-trip state of mind by reading John Steinbeck's classic Route 66 novel *The Grapes of Wrath*.

Survival of the Drive-In Theater

USA-WIDE / CARS & ENTERTAINMENT

Once upon a time people gathered in cars to watch movies under the stars. Drive-in theaters still pop up around the country, offering portals to a slower, simpler era, c 1950. But you'd better motor by soon, because they're disappearing from the landscape.

Pull into a drive-in theater on a warm summer night and – wham! – you're time-warped back a half century to vintage USA. A neon sign beckons you towards the enormous movie screen rising from the middle of a field. The sounds of staticky car radios and chirping crickets fill the air. Tubs of popcorn and Nutty Buddy ice-cream cones fly out of the concession stand. Meanwhile, folks get comfy on lawn chairs and car hoods to see two flicks for the price of one. The double feature lives on.

Some 320 drive-ins brighten the night sky these days. New York, Pennsylvania and Ohio have the most, while states in the west and northeast have the fewest. Compare this to the 1950s, when the concept peaked and more than 4000 drive-ins speckled the nation. It was the decade's main form of entertainment, and it's why many of the theaters that remain waft vibes from the Elvis era.

Drive-ins began to lose their luster in the 1970s. Some say it's because they became 'passion pits' – that the privacy of the car made way for naughty pursuits, and they garnered a bad reputation. The real reason has more to do with the rise of television and home entertainment. Theater numbers plummeted, and then kept on dropping in the decades that followed.

Yet groovy drive-ins are still out there. You'll just want to visit these top five picks for retro goodness sooner rather than later.

66 Drive-In

Drive-ins were all the rage along Route 66 during the road's heyday. Now most stand abandoned in ghostly overgrown fields. Not so at the 66 Drive-In in Carthage, Missouri. The art-deco-style theater looks just the same as when it opened in 1949, which is why it's on the Register of Historic Places.

Ford Drive-In

That the world's largest drive-in sits on the outskirts of Detroit, the nation's automaking hub, is fitting. Three thousand cars can fan around the five screens at this 1950s-era whopper in Dearborn, Michigan. Namesake industrialist Henry Ford would be very proud.

Best Western Movie Manor

Monte Vista, Colorado, offers a novel one: it's a drive-in next to a motel, where most rooms have a view of the screen and speakers inside. Yes, you can watch the double feature from the comfort of your bed. Families love it. The mountain scenery adds to the pleasure.

Shankweiler's Drive-In

Shankweiler's wins the prize for being the USA's oldest continually operating drive-in. The screens at the Orefield, Pennsylvania, institution have been flickering throughout summer evenings since 1934. Talk about survival of the drive-in!

Delsea Drive-In

The Delsea is New Jersey's only drive-in left. That's a shame, because Jersey is where Richard Hollingshead Jr invented the concept in 1933. He put a projector on the hood of his car and aimed it at a sheet tied to some trees. Voilà. The Delsea remains an exemplar of the genre.

To read about:
Iconic Candy see page 56
Hiring a Classic Car see page 98

Roaming with Bison on the Tallgrass Prairie

In the rocky Flint Hills of Kansas stands the only preserved patch of tallgrass prairie in the US National Park System. The virgin prairie used to cover a huge swath of the heartland from Texas to Minnesota, but during settlement it was uprooted by plow and grazed by cattle. Only 4% of this rare ecosystem remains.

KANSAS / WILDLIFE

The 11,000-acre (4452-hectare) stretch at the Tallgrass Prairie National Preserve is one of the last remaining fragments of an environment that bisected the American continent in centuries past. Thanks to its thin, rock-strewn soils, it was spared the plows that converted much of the rest of this area into farms.

Entering the native tallgrass prairie is like taking a step into the past. Towering stalks of grass, which can grow nearly 10ft (3m) tall, and a patchwork quilt of wildflowers dance in the nearly constant breeze. Forty miles of trails braid their way through rolling hills (yes, Kansas has hills!) and flower-cloaked prairie. The best is the 3.2-mile (5km) Scenic Overlook Trail, which climbs 300ft (91m) to a viewpoint over open land and swaying grasses all the way to the horizon. Best of all, the trail skirts through Windmill Pasture, where a free-roaming herd of huge, rugged American bison graze. Once teetering on the verge of extinction, the American bison, an icon of the West and now the country's national mammal, again flourish on their native prairie stomping grounds. They were reintroduced to the preserve in 2009 after a 140-year absence, on land that was once the hunting grounds of the Kaw, Osage, Wichita and Pawnee tribes. The Tallgrass Prairie National Preserve is one of the best places to encounter these majestic creatures and has a fraction of the visitor numbers of more well-known options, such as Yellowstone National Park.

The Flint Hills have more ups and downs than anywhere else in Kansas, but the hikes at the Tallgrass Prairie National Preserve are mostly easy going, ranging from a one-hour stroll to a 13-mile option. The trails are open 24 hours, for spectacular views of a star-studded night sky that's free of light pollution, or to revel in the silence of the sunrise with only the company of prairie chickens, meadowlarks and quiet bison lounging in the pasture.

Another popular (if you can call anything in this wonderfully rural and serene place popular) trail is the Southwind Nature Trail, named after the Kansa tribe (Kansas means 'the people of the Southwind'). This easy 1.75-mile (3km) trail, speckled with stalks of wild blue indigo and red splotches of butterfly milkweed, distills the best of the preserve into a single loop path that crawls over chalky limestone hills and across tree-lined streams. It's worth detouring from the loop for a short venture to Lower Fox Creek School, a one-room schoolhouse used from 1884 to 1930 that still has its original chalkboards.

The most thrilling time to visit the Tallgrass Prairie National Preserve is in spring, when intimidating walls of fire as tall as a two-story building lap hungrily at the pastures, charring the landscape and exposing the gleaming white ridges of limestone underneath the black ash. These controlled burns, once naturally caused by lightning but later deliberately

Bison vs Buffalo: What's the Difference?

Bison bison, the scientific name for these creatures covered in a shaggy dark brown coat, are unique to North America. But why are they so often called buffalo?

European settlers are to blame for the confusion. They thought this animal resembled the Asian water buffalo or the African Cape buffalo, and the name stuck, even though technically no buffalo have ever lived in North America. The state song of Kansas, 'Home on the Range,' even gets it wrong in the very first line: 'Oh, give me a home where the buffalo roam.' Unfortunately, if that's what you're after, you'll have to head to another continent.

set by Native Americans and ranchers, rejuvenate the prairie each year by weeding out fledgling trees and reducing the old growth to powdery dust. Within just a few weeks, green sprouts shoot through the ground, and the prairie once again blossoms to life.

The Tallgrass Prairie National Preserve is off the Flint Hills National Scenic Byway, 2 miles (3km) from the ever-hopefully named Strong City, population 455.

To read about hiking:
The John Muir Trail see page 64
The Appalachians see page 284

Alaska Native Celebration

In June of even-numbered years, Southeast Alaska's three main tribal groups, the Tlingit, Haida and Tsimshian, gather for what is aptly known as 'Celebration,' the largest Native cultural event in Alaska. The festival's sentiment is as simple as its name: to celebrate and revitalize ancient traditions in Native dance, music and art which, by the early 20th century, were in danger of extinction.

ALASKA / PEOPLE & CULTURE

Inaugurated by Sealaska, a Juneau-based heritage institute, in 1982, the four-day festival is spearheaded by the Pacific Northwest's three main coastal tribes, all of whom share important cultural similarities including totem carving, decorative clan houses, complex weaving skills, potlatches (gift-giving feasts) and salmon-fishing. By far the largest tribe is the Tlingit, denizens of Southeast Alaska's thickly forested Alexander Archipelago. The Haida reside primarily on Haida Gwaii in British Columbia, Canada, with a small contingent on the southern half of Alaska's Prince of Wales Island. The Tsimshian inhabit tiny Annette Island near Ketchikan.

The centerpiece of Celebration is its masked dances. Up to 50 dance groups converge from all over Alaska and beyond to perform on the main stage of Juneau's Centennial Hall in full Native regalia from elaborate raven headpieces down to hand-made moccasins.

As a state capital, Juneau is unusual. Cut off from the main road grid, it is only accessible by boat or airplane. Many participants fly in for the festival; others arrive on the state ferry system. However, since 2008, small groups of enterprising Alaska Natives have paddled to the event in traditional canoes from settlements as far away as Haines and Angoon, a journey of up to seven days by oar.

The rowing tradition began with the aid of the One People Canoe Society, a nonprofit organization committed to rebuilding and utilizing colorfully attired wooden watercraft. Canoes were once a vital means of Native transportation in coastal Alaska but have been slowly dying out since the early 19th century. Over the last decade, they have reemerged as an important part of festival folklore and their arrival is warmly welcomed by hundreds of spectators who rush down to the harbor to greet them.

Numerous sideshows complement the festival's energetic dance performances. There are film screenings, Native language sessions, story-telling, an art market, and food competitions that showcase classic Native dishes such as seaweed (a Tlingit staple), and bitter-sweet soapberries which are usually beaten and whipped into a fruity cream.

On its last day (usually a Saturday), the festival culminates with a grand parade to Juneau's Centennial Hall for a final song and dance performance. A fitting finale is provided by the so-called Grand Exit Procession.

Not only has Celebration been highly successful in restoring pride

Right **Tlingit mask,** Haines, Alaska

Above **Tlingit attendants at Celebration,** Juneau, Alaska

and pageantry among Pacific Coastal people, it also serves as a significant income generator for Juneau's economy, pulling in over $2 million from the sale of 6000 tickets. Better still is the heritage value, the claiming back of a culture largely taken away from Alaska Natives by successive colonizers in the 19th and 20th centuries who brought with them the unstoppable tentacles of modern life.

You don't need to travel far to see Celebration's ripple effect. A major cultural renaissance has been taking place in Alaska since the mid-2010s, visible in a magnificent new cultural center in Juneau's Walter Soboleff building, a restored Chilkat-Tlingit Whale House replete with priceless 200-year-old totem poles in Haines, and a refashioned Haida clan house in Kasaan on Prince of Wales Island dating from 1880. With the reclamation of these noble artifacts, there's plenty to celebrate.

To read more about:

Volcanic National Parks see page 74
The Alaska Marine Highway System see page 80

Totem Poles: A Beginner's Guide

There is no finer manifestation of coastal Alaska's Indigenous culture than its intricately carved totem poles adorned with ravens, eagles, wolves, whales and carved countenances from Native mythology.

Totem poles are peculiar to the Pacific Northwest region, where they have been sculpted for centuries by the Haida, Tlingit and Tsimshian people. Although the presence of totems predates the arrival of European explorers, the poles became grander when Native people gained access to iron tools in the late 18th century.

Usually fashioned out of mature cedars found deep in the forest, totems have a natural lifespan of around 75 years before the sodden Pacific Northwest climate takes its toll. Traditionally poles are rarely touched up. Progressive deterioration is seen as a part of the natural life-cycle, and ideally they are left to rot and return to the earth.

Totems serve several non-religious functions. 'Welcome poles' are designed to greet visitors to houses and communities, 'memorial poles' honor the dead and 'mortuary poles' contain the remains of deceased ancestors.

Totem poles reached their artistic zenith in the mid-19th century, but by the beginning of the 20th century their presence had nearly died out. Carving was revived in the 1960s amid a renewed appreciation of America's Indigenous cultures.

Kentucky Bourbon

KENTUCKY / DRINKS

The state of Kentucky is synonymous with the US heartland, a patchwork of mountains, rivers, caves and rolling green hills dotted with racehorses. It's also home to 'America's Official Native Spirit': bourbon. While it's always been a US staple, the amber, smoky-sweet beverage has taken the world by storm in recent years, and to truly understand its cultural legacy, you've got to see the Bluegrass State for yourself.

LABROT & GRAHAM DISTILLERS COMPANY
DSP-KY-52
BOURBON WHISKEY
BOURBON RC 52.8 G
FILL DATE 06-07-03
LOT NO. 03-E-07
RC 52.8 G
FILL DATE 06-07-03
LOT NO. 03-F-07
LABROT & GRAHAM DISTILLERS COMPANY
DSP-KY-52
BOURBON WHISKEY
RC 52.8 G
FILL DATE 12-06-03
LOT NO. 03-L-06
LABROT & GRAHAM DISTILLERS
DSP-KY-52
BOURBON WHISKEY
RC 52.8 G
FILL DATE 06-07-03
LOT NO. 03-F-07
LABROT & GRAHAM DISTILLERS
DSP-KY-52
BOURBON WHISKEY
BOURBON 52.8 G
RC. 52.8 G
GRAHAM DISTILLERS
DSP-KY-52

What makes bourbon special? Whiskey, after all, is made around the world. In order to be officially classified as bourbon, whiskey has to meet five criteria. First, it must be made in the US. It must be at least 51% corn, distilled at less than 160 proof and put into a barrel at below 125 proof. Most importantly, it must be aged in charred white oak barrels that have never been used before, and no artificial color or flavor can be added.

Bourbon's origins are steeped in legend. It's unclear who the first bourbon distiller was (most people's money is on Elijah Craig, a minister from central Kentucky), and there's similar dispute over how the whiskey got its name. Some argue that it's derived from Bourbon County, Kentucky, but historians have challenged that fact. An alternative story credits two French brothers who settled in Louisville in the early 1800s and traded whiskey down to New Orleans, where it was sold on Bourbon St. Either way, Kentucky bourbon whiskey has long held the bar high in quality – many credit the state's limestone-filtered water as the secret ingredient that contributes to its excellence. Fun fact: Kentucky produces 95% of the USA's bourbon, and there are 1.5 barrels of Kentucky bourbon for every person living in the state. That's right, there are more barrels of bourbon than people in Kentucky.

Today, bourbon has become one of the USA's most prized exports – love for the liquor has spread worldwide, and it shows up on menus from Louisville to Tokyo. Bourbon experienced a previous heyday in the 1950s before it was pushed aside in the '60s for trendier beverages such as vodka and gin. Now, the taste for that

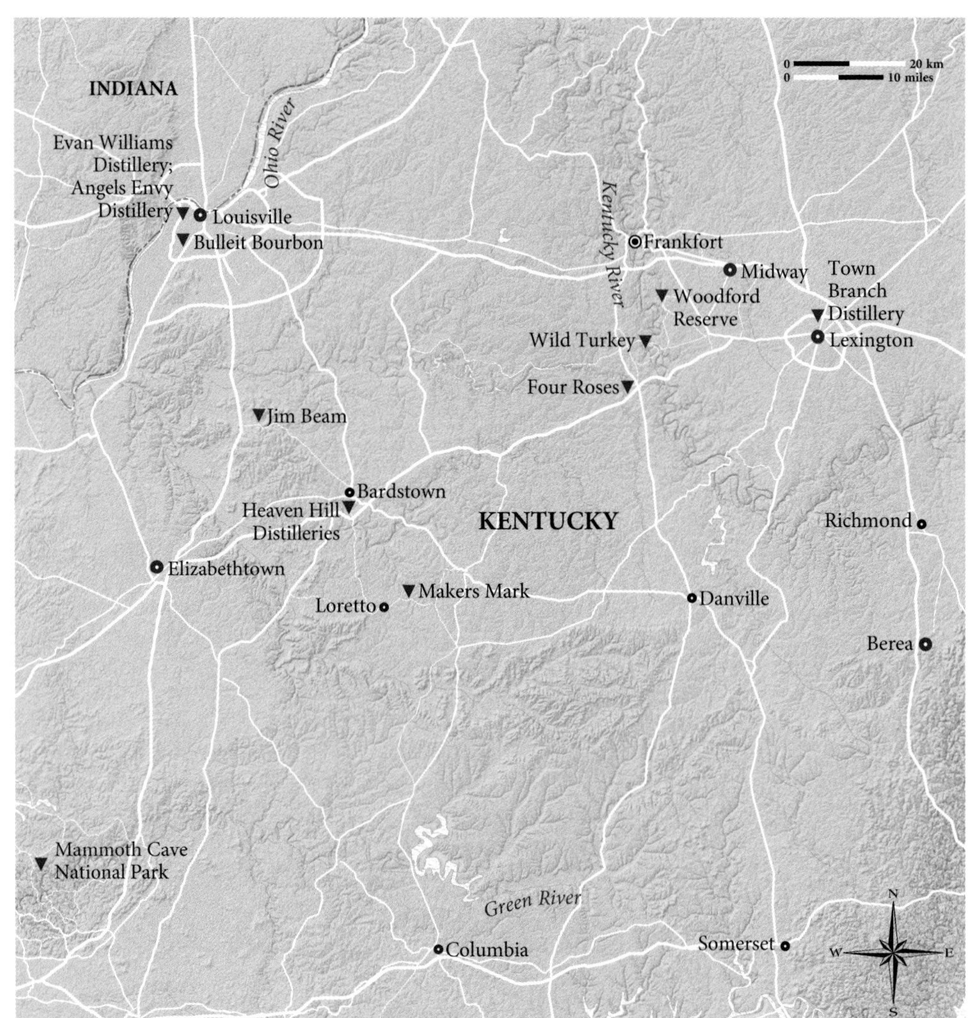

classic whiskey warmth has returned in full force; in fact, the spirit has experienced a certifiable boom in the last few years, leaving some distillers scrambling to meet public demand.

As expected, Kentucky has fully embraced bourbon's history, and it is deeply ingrained in the state's culture. Go to any barbecue or visit any cocktail bar and the bourbon is sure to be flowing. In 1999, the Kentucky Distiller's Association founded the Bourbon Trail, a network of distilleries across central Kentucky designed to show off bourbon's indelible impact and lead enthusiasts on a unique road trip through the state. Most points of interest lie within the geographic triangle formed by Elizabethtown, Louisville and Lexington.

After your distillery tours, hit Kentucky's biggest cities to see the bourbon scene walk the walk. At Louisville's historic Brown Hotel, sample a few snifters in the stunning lobby bar and taste the famous 'Kentucky Hot Brown' (a hot open-faced sandwich), the unofficial state dish that was first prepared in the hotel's kitchen. Those who love all things art deco should hightail it over to the Seelbach Hotel and sample its namesake cocktail (bourbon-based, of course); this historic spot was a favorite of Al Capone and many say it served as F Scott Fitzgerald's inspiration for the decadent setting of *The Great Gatsby*.

Once you're done with this hip riverside town, head east through acres of undulating horse farms to Lexington, heart of the Bluegrass. There you'll find Bluegrass Tavern, which serves more than 400 types of bourbon, including some rare selections; if you want a little slice of Lexington history along with your libation, pop over to Belle's

Cocktail House to sip on boozy creations and learn about the infamous madam who inspired the bar's name.

That said, Kentucky isn't just bourbon – it's also home to a burgeoning food and drink scene, and thriving local art and music movements. Seek out top-notch craft cocktails and locally inspired menus in Louisville, or tour the sprawling horse farms and creative craft breweries around Lexington. Learn about the state's long crafting tradition at the Kentucky Artisan Center in Berea or explore the quaint train track hugging the downtown area of Midway. If outdoor adventure is more your style, head east from central Kentucky to hike some of the prettiest parts of the Appalachian mountain chain, or veer south to go spelunking at Mammoth Cave, the world's longest cave system.

To read about:
Craft Beer see page 200
Lobster Shacks in Maine see page 256

Above **Bourbon barrel manufacturing,** Brown-Forman Cooperage Facility

Mint Julep Recipe

Serves 1

If one's going to drink a true-blue Kentucky liquor, it better be in an equally Kentucky cocktail. The mint julep usually makes its big appearance during the festivities surrounding the famous Kentucky Derby. This springy cocktail is a tasty tipple year-round, though, so grab that mint, a Derby-worthy sunhat, and stir up a genuine taste of the Bluegrass.

→ two sprigs of mint
→ 1 tablespoon simple syrup
→ crushed ice
→ 1.5oz (45mL) bourbon
→ splash of soda water (optional)

1. Start by pouring simple syrup into the bottom of the glass, and then add several mint leaves.

2. Muddle the syrup and the mint, and add crushed ice. Pour the bourbon over the ice and add a sprig of mint for garnish.

3. If you want a cocktail with a little fizz, add a splash of soda water.

4. Serve in a highball glass or silver julep cup.

Texas Barbecue

TEXAS / FOOD & CULTURE

Make no bones about it – Texas barbecue is an obsession. It's the subject of countless newspaper and magazine articles, from national press (including the New York Times) to regional favorite Texas Monthly. Some of central Texas' smaller towns maintain reputations for their smokehouse cultures, and routinely draw dedicated pilgrims from miles around.

Where to Eat Texas Barbecue

Central Texas Franklin Barbecue in Austin; Black's Barbecue in Lockhart

Dallas & the Panhandle Plains Tyler's Barbeque in Amarillo; Sonny Bryan's Smokehouse in Dallas; Heim Barbecue in Fort Worth; KD's Bar-B-Q in Midland; Vitek's BBQ in Waco

East Texas Truth BBQ in Brenham; Fargo's Pit BBQ in Bryan-College Station; Killen's Barbecue in Houston; New Zion Missionary Baptist Church in Huntsville; Joseph's Riverport Barbecue in Jefferson; Country Tavern in Kilgore; Stanley's Famous Pit Barbecue in Tyler

Gulf Coast & South Texas McMillan's BBQ in Fannin/Goliad

West Texas Rib Hut in El Paso

No self-respecting Texan would agree with another about who has the best barbecue, but most do see eye to eye on a few things: brisket is where a pit master proves his or her reputation; seasoning is rarely much more than salt, pepper and something spicy; and if there's a sauce, it's probably made from ketchup, vinegar and the drippings of the wood-smoked meat.

The best Texas barbecue often comes from famous family dynasties that have been dishing up the same crowd-pleasing recipes for generations. Tell-tale signs that you've located an authentic barbecue joint include zero decor, smoke-blackened ceilings, and laid-back table manners (silverware optional). At most places, you can order a combination plate or ask for specific meats to be sliced by the pound right in front of you. Of course, there are variations on this nowadays, but in Texas, where barbecue baiting is a bit of a pastime, some swear this down-home style is the only way.

However you like it – sliced thick onto butcher paper, slapped on picnic plates, doused with a tangy sauce or eaten naturally flavorful right out of the smokehouse barbecue pit – be sure to savor it...and then argue to the death that *your* way is the best way. Like a true Texan.

History

The origins of central Texas barbecue can be traced to 19th-century Czech and German settlers, many of whom were butchers. These settlers pioneered methods of smoking meat, both to better preserve it (before the advent of refrigeration) and also to tenderize cuts that might otherwise be wasted.

Credit also goes to Mexican *vaqueros* (Spanish-speaking cowboys), especially in Texas' southern and western borderland regions, who dug the first barbecue pits in about the 16th century, then grilled spicy meats over mesquite wood. African Americans who migrated to Texas brought with them recipes for a 'wet' style of barbecue, which involved thick marinades, sweet sauces and juicier meats.

Somewhere along the way, slow-smoked barbecue crossed the line from simple eating pleasure to statewide obsession. Maybe it's the primal joy of gnawing tender, tasty meat directly from the bone, or the simplistic, sloppy appeal of the hands-on eating experience. Whatever the reason, dedicated barbecue eaters demonstrate nearly religious devotion by worshipping at the pits of Texas' renowned smokehouses.

In today's Texas, barbecue recipes are as varied as central Texas summers are long. Most folks agree on the basics: slow cooking over a low-heat fire. A cooking time of up to 12 or 16 hours isn't unheard of – anything less and you're just too darn impatient. It allows the meat to be infused with a rich smoky flavor of usually hickory or pecan in the eastern part of the state, oak in central Texas and mesquite out west. (Mesquite was considered all but a weed until someone realized what a nice flavor it lent to wood chips.)

The Meat

When it comes to meat choices, Texas barbecue leans heavily toward beef – a logical outgrowth of the state's cattle industry – and most signature dishes come straight from the sacred cow. The most common is beef brisket, a cut often used for corned beef. With a combination of patience, experience and skill, a seasoned pit boss can transform this notoriously tough meat into a perfectly smoked, tender slab of heaven. Even tougher cuts of meat enter the smokehouse and emerge hours later, deeply flavorful and tender to the tooth. Sliced thin and internally moistened by natural fat, a well-smoked brisket falls apart with the slightest touch and can rival more expensive cuts for butter-smooth consistency.

Carnivores seeking a more toothy challenge can indulge in beef ribs – huge meaty racks that would do Fred Flintstone proud – or relax with a saucy chopped-beef sandwich. Word to the wise: if you need to stay presentable, think twice about the ribs, which tend to be a full-contact eating experience (even as part of a three-meat sampler plate).

Lone Star cattle worship stops short of excluding other meats from the pit. The noble pig makes appearances in the form of succulent ribs, thick buttery chops and perfect slices of loin so tender they melt on the tongue. In recent years, chicken has shown up on menu boards, mainly to provide beginners with a non-hoofed barnyard option. Traditionalists, however, stick with the good stuff – red meat and plenty of it.

Every self-respecting barbecue joint will also serve sausage. Texas hot links, the peppery sausage of regional renown, are created with ground pork and beef combined with pungent spices. Although it's not technically in the barbecue family, sausage is cooked over the same fire so has the same smoky flavor. If nothing else it makes an excellent meaty side dish to go alongside your meaty main dish.

The Rub

Everyone knows that the word 'barbecue' is usually followed by the word 'sauce.' But not so fast, there. Good barbecue is more than just meat and sauce. The other key component is the rub, which is how the meat is seasoned before it's cooked.

There are wet rubs and dry rubs. A dry rub is a mixture of salt, pepper, herbs and spices sprinkled over or painstakingly rubbed into the meat before cooking. A wet rub is created by adding liquid, which usually means oil, but also possibly vinegar, lemon juice or even mustard. Applied like a paste, a wet rub seals in the meat's natural juices before cooking. This key step is as important as the slow cooking in getting the flavor just right.

The Sauce

Wisdom about barbecue sauce varies widely from region to region and sometimes joint to joint. There's huge debate over what kind, how much or whether you need it at all. In Lockhart, Kreuz Market's meat is served without any sauce at all, and it's so naturally juicy and tender you'll agree it's not necessary. But excellent, sauce-heavy barbecue is divine as well. We'll leave it to you to make up your own mind.

Texas barbecue sauce has a different flavor from other types – that's why it's Texas barbecue, y'all. It's not as sweet as the kind you'll find gracing the tables of barbecue joints in Kansas City and Memphis – more a blend of spicy and slightly sweet. There are thousands of variations and no two sauces are exactly alike, but recipes are usually tomato-based with vinegar, brown sugar, chili powder, onion, garlic and other seasonings.

The Sides

Side dishes naturally take second place to the platters of smoked meat. Restaurant-style sides usually include pinto beans, potato salad or coleslaw, while markets sometimes opt for simpler accompaniments like onion slices, dill pickles, cheese slices or whole tomatoes. (If your meat is served on butcher paper, the sides will come in a bowl or on a plate.)

Etiquette

The first question that comes to most people's minds is, 'How do I eat this without making a mess?' You don't. Accepting the fact early on that barbecue is a messy, messy venture will give you the attitude you need to enjoy your meal. One coping mechanism is to make a drop cloth of your napkin. Bibs haven't exactly caught on in the barbecue world – this is a manly meal, after all – but tucking your napkin into your shirt is never frowned upon, especially if you didn't come dressed for it.

So how does one dress for barbecue? First off, don't wear white. Or yellow, or pink, or anything that won't camouflage or coordinate with red. At 99% of barbecue restaurants (the exception being uppity nouveau 'cue) you will see the most casual of casual attire, including jeans (harder to stain) and shorts, and maybe even some trucker hats.

Whether you eat with your hands or a fork depends on the cut of the meat. Brisket and sausage are fork dishes, while ribs are eaten prehistoric-style. (It also depends on the restaurant. Kreuz Market doesn't offer forks. As the restaurant says, Texas barbecue was served on wax paper over a century ago and that's how they're gonna keep doing it.)

Texas Cook-Offs

At the many cook-offs around the state, amateurs and pros alike come together to seek barbecue perfection and, if they're lucky, bragging rights. Cook-offs generally start on Friday afternoon so the pit masters have plenty of time to get their meat just right before the judging on Saturday. Once that's complete, the public can swoop in and judge for themselves.

One of the largest is the Taylor International Barbecue Cook-Off, with up to 100 contestants competing in seven different meat categories. If you can't make that one, a quick search on www.tourtexas.com will lead you to many more events.

If you're eating with your hands, grab extra napkins. Ah, heck, grab extras anyway. You might also be provided with a small packet containing a moist towelette, which will at least get you clean enough to head to the restrooms to wash up.

A final thought on etiquette: if you're at a restaurant that uses a dry rub and you don't see any sauce, it's probably best not to ask – it would be a bit like asking for ketchup to put on your steak.

To read about:
NYC Cuisine see page 190
Lobster in Maine see page 256

Order Up! Diners & Diner Slang

USA-WIDE / FOOD & CULTURE

You know the place: long and narrow, with chrome stools dotted along the counter. It's open 24 hours, the fluorescent lights unyielding. Newspapers rustle, silverware clatters, and jumbo plates of eggs or fries thud onto tables. The waitress calls you 'honey.' Whatever city you're in or back road you're on, a diner beckons, comforting and familiar as apple pie.

Diners loom large in US culture. They've been around for more than a century, but it was the 1930s when the concept really took off. The little restaurants – many designed to look like 'modern' rail cars – began to appear in working-class communities where residents wanted a cheap, filling meal regardless of the time of day. By the 1950s diners had gone viral, spreading from cities to suburbs to roadways such as Route 66, where neon signs flashed to lure passing motorists.

Today's diners stick to the original formula. Portions are huge, while prices are moderate. The homey menu goes on for pages: a tuna melt, strawberry milkshake or cheeseburger with fries? Meat loaf, a turkey sandwich or split pea soup? Waffles, pancakes or eggs with bacon? Name it and it's served around the clock, hot off the grill.

Breakfast foods are a diner specialty. So are desserts. Go ahead, try to resist the banana cream pie, chocolate layer cake and raspberry cobbler rotating in the glass case. A cup of coffee is de rigueur with whatever you order. Or on its own, to fuel newspaper reading.

Diners are communal spots. Plunk down on a stool at the counter and soon you'll be chatting with the cook about his kids. Ballcap-wearing regulars give you the neighborhood gossip. Then the waitress joins in. She has a name like Margie or Virginia, sewn in big letters on her apron, and she's wise as Solomon, dispensing relationship advice while delivering your biscuits and gravy.

Thankfully, diners remain thick on the ground. The Northeast and Midwest have the mother lode, but no matter what region you're in, one of these mom-and-pop eateries will be cooking nearby, offering a bit of home away from home.

Diner Lingo Translator

Butcher's revenge – meat loaf

Make it cry – add onions

Bow-wow or bun pup – hot dog

Frog sticks – French fries

Cluck and grunt – eggs and bacon

Sinkers and suds – doughnuts and coffee

Wreck 'em – scramble the eggs

Moo juice – milk

Twins – salt and pepper

Cow paste – butter

To read about:
LA's World Food see page 88
Coffee in Three Waves see page 154

Southern Manners: Charleston & Savannah

SOUTH CAROLINA & GEORGIA / CULTURE

Charleston and Savannah have long had the friendliest of rivalries over which is the Most Mannerly City in the USA. Neither are the kind to boast – it just wouldn't be neighborly – but both are bastions of civility and charm, as welcoming as a Mason jar full of sweet iced tea on a hot, summer day.

Right **Charleston,** South Carolina

We're tickled pink, as they like to say in the South, to introduce you to two of our favorite Southern cities: Savannah, Georgia, and Charleston, South Carolina. Just a couple hours' drive from each other, these supremely gracious coastal towns ooze Southern charm, with friendly locals who invite you to come sit for a spell.

Both cities are steeped in the traditions of the past, and good manners and social graces are passed down from generation to generation. But it's more than just finishing-school etiquette you'll experience. Here, people take the time to look you in the eye, greet you properly, and make you feel like a cherished friend.

The pace is a lot slower in the South, which can be a little maddening or utterly charming, depending on how big a hurry you're in. Best to just relax into it. You can't quickly ask for directions without being expected to make a little polite chitchat first, but on the plus side, think of all the friendly conversations you'll have. Play your cards right and you might just get invited for supper.

Speaking of supper, Charlestonians and Savannians have raised table manners to an art form. Everybody knows not to talk with their mouth full or put their elbows on the table. But you should also be aware that setting your fork down between bites is considered the proper thing to do – and heaven forbid you drag your soup spoon *toward* you when everyone knows you should only spoon your soup *away* from you.

The locals, of course, know what each and every one of those multiple utensils is for. But what happens if you upset the natural order by using the wrong fork? Don't worry; embarrassing someone isn't considered good form in the South. (However, if a waiter discreetly presents you with a fresh fork when you already seem to have plenty, you're probably being given a hint.)

A Southern drawl isn't strictly necessary, but there is a certain etiquette to the way Southerners talk. 'Please' and 'thank you' are de rigueur. 'Yes, ma'am,' and 'No, sir,' are also considered the polite way to answer a direct query. Of course, formality is reserved for elders and people you don't know all that well. If you get called Sugar, Sweetheart, or Hon, that just means they're mighty glad to see you.

Savannah: Visiting the Hostess City

Much has been written about Charleston's virtues as a travel destination, but when it comes to tourism, Savannah is a little newer to the social scene. One of the great joys of visiting is simply strolling around the elegant townhouses, antebellum mansions, mammoth live oak trees and green public squares draped in Spanish moss. The best time to visit is in March, when it's warm but not too warm, the azaleas and dogwoods are blooming, and you can get a peek into local life during the annual home and garden tour.

To read about:
Gullah Culture in Charleston see page 162
The Appalachians see page 284

Top left **Azalea Inn & Gardens,** Savannah, Georgia
Bottom left **The Pink House,** Savannah, Georgia

Highway 61 Re-Revisited

Highway 61 inspired Bob Dylan and countless legendary American musicians. Drive it and experience the region that shaped rock and roll.

SOUTH / ROAD TRIPS & MUSIC

Highway 61 runs from the chilly northern plains of Wyoming, Minnesota, to the steamy southern swamps of New Orleans, Louisiana. If Hwy 61 has any claim to being the world's most famous road, this is due to Bob Dylan's celebrated 1965 album *Highway 61 Revisited*. Both before and after Dylan gave the road iconic status, many a blues, soul and country musician traveled it in search of bright lights, big cities and maybe a record deal.

Highway 61 spans 1407 miles (2264km) and while driving the entirety of this epic trip would be fascinating, you can also opt to stick with just the southern end – nicknamed 'the Blues Highway.' And what a pleasure it is to drive.

Beginning in Memphis, Tennessee, take a couple of days to explore the city's rich music heritage: Sun Studio, where BB King, Howlin' Wolf, Elvis Presley and Roy Orbison started out; 'Soulsville USA,' the neighborhood that's home to the pioneering soul label Stax Records, which launched the careers of Otis Redding and Isaac Hayes; and then, of course, there's Graceland. Visit the National Civil Rights Museum to put into context the lives and struggles of African Americans throughout this era. And don't miss out on BBQ ribs – a Memphis specialty – before hitting the bars and clubs of downtown, soaking up the sound of the city that helped create blues, soul and rock and roll.

Leaving Memphis on the 61 is easy and once outside the city limits, you'll cross the border into Mississippi. During the 1960s and the Civil Rights Movement, Mississippi gained a reputation for murderous racism, somewhere people fled from rather than traveled to. Today, the state remains one of the poorest and most racially divided in the US, but it is peaceful. And the music that crystallised here a century ago continues to draw blues tourists from around the world.

Cotton, which was once the dominant local industry, is still grown on vast plantations, but it's the sprouting casino signs that suggest the state's new growth industry. Once past Tunica, a mini–Las Vegas situated on the Mississippi River, you will start to see the roadside Blues Trail markers, which acknowledge the places where so many legendary blues men and women once lived, worked, recorded and died.

Around 90 minutes south of Memphis is Clarksdale, a run-down cotton town turned mecca for blues pilgrims. The first port of call is the excellent Delta Blues Museum, which tells the story of how the sound that was to become rock and soul took shape here. Pay homage to the city's blues sites – it's where Bessie Smith died (take note: after a car crash on Hwy 61) and Ike Turner and Sam Cooke were born, and you can even drive over the actual crossroads where Robert Johnson sold his soul in 'Cross Road Blues.' That certainly provides plenty of food for thought, though make sure to head to a diner for some tamales (a local favorite) to fill your belly.

Clarksdale's epicenter is Cat Head, a blues and folk art store. Pick up tips from its amiable proprietor, Roger Stolle, and head into town for the evening. Start out at Ground Zero Blues Club, a sumptuous live music bar owned by actor and Mississippi resident Morgan Freeman, before wandering down to Red's, a juke joint that looks as if it was due for demolition sometime during the last century. Juke joints – the African American drinking and dancing clubs that were once prominent across much of the rural South – were the breeding grounds for blues. A few still stand, and those that do often play host to local talent. Clarksdale also hosts the Juke Joint Festival every April: three days of beer, BBQ and blues.

If by now you're in need of some fresh air, sign up for a guided canoe trip down the

Right **Sun Studio,** Memphis, Tennessee

SUN Studio
SUN STUDIO
FREE PARKING IN REAR
Sam Phillips
AVENUE
WALKER
RADIATOR
WORKS
BIKE LN
Elvis LIVES
GRACELAND
ominos
The Legendary
SUN STUDIO
Open Every Day
10:00 till 6:15
Guided Tours Hourly
At Half Past
10:30 till 5:30

Mississippi – you'll feel as happy as Huckleberry Finn paddling down the mighty river. Later, back in Clarksdale, head east to Oxford, home of the celebrated University of Mississippi – aka Ole Miss – and Rowan Oak, William Faulkner's house from 1930 until he died in 1962. A little further east is Tupelo, where a certain Elvis Aaron Presley was born in a two-room shack in 1935.

Your next stop is Indianola, now home to a museum honoring its most famous son, BB King. Close by is Greenville, a small, impoverished city that hosts the longest-running blues festival in the US every year, at the very height of summer. Where Clarksdale's juke joints are accommodating to visitors, Greenville's are rough: only seek them out alongside a local guide.

Continuing south, drop into two more towns: Vicksburg is a small city that played a leading role in the American Civil War and, just east of here, Jackson is the state's sleepy capital.

However, it's the swampy and near-empty rural Mississippi landscape where the 61 really gets evocative. The cotton plantations where musical legends were born and worked still stand, often seemingly unchanged, and the small towns that have been immortalized in blues songs – Natchez, Yazoo City, Sunflower, Merigold, Shelby – are still working towns, even if some of them seem to be on the verge of becoming ghost towns.

In *On the Road,* Jack Kerouac and Neal Cassady drove Hwy 61 to visit William Burroughs. When this task was complete, they carried on to New Orleans. Having soaked up Mississippi's small-town lassitude and blues bars, follow their lead and drive on to the Big Easy.

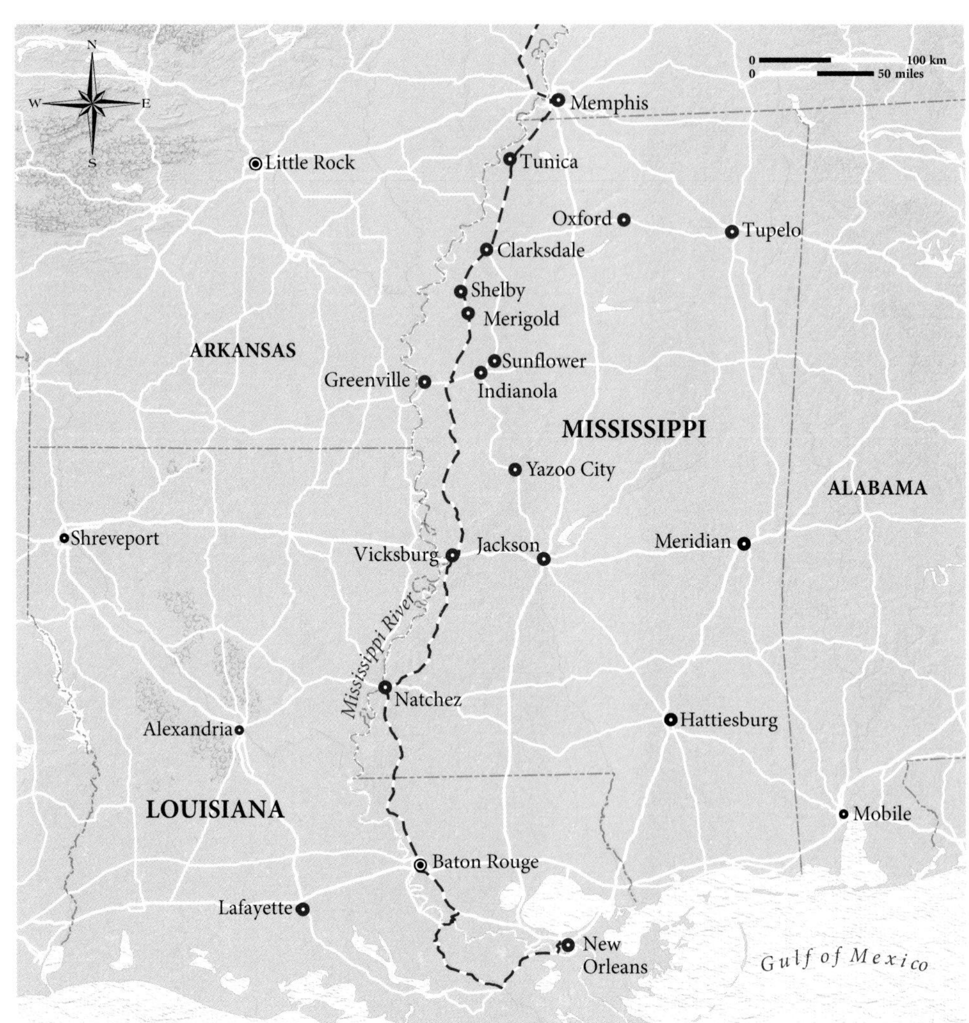

Right **Beale St,** Memphis, Tennessee

Road-Trip Toolkit

When to Drive Spring to autumn finds the Blues Highway at its most lively, but June to August can be extremely hot and humid. Live music generally happens at weekends, except in New Orleans where the good times roll every day.

Where to Stay Mississippi is the land of cheap motels. Both Memphis and New Orleans can be expensive; book accommodations in advance.

Detours When entering Louisiana drive west to Lafayette: the capital of Cajun Country is home to great Cajun and zydeco music.

Mississippi Blues Trail Since 2006, more than 200 Blues Trail markers have been placed across Mississippi. The plaques stand outside everything from cemeteries where musicians rest to juke joints, studios, record labels, homes, streets and even Parchman Farm, where many an unlucky musician did time. Maps are available and it's a fascinating drive as you explore the humble settings where one of the most atmospheric musical genres took shape.

To read about:

Driving the Great River Road see page 52
African American Music see page 164

Saddling Up in the American West

MONTANA / HORSEBACK RIDING

Fancy learning horseback-riding skills, herding cattle across plains with bona fide cowgirls and cowboys, and sleeping in century-old homestead cabins? Experience the real American West at a working cattle ranch in southwestern Montana's remote Centennial Valley.

Guests who make the long drive to J Bar L, a ranch with some 400 head of cattle, can look forward to being welcomed by a latter-day Marlboro Man, an honest-to-goodness cowboy who doffs his hat and greets female visitors as 'ma'am.' It's like a scene out of a John Wayne film, minus the shootouts.

During weeklong working-ranch vacations, up to eight guests get to accompany the cowhands on their daily rounds, herding cattle, administering medication, fixing fences and whatever other chores need to be done. Then they eat a hearty, home-cooked dinner together, sharing stories with people who lead a completely different way of life. The peace that comes from sauntering across limitless prairies with snow-speckled mountains in the distance is a tonic for desk jockeys who wonder if their information-age jobs serve any actual purpose. Cowboying is good old-fashioned work: the animals depend on you. And at the end of the day, your hunger is well earned and your tiredness well deserved.

Sleep comes easily here, both because of the outdoor exertions and because the ranch is impossibly quiet – it's 22 miles (35km) from pavement, and two hours from a city of any size. The cabins might be 4 miles (6km) from the dining hall. It's just you and the lonesome prairie – you're more likely to spot a wolf or an elk than another human being. It's rugged and difficult, and it forces you to contemplate what it was like for pioneers a century ago, before Gore-Tex and gas stoves. It has quite a way of putting things into perspective.

In addition to the working-ranch weeks, J Bar L opens its cabins and historic homes to visitors throughout the summer. During non-working weeks, guests use the lodging as a base for pursuits like fly-fishing, bird-watching – there are more than 230 species in the nearby Red Rock Lakes National Wildlife Refuge, considered one of the United States' most beautiful reserves – hiking, mountain biking and horseback riding, or making day trips to nearby Yellowstone or Grand Teton National Parks. And don't underestimate the pleasure of sitting on the porch and watching the sun crest the mountains on a clear, crisp morning.

Essential Experiences

→ Mounting a spirited steed for horseback-riding training with the ranch hands before heading out onto the plains, taking in unfathomably vast prairies and mountain ranges.

→ Dining with ranch staff: Montana cowgirls and cowboys break bread with city-slicker guests, and conversations can go in any number of fascinating directions.

→ Eating grass-fed steak straight from the ranch – the epitome of farm-to-table and undeniably delicious (as well as healthier than most beef).

→ Sleeping in the middle of nowhere – and remembering the pioneers who did it not for a vacation but because it was their only choice.

To read about:

Where to Spy a Bear (and a Moose) see page 60
Bison on the Tallgrass Prairie see page 112

AUSTIN

Live Music Capital of the World

Austin is a big city with a small-town heart, a place where visitors fall head-over-cowboy-boots for the thriving music scene, world-class culinary culture and whip-smart locals with an irresistible social streak. This is a place where you can eat the best meal of the week at a rusty food truck, hear a life-affirming band for a $5 cover charge and follow a session of yoga with a smoky plate of ribs. It's an easy place to fall in love with.

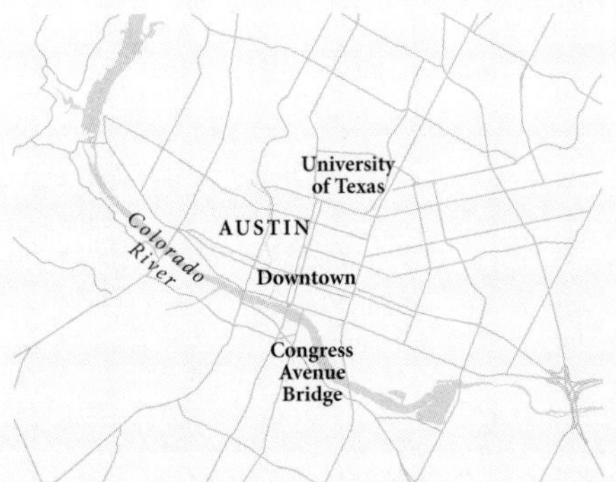

Maybe too easy. You'll see locals in T-shirts that say 'Welcome to Austin. Please don't move here.' They're only half-joking. Why is it so easy to love? First, there's always something going on. The city easily earns its title of 'Live Music Capital of the World' with two big music festivals and quality live performances every single night of the week. Downtown is home to two art museums, both noted for bold avant-garde and thoughtful temporary exhibits. Its *other* T-shirt slogan, 'Keep Austin Weird,' is evident in its share of offbeat attractions, from the flight of the bats from the Congress Avenue Bridge to niche museums spotlighting everything from pop culture to oddities from around the world. The University of Texas is here too, adding youthful energy to the nightlife.

Those smoky ribs are only the start of the city's world-class food scene, which never takes itself too seriously. When the lines for the best barbecue joints stretch out the door, staff sell beer to the folks in the queue and it becomes a communal party. And menus at the fanciest farm-to-table restaurants often get downright whimsical. There's not much foodie snobbishness here. But passion? Yes. Boutique ice cream and smoky Tex-Mex. All that barbecue and to-die-for breakfast tacos. Locals love to opine. Take a few bites, join the conversation.

Don't be surprised if that conversation gravitates back to the challenges that come along with a booming city that's trying to hold on to the things that make it so special. As the most open-hearted city in Texas, Austin is a bastion for progressive politics and a cooperative and hospitable social atmosphere – a place where people of all ages will socialize with the merest of provocation and no one is a stranger for long. But despite its popularity, Austin hasn't forgotten where it came from. Welcome to Austin. You're going to want to move here.

BAT CITY SPECTACLE

AUSTIN / WILDLIFE

Every year up to 1.5 million Mexican free-tailed bats make their home upon a platform beneath the Congress Avenue Bridge, forming the largest urban bat colony in North America.

It's become an Austin tradition to sit on the grassy banks of Lady Bird Lake and watch the bats swarm out to feed on an estimated 30,000lbs (13,600kg) of insects per night. It looks a lot like a fast-moving, black, chittering river. Don't miss this nightly show, best viewed in August.

The colony is made up entirely of female and young animals. Such is the bat-density that bat-radars have detected bat-columns up to 10,000 bat-feet (3050m) high. In June, each female gives birth to one pup, and every night at dusk, the families take to the skies in search of food. Capitol Cruises, behind the Hyatt Hotel, offers bat-watching cruises on Town Lake below the bridge.

To read about:
Wildlife Spotting see page 60
Caves see page 290

AUSTIN, MUSIC CITY

AUSTIN / MUSIC

It's in the air when you step off the airplane or stroll under the neon lights of 6th St, it lingers on the breeze along the Congress Avenue Bridge and from the corner of your new favorite barbecue joint. In Austin, music is everywhere.

Right **Anderson .Paak performs at South by Southwest (SXSW),** Austin

The city's official motto – 'Live Music Capital of the World' – is no overstatement. Texas' capital city is home to more live music venues per capita (250, give or take) than any other city on Earth and boasts some 2000 bands and recording artists. That tight-knit community forms one of the nation's most diverse, concentrated destinations for music, playing everything from Texas two-step to sludge metal. Even though live performance is a seven-days-a-week-365-days-a-year fixture of city life, Austin really gets loud during its world-famous music festivals, South by Southwest (SXSW) in the spring and Austin City Limits Festival in the fall, when big-name musicians, industry bigshots, and fans from around the world descend on the city.

If Austin is the heart of music in Texas – and maybe the USA – then 6th Street is its main artery. Lined with bars, clubs and restaurants, Dirty Sixth (as it's known to locals) is an electrifying stretch where live rock, blues and country pour out of nearly every address. The street closes on the weekends, when college students and buskers take over. During SXSW, the stretch is absolute chaos, as conventioneers wobble from one showcase to the next, aspiring hip-hop stars hock promotional CDs, and the shows start at noon and end in the wee hours of the morning.

But even if the sound of Austin is wildly eclectic, the traditions of music in this town run deep. To get a taste of the old days, head to the Broken Spoke, a honky-tonk roadhouse that has been around for over half a century. Sandwiched between the hulking condos that have popped up all over Austin in more recent years, the landmark venue has hosted legends including Ernest Tubbs, Bob Wills and Willie Nelson (who lives just outside of town, and who hosts a helluva 4th of July picnic that's open to the public). Regardless of who's in the limelight, the action is on the dance floor, as sharp-dressed cowboys and gals twirl to the sound of wilting fiddles and shuffling guitars.

Another taste of vintage Austin is available at Ginny's Little Longhorn Saloon. Local music icon Dale Watson rescued the place from bankruptcy and hosts the city's inimitable Chicken Shit Bingo, a Sunday tradition that sends a hapless fowl clucking around a large bingo board. To find yourself on the back patio of Ginny's with a cold bottle of Lone Star in hand while Dale and the boys reel through the country classics is one of many musical experiences that can only happen in Austin, Music City. And it'll make your heart sing.

The Armadillo

In this part of the state you can see any kind of musical performance, from a four-piece bluegrass band kicking out jug tunes to a lone DJ spinning the latest trance grooves. The area's unique prominence on the country's musical stage can be traced all the way back to the German settlers who immigrated to the area in the mid-1800s, as well as to the rich musical heritage Texas has always shared with Mexico. Austin's modern sound first took shape in the early 1970s at a barnlike venue known as the Armadillo World Headquarters.

The Armadillo of the 1970s was a hippie haven. The club's owners included Eddie Wilson, former band manager for Shiva's Head Band, and Jim Franklin, a local muralist and poster artist. They created a place that quickly became known as a

PACIFIC
RING

counterculture hangout, a bar frequented by bikers, cowboys, hippies and college kids alike. They played a wide variety of music, but it was here that Texas singer-songwriters pioneered what would be called 'outlaw country.'

Willie Nelson had come home to Texas looking for more creative freedom than Nashville allowed. He, Waylon Jennings and Kris Kristofferson started writing music that mixed softer, traditional Nashville country with blues and rock, rhythms reminiscent of honky-tonks' early days. Though there was an edge to the music, the term 'outlaw' had a lot more to do with the singers' personal lives than with the music.

Tunes such as 'Luckenbach, Texas' and 'Mammas, Don't Let Your Babies Grow Up to be Cowboys' forced the industry to take notice. Musicians and bands who had been hard-pressed to find an audience for their country-rock songs began to flock to the Armadillo. Acts like Asleep at the Wheel and Kinky Friedman regularly played to packed crowds.

Though the Armadillo as it was closed its doors in the 1980s, its legacy continues in *Austin City Limits,* a live Texas public-radio music program that debuted in 1976 with Willie Nelson playing on the first episode.

To read about:

African American Music see page 164
Motown see page 302

Melting Pot

A Multicultural Blend of Irresistible Cuisine, Music & Customs

From the get-go, America was called a 'melting pot,' where immigrants came and blended into the existing community. The first new arrivals in millennia were from Europe, and they were joined later by waves of people from Asia and Latin America. Hundreds of thousands of Africans also became part of the mix – not willingly, but through the institution of slavery – during the nation's early years.

Today the USA's 325 million people comprise the globe's third-largest population, an ever-changing behemoth fed by a steady stream of new cultures and creeds. While this massive mingling of individuals has had its up and downs, there's no denying some extraordinary things have come out of the blend.

Blues music, for one, shows the inspired results. The genre developed out of black communities in the South, from their work songs, field chants and spirituals that were adaptations of African music. Jazz similarly originated in New Orleans, where ex-slaves combined African and European notes to create fresh sounds. And it's thanks to the US crucible that salsa music emerged. Performers from around Latin America crossed rhythms while living in New York City, and the nation's hips haven't stopped shaking since.

The list of new-forged types goes on. Consider the French-African-Cajun mash-up of Mardi Gras. Or Charleston's outsized food scene and how the cooking of the Gullah people transformed it. Chinatowns pop up around the country, bringing mooncakes and pork buns to Boston, Seattle and spots in-between. Even a small town like Tarpon Springs, Florida, becomes a unique fusion in the USA – in this case an idyllic place to watch fishing boats cast off as you fork into a plate of moussaka and learn the peculiar history of sponges.

Amexica: Border Towns of the South

SOUTH / PEOPLE & CULTURE

Any seasoned traveler knows the elusive charm of a border town, where traditions blur and time moves at a different pace. On the US–Mexico border the vibrant cultural commingling can be every bit as disarming as the transnational residents of these little towns, who often disregard the geopolitical line with a good-natured shrug. This region holds an abundance of natural splendor – including the remote Cabeza Prieta National Wildlife Refuge and the canyon-filled wilderness of the Coronado National Forest – along with many towns that are worthy sites unto themselves.

Right **El Paso,** Texas

PRESTAMOS
Teresa
FINANCE II
LOTTO $ CAR TITLES $ LOANS
410
ABIERTO - OPEN
RASPADITOS
PRESTAMOS
LOANS
TEXAS
LOTTERY
Restaurant
Fine Food
Phone
the
Tap
SUNDAYS
The Tap LOUNGE
AND RESTAURANT
408 E. SAN ANTONIO ST.
"The Downtown Bar"
EST. 1956
EXCLUSIVO CLIENTES
CORTESIA RESTAURANT TAP
ROYAL CHINESE
RESTAURANT
ROYAL
ROYAL ROYAL

Above Chili cooking contest, Terlingua, Texas

San Diego/Tijuana

Tijuana and San Diego are sister cities that serve as the de facto capital of Amexica. To get a real feel for Mexican culture, cross the border for a day. A passport is required to cross the border and to re-enter the United States. Several companies run tours from San Diego to Tijuana, but you can also travel by car.

For decades, TJ was a cheap, convivial escape for hard-partying San Diegans, Angelenos, sailors and college kids until a double-whammy of drug-related violence and global recession nearly shuttered the once-bustling tourist areas. But TJ is making a flourishing comeback.

Avenida Revolución ('La Revo') is the main tourist drag, though its charm is checkered with cheap clothing and souvenir stores, strip joints and pharmacies selling bargain-priced meds to US visitors. It's worth taking a short ride from here to the Museo de las Californias, inside the architecturally daring Centro Cultural Tijuana. 'El Cubo,' as locals call it, offers an excellent history of the border region from prehistory to the present. If you're in town on a Friday night, check out a *lucha libre* (Mexican wrestling) match at the Auditorio Municipal Fausto Gutiérrez Moreno. You can also get your bearing with Turista Libre, which runs a variety of public and private tours in English, led by a US expat with endless enthusiasm for the city and its lesser-known nooks and crannies.

El Paso

El Paso is the coolest border stop in Texas. Long considered a sleepy western town, El Paso moseyed along, keeping its head low while sketchy Ciudad Juárez (just over the Rio Grande) grabbed headlines. But no more. With a sleek new hotel downtown, El Paso has lured locals back to the city's core for socializing and dining. A streetcar line linking downtown and the University of Texas at El Paso (UTEP) is underway and the new Montecillo entertainment and residential district to the west is booming. The city even has a new baseball team, the El Paso Chihuahuas.

Outdoorsy types have it made here: there's cycling and hiking in the largest urban park in the US, and the nearby Hueco Tanks State Park is ideal for wintertime rock climbing. Prefer the indoors? The city's top museums are free. Best of all is the hospitality of the locals, which makes this city of nearly 700,000 feel a whole lot smaller.

They're not always mentioned in guidebooks – maybe because they're primarily in the poorest areas of town – but Los Murales, the street murals of El Paso, are perhaps the city's preeminent cultural treasure. Of the more than 100 murals in the city, the greatest concentrations are south of downtown between Paisano Dr and the Border Hwy, and north of Paisano Dr near Douglass Elementary School.

Terlingua

Tucked into a quiet corner of southwest Texas, this remote little town sits in the shadow of the massive Big Bend National Park. Square in the middle of the Chihuahuan Desert near a lazy stretch of the Rio Grande, Terlingua is an oasis town among the breathtaking landscape of dusty canyons, barren desert, and the distant Chisos Mountains. The little place came to existence in the 1890s as a mercury-mining town, and you can find the remnants of its history in the ghost town just outside the city's center. Today hippies and desert bohemians have taken the place of the miners, and thrill-seekers come to ride the rapids in Santa Elena Canyon. Consider yourself lucky if you happen on one of the town's major festivals in November: Dia de los Muertos, or the renowned international chili cook-off, which has been going strong for five decades.

To read about:
Texas Barbecue see page 124
San Diego Comic-Con see page 224

Tortilla Soup

Serves 4

This spicy, hearty soup is standard fare along the Texas–Mexico border. It is served over tortilla strips for a chunky, satisfying meal.

- → 1 large pasilla chile
- → 15oz can diced tomatoes
- → 2 tablespoons canola oil
- → medium onion, chopped
- → 4 cloves garlic
- → 8 cups chicken or vegetable stock
- → 1.5lb (700g) boneless chicken breast or thigh, cut into half-inch pieces
- → salt and black pepper
- → 2 avocados, diced
- → handful crushed tortilla chips
- → Monterey Jack cheese, shredded, for serving
- → sour cream, for serving
- → lime wedges, for serving

1. Hold the chile in tongs and toast it over an open flame (or, alternatively, in a saucepan) until slightly blackened on all sides. Remove stem and seeds, break into pieces and transfer to a blender with the tomatoes.

2. Heat oil in saucepan and add garlic and onion. Cook until translucent, 8–10 minutes. Add to blender with chile and tomatoes.

3. Blend mixture then pour into saucepan and cook on medium-high until thick, about 10 minutes. Add stock and bring to the boil. Reduce heat to low and simmer for 15 minutes. Add the chicken, salt and pepper and cook until chicken is cooked through (about 8 minutes).

4. Ladle over a handful of crushed tortilla chips and sprinkle with cheese, a dollop of sour cream and avocado. Add a squeeze of lime.

Coffee in Three Waves

USA-WIDE / DRINKS

The coffee plant isn't grown in the mainland United States, but that hasn't stopped the country from having a major influence on the way the drink is prepared and consumed around the world today. From the functional instant granules that kept US troops awake during WWII, to the bucket-size throwaway cups of Starbucks, to the flowery latte art of 21st-century hipsters, it's a tale of entrepreneurship and experimentation that came in three distinct waves.

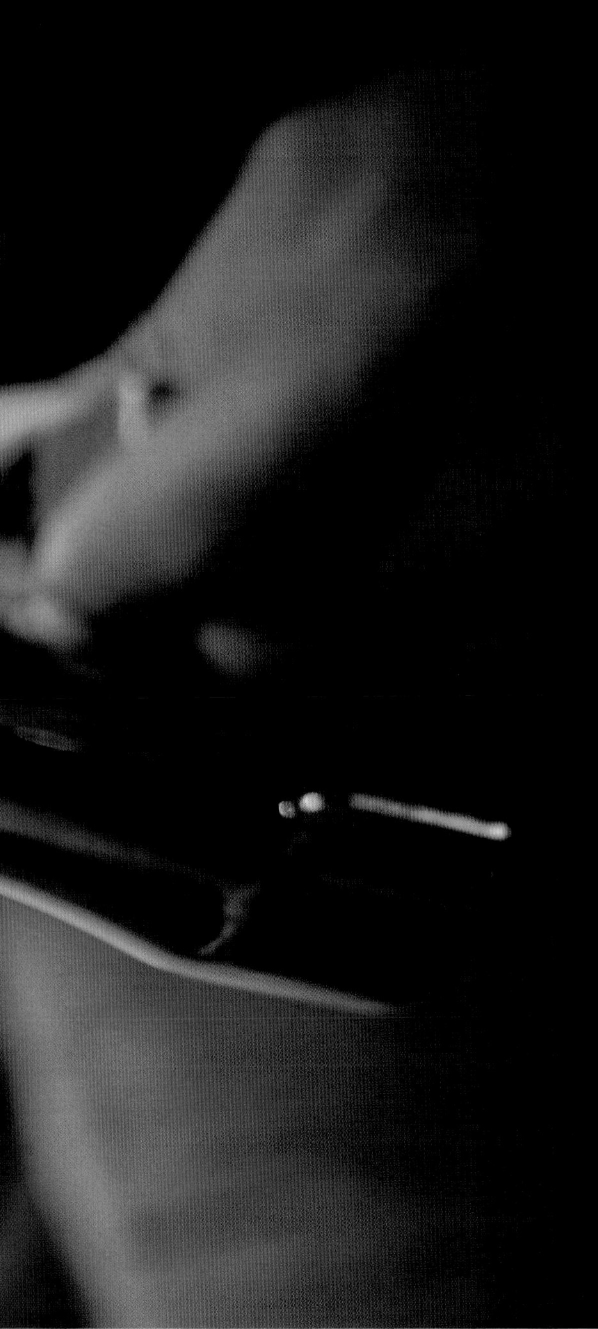

Before coffee there was, well, tea. As denizens of a restless British colony in the 18th century, most American settlers favored pouring boiling water over cured tea leaves to get their caffeine fix.

Then came a revolution. Some say it was the Boston Tea Party in 1773 that led Americans to jettison the drink of their British colonizers in favor of coffee. In a letter to his wife in 1774, future US president John Adams shrilly declared that tea drinking was unpatriotic. From that moment on, the soon-to-be United States was destined to become a nation of coffee drinkers.

When people talk about coffee's 'first wave' they are generally referring to the era of vacuum-packed low-quality instant coffee that peaked in the era of WWII rationing. The favored drink of US servicemen and women, epitomized by brands such as Maxwell House and Folgers, continued to be popular in the 1950s and '60s when consumer commercials sold it as a time-saving device to busy 'housewives.'

Time-saving it may have been, but tasty it wasn't. First-wave coffee, rather like TV dinners and mass-produced beer, was about as nuanced as water. There were no varieties, just brands; no specialist cafes, just diners and restaurants.

Coffee's second wave can be summed up in one word: Starbucks. The global behemoth was founded as a bean-selling operation in Seattle in 1971, but didn't take off nationwide until the early 1980s. Starbucks got much of its inspiration from Italy, where all coffee emanated from the magical espresso machine. Ultimately, Starbucks and its followers didn't just brew coffee, they changed its culture, educating people about the beans, serving it in numerous ways, and infusing it with love, variety and, above all, taste.

The second wave emerged, naturally enough, in the Pacific Northwest, but quickly spread around the US. From now on, every coffee shop that mattered had an espresso machine, a menu of available drinks, and a cozy interior in which to relax and imbibe your favorite concoction.

In the late 1990s, producers had another epiphany. Coffee's third wave endowed the drink with the mythology of wine. In contrast to the macro-tactics of Starbucks, smaller-scale coffee makers went back to the drawing board, analyzing everything from the growing process to the roasting and preparation of coffee in order to wring the best possible flavors from the beans. Three of the earliest proponents of this new approach were Intelligentsia in Chicago, Stumptown in Portland, Oregon, and Counter Culture in Durham, North Carolina, all of whom micro-roasted beans carefully sourced from individual farms.

Today, third-wave coffee and the hip people who make it have spread to urban centers in every corner of the US. Seattle consistently ranks as one of the world's classiest coffee cities, but is closely shadowed by New York, Austin, Portland, Honolulu and Anchorage, Alaska. By the 2010s, half the US populace were coffee aficionados and the person dispatching your 'joe' was no longer a congenial old lady named Beryl in a checkered apron, but a nerdy-looking twentysomething called Gulliver with ironic tattoos.

To read about:
Craft Beer see page 200
Urban Farming see page 306

Willamette Valley Wine Tour

OREGON / WINE

It is remarkable what has been achieved by Oregon's wine producers in the last 50 years. Burgundian expats and Portland hipsters have helped turn the northwest of the USA into a food and wine powerhouse in just a few decades.

MONTINORE ESTATE, OREGON / ANDREA JOHNSON PHOTOGRAPHY ©

Before the 1960s, there was hardly a vineyard to be found in this densely forested state, but today its foremost wine region, the Willamette Valley, is renowned as one of the best places in the world to grow pinot noir. Anyone doubting this claim should talk to one of the numerous Burgundian expats who have enthusiastically established wineries here to produce delicate, elegant reds that bear more than a passing resemblance to the wines of their homeland. White-wine lovers need not worry, as pinot noir is not the only game in town – pinot gris and chardonnay also perform well here, and aromatic whites like riesling and gewürztraminer are getting better with every vintage.

The 6070 hectares (15,000 acres) of vineyards in the Willamette Valley (the vast majority of which are pinot noir) stretch to the south and southwest of the state's largest city, Portland, which serves as an ideal staging post for visits to the region. Portland has a reputation for eccentricity and is rumored to be the birthplace of the hipster, but it is also a vibrant city that offers visitors a dazzling array of great restaurants and places to drink. An abundance of organic produce, artisanal coffee, craft beer and street food are evidence of a foodie culture in which wine plays a leading role, and more than 250 wineries are just a short drive away, making a trip to Oregon the ideal combination of a city break and rural wine-tasting experience.

David Hill

This beautiful estate has more history than most in the Willamette Valley – wine was being made here way back in the late 1800s, long before it was considered a sensible pursuit for an Oregonian. In 1919 Prohibition put paid to all that, though, and it wasn't

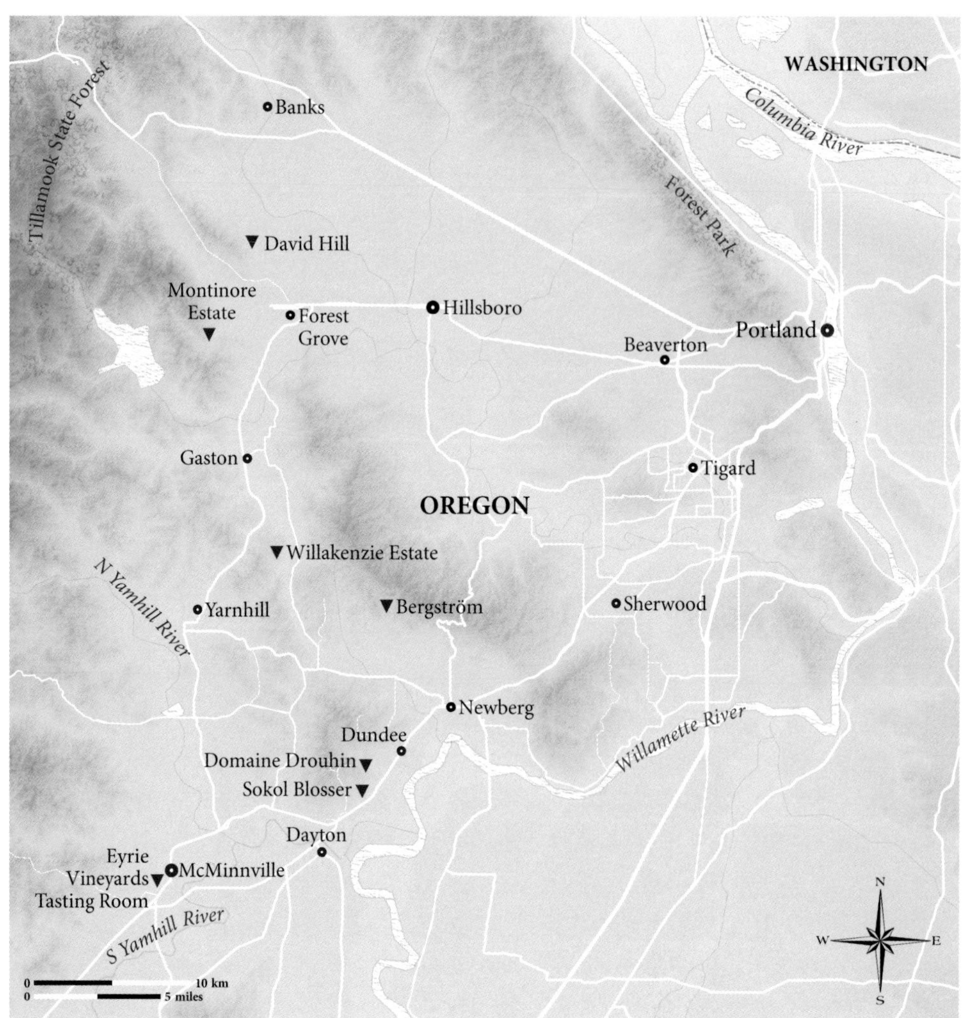

Above **Eyrie Vineyards,** Oregon

Portland Celebrations

A packed calendar of events in Portland includes the Portland Rose Festival (May/June), World Naked Bike Ride (June) and the Adult Soapbox Derby (August). Weekly markets are also important to Portlanders and the best are the Saturday Market and the Farmers Market, which has a weekly program of live music and cooking demonstrations by top chefs.

until the mid-1960s that people started planting vineyards again. When that happened, the place originally known as 'Wine Hill' (the name was later changed to honor the local David family) was one of the first to see grapevines and it continues to thrive to this day, with many of the original vineyards still intact. Pinot noir wines form the bulk of the lineup, but David Hill also produces wines from a range of other varieties and even has some fortified port-style wines. Visiting the winery is worthwhile as much for the stunning views as the wines.

Montinore Estate

Established in 1982, Montinore is a great place to get to grips with what makes the Willamette Valley special. Pinot noir is the most important variety here, as it is throughout the valley, but owner Rudy Marchesi is also very fond of aromatic white wines and their riesling, gewürztraminer and pinot gris are some of the region's best. The estate is Demeter-certified, so anyone interested in seeing the realities of biodynamic agriculture can learn more about this fascinating way of farming; the

Willamette Valley has a remarkably high number of biodynamic practitioners. The tasting room overlooks the estate's 210 acres (85 hectares) of vines and if the weather is good, Montinore is also the perfect place to bring a picnic and spend some time wandering through the vineyards.

Willakenzie Estate
Willakenzie is a splicing together of the names of the Willamette and McKenzie Rivers, which between them are responsible for the distinctive soil type found in this part of the region. The Lacroute family that founded the estate back in 1991 have French roots (Burgundy, naturally) and their belief in the Willamette Valley's terroir (translated into the local parlance as 'dirt matters') prompted them to adopt the practice of making single-vineyard wines from their most interesting parcels of vines. Willakenzie Estate is considered to be one of the foremost players in the drive for quality in the Willamette Valley, and it is also one of the best set up to receive visitors.

Bergström
When many Burgundians were coming over to Oregon to establish wineries, Josh Bergström (son of the founders of Bergström Wines) was heading in the opposite direction. After learning to make wine in pinot noir's spiritual home, Josh returned to the Willamette Valley and has since established a reputation as one of the very best winemakers in the state. He will tell you that the secret is conscientious farming – the 36 acres (15 hectares) of vineyards are organically certified, but Josh also farms biodynamically to ensure the fruit is perfect.

If you want to get to grips with how good Oregon pinot noir can be, this is the place to do it, as everything from their Cumberland Reserve up to the Bergström Vineyard is superb. Josh is a dab hand with chardonnay too, so be sure to taste the whites while you are there. No reservation is required to pop into the charming winery and tasting room for a flight of these benchmark wines.

Domaine Drouhin
The Drouhin family are a big name back in their native Burgundy, so their decision to plant vineyards in the Willamette Valley was critical in legitimizing the idea that Oregon can grow world-class pinot noir. Since they arrived in 1988 many more have followed, but Véronique Drouhin's pinot noirs still set the standard and their Cuvée Laurène is a contender for the state's best wine.

Visitors can swing by the idyllic tasting room and terrace without an appointment to taste a flight of three wines. Those with a bit more time (and some forward planning – a reservation is essential) can take part in the Drouhin Experience, a fascinating tour of the winery that culminates in a comparative tasting of Oregon and Burgundy wines (with cheese).

Sokol Blosser
This family-run winery was established in 1971 by Bill Blosser and Susan Sokol-Blosser, and has always played a pioneering role in the Willamette Valley's wine scene. Sure, it was one of the first wineries in the region, but it was also the first to open a tasting room to welcome visitors, back in 1978, and its innovative range of wines has always kept it at the forefront of the region's wine scene. The customary pinot noir forms the core of the Sokol Blosser range, but there are other varieties available and its Evolution red

and white blends are some of the best-value wines in Oregon.

Guests at the winery are not just in for a sensory treat with the wines – the visitor center itself is an architectural gem. Beautifully designed, with incredible views of their vineyards and the Cascade Mountains, it has tasting flights on offer, a tour of the winery with a flight and nibbles and, in summer, a two-hour educational hike through the estate with (much-needed) wine tastings, followed by food. If there's one winery that you must visit during your trip to Oregon, this is it.

Eyrie Vineyards

In 1965, David Lett was among those planting the first pinot noir cuttings in Oregon, which he did against the advice of every 'expert' in the USA at the time. He followed this by planting the first commercial vineyards of pinot gris in the New World. People thought he was mad, but by the mid-1970s his wines were winning international acclaim and his bravery served as an inspiration for the entire Oregon wine industry. A recent tasting of old Eyrie Vineyards wines was greeted with widespread praise by the critics that were present, proving that this really is a special wine estate. Today Eyrie is run by David's gifted son, Jason Lett, and the wines are as good as ever.

The tasting room for the winery is in downtown McMinnville. These are some of the most age-worthy wines in the New World, so be sure to get a couple of bottles and save them for a special occasion.

To read about:
Pacific Coast Highway in Oregon see page 42
Columbia Valley Wine Trail see page 278

Haunted South: The Spirits of Charleston

SOUTH CAROLINA / PEOPLE & CULTURE

The grand mansions of Charleston – an exceptionally beautiful, walkable city – are a testament to the vast wealth that was generated from the area's rice, indigo and cotton plantations. Generations later, descendants of the slaves who were brought here to make that fortune keep alive many of the traditions and customs of West Africa. Among them are the spiritual beliefs of the Gullah.

Right **Carolyn 'Jabulile' White,** Gullah storyteller, Charleston, South Carolina

Alphonso Brown is a guide of Gullah heritage whose award-winning tours of Charleston focus on the African inheritance of the area. The origin of the word Gullah is uncertain (it might come from Angola), but it has come to refer to a distinct African American culture that belongs to this region, with a very recognizable dialect and traditions. Brown dips into Gullah speech for part of his tour and it's reminiscent of West Indian. He points out other aspects of African culture that have persisted in the area: the cuisine – okra, rice, seafood – and the sweet grass baskets that are being woven by hand and sold on Broad St.

When asked about the work of white folklorist John Bennett, who writes about Gullah ghost stories, Brown shakes his head. In white culture ghosts are a novelty but they are real to the Gullah, a subject too serious to be trifled with. African folklore has penetrated deeply into this region. The low-lying land that arcs along the coast between Charleston and Savannah, 100 miles (161km) to the southwest, is made up of swampy islands, divided by tidal creeks. In these once-remote places, African customs flourished and fused with European superstitions.

Brown warns about the twin threats of haints (ghosts) and hags, the spirits that belong to a shape-changing practitioner of the dark arts. He explains how to survive being 'hag-rid,' that you must find the skin of the hag at midnight and sprinkle salt on it so it shrivels up. Brown's belief echoes superstitions recorded by folklorists more than a century ago when working among the Igbo of Nigeria and the Vai people of Liberia and Sierra Leone.

To further deter hags, brooms and sieves can be left in a corner or on a doorknob; hags compulsively count the bristles and holes, a time-consuming task that can take up all the hours of the night. As an added precaution, window frames and ceilings are painted 'haint blue' – a precise shade of aquamarine that is said to have the dual power of repelling both evil spirits and wasps.

A 15-minute drive away, Gullah storyteller, Carolyn 'Jabulile' White has a bungalow freshly painted in haint blue and a wrought-iron tree hung with blue glass bottles – a traditional method for trapping evil spirits and protecting the home. White lives on James Island, and is a stone's throw from McLeod Plantation, named after owners who arrived from Scotland and grew rich farming cotton – or rather, using slaves who farmed it for them. The gracious white timber home sits next to a row of slave shacks. It seems an unimaginably cruel and distant world, and yet at the time the last McLeod died here, in 1990, descendants of slaves were still renting the shacks on the property for $20 a month.

When planned construction on the island revealed an old African American burial ground, White was one of the first who demanded that building cease. The preliminary dig had disinterred bodies that had been buried with glass beads, tiny bottles and shells. These burial practices connected the African Americans with the West African traditions of their distant homelands. As White explains over a meal of Gullah food – red rice, shrimp and flounder, green beans cooked with bacon – the protests were successful and all further building stopped.

Charleston is also voodoo country, though the degree to which it's practiced is hard to determine. Unlike New Orleans, where the grave of the voodoo priest Marie Laveau is a site of pilgrimage, the subject here is veiled in secrecy. The voodoo practitioners of the Lowcountry are known as root doctors, and the most notorious was a man named Doctor Buzzard. When he died in 1947, he was buried in a secret location, for fear that other people would dig him up and use his remains for casting spells.

To read about:

Alaska Native Celebration see page 114
Rituals of New Orleans see page 178

From the Delta to the DJ: African American Music

USA-WIDE / MUSIC

Shaped over 400 years of triumph and tragedy, African American music is a poignant, powerful reflection of the nation. From the field songs and spirituals that laid the foundation of rock and roll, to the revolutionary verses of visionary MCs, African American music is American music.

Right **Saxophone players**
Far right **Flavor Flav,** Public Enemy

Landing on the shores of America with slaves from Africa, the original African American music came with field chants of workers in the South. Raised in poverty and pain, it has flourished for more than a century, evolving from tarpaper shacks and ramshackle dives into concert halls and the White House. Along the way it shaped the sound of jazz and rock and roll, supplied key strands to the DNA of swing and hip-hop, and penned whole chapters of the Great American Songbook.

The Blues & the Beginning

Unlike the genres it helped create, the blues has preserved its essential spirit for a century. Maybe that's because from its earliest days there's always been purity to the art form: a simple structure that allows anyone who can play three chords on guitar to speak to the depths of the human condition. Both its pioneers and contemporary icons dig this music for its primal appeal: something that just *feels* right, even when its subject is hardship and heartbreak.

Although the cradle of the blues is the Mississippi Delta – where legendary musicians such as Robert Johnson, John Lee Hooker and Muddy Waters shaped the sound – it traveled through the nation with the meandering flow of that mighty river and found distinct regional dialects in Chicago, St Louis and Nashville. Today, all of these cities have at least a few blues clubs that proudly carry on the tradition.

Above **The Supremes,** 1968

Jazz

Forged in the chaotic multicultural melting pot of 1900s New Orleans – a place where European classical music merged with the blues of the American South and Caribbean rhythms – jazz began as a fundamentally African American expression. The music developed in ethnically integrated speakeasies and nightclubs, where musicians from all backgrounds had an opportunity to play together and learn from each other. No wonder it's called 'America's classical music.'

New Orleans was home to geniuses including Louis Armstrong, who created a new improvisatory language, and eventually jazz became a staple of glittering ballrooms and dance floors with the sophisticated compositions and arrangements of Duke Ellington. Taking tunes from popular white songwriters like George and Ira Gershwin and Irving Berlin, African American vocalists including Billie Holiday and Ella Fitzgerald gave jazz its powerful voice.

But jazz as we know it today took its most ambitious creative leaps in the 1940s and '50s, placing improvisation and free expression center stage. Small groups became nimble vehicles for the likes of bebop pioneer and saxophonist Charlie Parker and trumpeter Dizzy Gillespie. Miles Davis continued the mid-century evolution – from his cool-jazz landmark *Kind of Blue* to the rock fusion of *Bitches Brew*. The radical experimentation of John Coltrane in the 1960s took jazz to new heights.

The most active jazz scene in the United States is unquestionably in New York City, a place that draws the best players from around the word. But every major city in the US will have a creative harbor for jazz, such as Los Angeles' Blue Whale or Wally's Café in Boston (the first nightclub in New England to be owned by an African American). One of the most exciting new spots for jazz in the world is San Francisco's SFJAZZ, an acoustically pristine addition to San Francisco's cultural district, with forward-thinking programming and educational programs.

Motown & Soul

It was the heart of the '60s, the eye of a countercultural storm the likes of which the US had never experienced: political assassinations, an unwinnable war halfway around the world and racial unrest in the street. African Americans simultaneously fought for civil rights in the streets and the dominance of the US pop charts (listen closely to Martha and the Vandellas' 'Dancing in the Streets' and you might even hear the clever double entendre). This era was defined by a pair of African American record labels: Detroit's Motown and Memphis' Stax.

These titans of American soul and R&B were like rival sports teams with impeccable rosters – Motown boasted the polished stars Diana Ross and the Supremes, Smokey Robinson, Stevie Wonder and Marvin Gaye. Stax, its grittier Southern rival, had a harder, funkier sound, emblematic in the wail of Otis Redding, Isaac Hayes, Booker T & the MGs and Sam & Dave.

Like every other form of African American music, soul found distinctive variations in cities around the country, with funky offspring in the form of Philadelphia's so-called Philly Soul, which dominated airwaves of the early '70s. With sweeping strings, gleaming horns, and lush arrangements, it laid the smooth groundwork for disco.

Iconic African American Music Landmarks

Preservation Hall, New Orleans In the heart of the city's historic French Quarter, this site is dedicated to preserving the rich traditions of New Orleans' jazz.

Village Vanguard, New York This stage has seen performances by every icon in jazz, including John Coltrane, Elvin Jones and Dizzy Gillespie.

The Blue Note, New York One of the most legendary rooms for jazz in New York, where you can get an intimate view of the city's best talent.

SFJAZZ, San Francisco The nation's new capital for live jazz performance, with a stunning roster of performances and impeccable acoustics.

Blues City Café, Memphis An old-school juke joint that makes the perfect jumping-off point to explore the Mississippi Delta's blues heroes.

Buddy Guy's Legends, Chicago The best place to catch electric blues in the Windy City. The iconic owner sometimes takes the stage.

Bradfordville Blues Club, Tallahassee An authentic juke joint that will transport you back in time to the swampy, soulful heart of Southern Blues.

Stax Museum, Memphis A brilliantly curated small museum with more than 2000 cultural artifacts celebrating the music of Al Green, Isaac Hayes, Otis Redding and Aretha Franklin.

The Hip-Hop Revolution

Although hip-hop seemed like a passing fancy when it rose out of New York City in the late 1970s, it's the most consequential US art form in a generation. In the so-called Golden Age – six magical years between Run-DMC's *Raising Hell* and Dr Dre's *The Chronic* – the movement exploded into a culture-shifting, moneymaking, riot-instigating revolution.

DJs evolved into producers. Sequenced breakbeats gave way to polyphonic textures. Old-school mike-rocking turned to messages of spiritual liberation and political rebellion. Just like that, hip-hop busted out of the inner city and infiltrated the suburbs.

The record industry wanted to cash in, but A&R execs didn't know where to begin, leaving creative decisions to hip-hoppers themselves. The result? Public Enemy's *It Takes a Nation of Millions to Hold Us Back* and NWA's *Straight Outta Compton,* two of many incendiary releases from the late 1980s that gave a voice to an entire generation of poor African American kids who came of age under the nightstick of poverty, racial profiling and police brutality.

Early on, politicians and censors tried to push back but Pandora's box was open: hip-hop became a worldwide phenomenon. In the generations since, the micro-evolutions of hip-hop have come at a blistering pace, evidenced by MC/producers who constantly push the envelope and dominate the pop culture conversation.

To read about:
Music Festivals see page 212
Motown Music see page 302

Right **New York,** 1980

VIDEO
TRANSFER
INC.
XXX RATED
VIDEO
TAPES
WHOLESALE
& RETAIL
ROOM 401
JODEL PHOTO
CORP.
VIDEO TRANSFER INC
HAIRCUT
NEW

Salsa in South Florida

Put on your dancing shoes (with unreasonably high heels) and step out into the hot South Florida salsa scene. Beginners can learn how to tell their cha-cha from their mambo with group lessons. Then, once the band starts playing, it's everyone to the dance floor. There's something intoxicating about the sexy Latin rhythms – or is that just the mojitos talking?

FLORIDA / DANCE

Miami

Ball & Chain Head to Calle Ocho for open-air dancing, tapas and cocktails in Little Havana. After being closed for decades, this 1930s-era jazz club is back, embracing its past with a retro vibe and an outdoor band shell that looks like the inside of a pineapple.

Hoy Como Ayer The dance floor is small (some would say practically nonexistent) at this beloved Cuban hot spot, but you won't mind. The live Latin music is excellent, and it's enhanced by first-rate mojitos.

Salsa Mia Newcomers can get in the groove with nightly salsa lessons in the Mojito Room before heading downstairs to show off their new moves at Mango's Tropical Café in South Beach.

Club Tipico Dominicano Come for the food, stay for the dancing. Located in the Arts District, this authentic Dominican restaurant serves up salsa, bachata and merengue.

Salsa Fever at Yuca Lounge On Wednesday and Friday nights, Yuca lets you brush up on your salsa skills with lessons in a stylish Miami Beach setting. Or pony up for private lessons so you can groove with the best of them.

Tampa

Ceviche Tapas Bar and Restaurant Tapas, sangria and flamenco shows are all excellent reasons to come. And on Saturday nights you can shake it to live bands playing Latin jazz, salsa and Afro-Cuban music until the wee hours.

Amorama Latin Nightclub Head to nearby Clearwater for a Latin-music mash-up of salsa, barchata and merengue, and learn some new moves with classes from Simone Salsa Dance.

Hyde Park Café Friday nights at HPC are a staple of Tampa's Latin music scene. Head to its Velociti Bar, which is usually packed with dancers fueled by HPC's late-night happy hour.

Salsa Caliente Dance Studio Learn how to salsa from the pros with private lessons or drop-in classes on Monday nights.

Orlando

Mango's Tropical Café This over-the-top venue features Latin dancers who perform during dinner. Or you can just head straight to one of its eight bars and shake your booty to Latin tunes until late into the night.

Cuba Libre It's a restaurant by day, but on Friday and Saturday nights Cuba Libre turns into a Latin nightclub with merengue, salsa and bachata music until 2am.

Salsa Latina The space itself may be a little dated, but who cares when you're feeling the music? It's all salsa all the time at Salsa Latina, in the Orlando suburb of Kissimmee.

Salsa Heat It's not just the dance lessons that you'll love; this dance studio also hosts 'salsa socials' for practicing your moves in a low-pressure setting.

To read about:
Southern Border Towns see page 150
Music Festivals see page 212

Greek Town, USA

FLORIDA / FOOD & CULTURE

Experience a taste of Greece without leaving the US in Tarpon Springs, the closest thing to the Greek Islands in North America. The sponge industry drew Greek immigrants to this small town on Florida's Gulf Coast in the early 20th century, bringing families, food and culture with them. Thanks to this unique history, visitors will find some of the best eating in the state and an all-American dose of kitsch.

Right **Tarpon Springs,** Florida

Boom towns that draw immigrant populations aren't uncommon in the USA, but the tale of Tarpon Springs is one of the most colorful. In 1891, businessman John Cheyney noticed that sponges were being hauled up along with the fish in local fishing nets. Aware that the sponge industry was a major money-maker in Key West, Cheyney seized the business opportunity and started a sponge company in Tarpon Springs.

At the time, sponge harvesting in the US was done by hooking sponges up out of shallow water with a long, trident-like fork. But Greek immigrant John Cocoris, who teamed up with Cheyney in 1896, knew there was a better way. Sponge-divers in Greece had gone beyond scooping up sponges and were instead diving to harvest them, using metal helmets and rubberized suits not yet popular in the USA. Within a decade, Cocoris had recruited hundreds of Greeks from the Dodecanese Islands to use their talents – and superior equipment – to snatch sponges from the ocean floor.

Sponges have been harvested for hundreds of uses over thousands of years. Though they look like plants, they're actually animals, and draw nutrients from plankton and other organisms in the water. Young sponges often roll across the ocean floor like tumbleweeds, but once mature they are stationary, attached to pieces of rock or coral. Like earthworms, sponges have amazing regenerative powers: it's possible for even a broken piece of sponge to anchor itself and rebuild. Experienced divers slice the sponge free at least an inch from the base, leaving enough for regrowth – when an area is harvested properly, sponge density will increase.

As the sponge market boomed, more and more Greeks arrived in Tarpon Springs, both to dive and to support the growing industry, working to wash, dry, trim and sort sponges or to construct boats and diving equipment. By the 1920s, the city was known as the 'Sponge Capital of the World' and was raking in some $3 million in profits.

Though the industry suffered setbacks – an algae blight that decimated the sponge beds in the 1940s; competition from synthetic sponges – and is nowhere near the economic powerhouse it was in the early 20th century, Tarpon Springs is still a main player in the national sponge market.

Greek Life in Tarpon Springs

Just like the sponge industry, Greek culture is alive and well in Tarpon Springs. The town still boasts the highest percentage of Greek Americans in the United States and thanks to this cultural inheritance, the city has some of the best eating in the region. You'll find the expected Greek imports, like savory gyros wrapped in soft, homemade pita; rich moussaka with eggplant buried under layers of creamy sauce; and crunchy spanakopita. But the community's history also results in delectable Greek-American hybrids, like the creamy baklava cheesecake served up at Hellas Restaurant and Bakery.

It's not unusual to see women in headscarves mounting the steps of St Nicholas Greek Orthodox Cathedral, a 1907 landmark with a neo-Byzantine exterior inspired by Istanbul's St Sophia Cathedral. The 60-ton marble altar, a gift from Greece, is a highlight, and was part of an exhibition at the first New York State World's Fair in 1939.

Visitors to Tarpon Springs could stumble upon a Greek celebration year-round, but the most famous imported cultural ritual in Tarpon Springs is Epiphany, the Greek Orthodox celebration of Jesus' baptism. Every year on January 6, the city puts on a day-long celebration to rival any found in Greece. The event begins with services at 8am and climaxes with the Casting of the Cross. Dressed in his black robes and hat, the Archbishop stands on a dock and tosses a weighted wooden cross into the bay. Hundreds of teenage boys dive in pursuit of it, a tumult of kicking legs and jabbing elbows. The boy who claims the prize has the honor of returning the cross to the Archbishop and receiving a special blessing. After the Casting, there's an evening of song, dance and food for the community.

Above Sponge diver, Tarpon Springs

Tarpon Springs Today

Visitors can explore the community's unique history and watch the sponge harvest unfold before their eyes on the city's bustling docks or at the weekly sponge market. Boats laden with sponges arrive at the docks every day, and the divers sort and unload their hauls. It's very much a working city, so unlike many other waterfront areas on the Florida coast, Tarpon Springs is no slick, glossed-up theme park. It's more like a county fair, with vintage signage and cozy restaurants that are authentically mid-century.

The city's main commercial drag, Dodecanese Blvd, contains kitschy attractions such as the aptly named Spongeorama, a hybrid shop and museum. Up front, there are sponges of every shape and size alongside loofahs, jewelry and plenty of gaudy Greek- and Florida-inspired souvenirs. In the back, you can catch a very vintage 1950s film promoting the sponge industry, complete with an advertising jingle.

Not far from the sponge docks lies Greek Village, full of modest wooden houses and sponge-packing and -sorting buildings built by the city's original Greek immigrants. No surprise, many of these buildings are painted white, like the island homes their inhabitants left across the sea. The leafy streets along the bayou are lined with Victorian homes built by the wealthy Northerners who used to winter here – strolling by them is a pleasant way to spend the afternoon.

In a time when many cities are beginning to feel more and more alike, Tarpon Springs is refreshingly different. An unusual history, fascinating culture and natural beauty combine to make it an off-the-beaten-path delight.

The Master Helmet Maker

Once the Greeks arrived in Tarpon Springs, the industry soon found itself short of equipment for the growing community of divers. Enter Anthony Lerios, a 21-year-old machinist from Kalymnos who arrived in 1913. Lerios set to work making compressors, helmets, shoulderplates and more for the dive crews, using cast-iron molds and hand-made tools.

Though this equipment was sophisticated for the time, it looks a bit dated now – think the sort of dive helmet a villain on *Scooby Doo* would have pried off at the end of the show. Still, making one requires an astonishing level of craft. Each helmet is constructed of copper sheets, takes 150 hours to make and weighs more than 30lb (14kg). Every single piece, down to the bolts that hold it together, is made by hand.

Lerios continued to work until his late 80s, and passed the trade down to his grandson Nicholas Toth, before dying in 1992 at the age of 100. Toth is now considered the last practitioner of this 200-year-old art.

To read about:
World on a Plate in LA see page 88
Salsa in South Florida see page 170

Where to Find the Best Chinatowns

Visiting Chinese temples, shopping for embroidered silk goods, following a parade of dancing dragons – wait, where are we again? Many of the major cities in the United States are home to vibrant Chinatowns, which means you don't have to travel far to spend an afternoon immersed in a completely different culture.

USA-WIDE / FOOD & CULTURE

In the mid-1800s, an influx of Chinese immigrants began to arrive in the United States, fueled by tales of the California Gold Rush and the promise of jobs on the Transcontinental Railroad. They formed tight-knit communities where they lived and worked, allowing them to retain their cultural identities even while living in a new country.

While many Chinatowns have succumbed to gentrification, there are still thriving enclaves that offer you a glimpse into another culture. Chinese lanterns line the street, the clack of mahjong tiles fills the air, and the smell of roast duck wafts up to the pagoda-style rooftops.

San Francisco

Established in the 1840s, San Francisco's Chinatown is the oldest in the country. With its welcoming Gateway Arch in the middle of downtown, souvenir shopping and authentic cuisine draw visitors year-round, but the massive Chinese New Year Parade is one of the best times to visit. Learn more about the neighborhood with one of the fascinating Chinatown Alleyway Tours.

New York

With the largest Chinese population outside of Asia, the boroughs of New York City boast not one but six different Chinatowns. Manhattan's is the most famous, with noodle shops, teahouses and souvenir stores lining more than 40 square blocks. Visit the Museum of Chinese in America to learn more about the area's history.

Los Angeles

This is a relatively new Chinatown, built in the 1930s after the old one was razed to make way for Union Station. In true LA style, the east dragon gates are outlined in neon for a little Hollywood glamour, and the Broadway dragon gates have a dramatic, modern flair.

Boston

The third-largest Chinatown in the United States, Boston's was established in 1890 and is the only one remaining in New England. Lion statues guard the gate, welcoming visitors to events like the Lion Dance Festival and the August Moon Festival.

Chicago

Established in 1905, Chicago's Chinatown is about 20 minutes outside of downtown. Find a tour at the Chicago Chinese Cultural Institute, or visit the Chinese-American Museum of Chicago.

Washington, DC

Once home to a large number of Chinese immigrants, DC's Chinatown now occupies only a few square blocks. But it's worth checking out the Friendship Archway, the largest single-span arch in the world, sporting seven roofs and 272 painted dragons.

Seattle

Experience a diverse blend of Chinese, Filipino, Japanese and Vietnamese culture in the Chinatown-International District — aka the 'ID.' Don't miss the Wing Luke Museum of the Asian Pacific American Experience.

To read about:

Los Angeles see page 84
New York see page 182

Top left **Chinese New Year Parade,** San Francisco; Top right **Boston's Chinatown,** 1986; Bottom left **Chinatown,** Manhattan, New York City; Bottom right **Lanterns in Chinatown,** Los Angeles

PEKING CUISINE
SZECHUAN & MANDARIN

LI HING INC.
ARTS ANTIQUE
CHEUNG COMPANY

Rituals of New Orleans

With a festival or a parade every week of the year, no other place in the USA demonstrates such an unquenchable thirst for the sweet nectar of life. The celebrations and rituals of New Orleans are as much about history as hedonism, and every dance is as much an expression of tradition and community spirit as it is of joy.

NEW ORLEANS / FESTIVALS & CULTURE

New Orleans has always been a place for exiles and seekers: French aristocrats and Canadian frontiersfolk, Haitian slave owners and African slaves, American explorers, Spanish merchants and Jewish refugees. Each group brought their own traditions to bear on the most vibrant and idiosyncratic city in the USA. But no matter how strong those traditions may have been back in the old country, nothing stays unchanged in this white-hot melting pot at the mouth of the Mississippi. The same is true of the people. Together, they came to be classified as Creoles – a racial, religious, transnational, linguistic mix of folks who forged a unique identity, a sum of many parts that formed a greater whole.

Mardi Gras

No event encapsulates New Orleans like Mardi Gras. It's more than a wild party: it contains every thread of the colorful, complicated New Orleans tapestry. One of the event's most exciting traditions is the parading Mardi Gras Indians. All feathers and finery, you know that the party is reaching its peak when they come dancing and chanting down the street surrounded by their followers.

The Mardi Gras Indians are African American men who sew strikingly original, outrageously colorful 'suits' and parade in their 'tribes' on Fat Tuesday, Mardi Gras's climax. The tradition dates back to the late 19th century and is thought to reflect the kinship of recently freed African slaves and Native Americans. For decades the Indians were an underground movement who often fought pitched battles (tribe on tribe) on the street. But in recent decades several of the Mardi Gras Indian tribes (the Wild Tchoupitoulas, the Wild Magnolias) have embraced the wider world, making seminal albums and becoming a popular part of New Orleans folklore.

Also taking to the streets on Fat Tuesday is the Zulu Parade, when black New Orleans comes out to strut and celebrate. This parade starts early – be up and out by 8am to catch it – and moves across the central city. It's a feast of brass bands, elaborate floats and huge fun, with 'krewes' tossing beads and gifts to the throngs who line the streets. (Try and catch a painted coconut – exclusive to Zulu!)

The whole celebration precedes the Catholic celebration of Lent: Louisiana was first a Spanish and then a French colony (until 1803). The French allowed their slaves a degree of freedom to dance and perform music, providing the foundations for New Orleans as a hotbed of music-making. These days, Fat Tuesday's party is about witnessing a city that's survived hard times get up and shake its tail feathers.

Jazz Funerals & Second Line

In a place that so richly celebrates life, the festivities don't end with death. The tradition of jazz funerals began in the 19th century, when Social Aid & Pleasure (or S&P) Clubs collected annual dues to cover funeral arrangements for their members – which, for an additional fee, might include a brass band. The musical funeral tradition continues today. During the procession, musicians, family and friends of the deceased walk in the Main Line, while the crowd that marches behind is collectively known as the Second Line. At

the beginning of the procession, the band plays wilting dirges. After the body is laid to rest, the party begins.

Second Line parades have taken on a life of their own, and today they are more common than the jazz funerals. S&P members deck themselves out in flash suits, hats and shoes and carry decorated umbrellas and fans. This snazzy crowd, accompanied by a hired band, marches through the city pumping music and 'steppin' – engaging in a kind of syncopated marching dance that looks like a soldier in formation overcome by an uncontrollable need to groove. Hundreds, sometimes thousands, of people dance in the Second Line, stopping for drinks and food along the parade route.

Voodoo

Although it gets overhyped with sensationalistic clichés, voodoo is a religious practice that's woven deep into New Orleans culture. Voodoo stresses ancestor worship and the presence of the divine via a pantheon of spirits and deities. Slaves from Africa and the Caribbean brought voodoo to Louisiana, where it melded with Roman Catholicism. One faith stressed saints and angels, the other ancestor spirits and supernatural forces; all came under the rubric of voodoo. Voodoo became wildly popular in New Orleans after it was introduced by black émigrés from Saint-Domingue (now Haiti) at the beginning of the 19th century.

One of its most famous practitioners is now-legendary 19th-century voodoo queen Marie Laveau, who gained fame and fortune by shrewdly exploiting voodoo's mystique. Though details of her life are shrouded in myth and misconception, what has been passed down from generation to generation makes for a fascinating story.

Laveau was born in 1794, a French-speaking Catholic of mixed black and white ancestry. Invariably described as beautiful and charismatic, at age 25 she married a man named Paris. He died a few years later, and Laveau became known as the Widow Paris. She had 15 children with another man, Glapion, who is believed to have migrated from Saint-Domingue, and may have been Laveau's first connection to voodoo.

In the 1830s Laveau established herself as the city's preeminent voodoo queen, and her influence crossed racial lines. Mostly she reeled in stray husbands and helped people avenge wrongs done to them. According to legend, she earned her house on St Anne St as payment for ensuring a young man's acquittal in a rape or murder trial.

Laveau apparently had some tricks up her sleeve. She is said to have worked as a hairdresser in the homes of upper-class white women, and it was not uncommon for these women to share local society gossip while having their hair done. At the peak of her reign as voodoo queen, she

Above **Mardi Gras,** New Orleans

Above **Anthony Dopsie and Rockin' Dopsie Jr,** New Orleans Jazz & Heritage Festival

Zydeco: The Music of New Orleans

New Orleans has birthed more musical movements than you can count, but one of the city's signature sounds is zydeco. The ensembles that play it originally comprised a fiddle, diatonic button accordion, guitar and triangle (the metal percussion instrument common to symphony orchestras and kindergarten music classes); the rhythm section usually included a *frottoir,* a metal washboard-like instrument that's worn like armor and played with spoons. The result is a genre of music that is made for dance accompaniment, and one that, like the city itself, pulses with energy.

employed an entire network of spies, most household servants in upper-class homes.

Her supposed grave is among the massive labyrinth of mausoleums at St Louis Cemetary No 1, scratched with 'XXX's from spellbound devotees. Debates over *which* Marie Laveau – mother or daughter, if either – was actually buried here will never be resolved.

To read about:
Driving the Great River Road see page 52
African American Music see page 164

NEW YORK CITY

The Big Apple

If you were going to show aliens the best example of human ingenuity and achievement on Earth, New York City would be a good place to start. Welcome to the glittering metropolis that gifted the world with bebop, hip-hop, the Village Voice, Rhapsody in Blue, eggs Benedict, the Yankees, toilet paper, air-conditioning, the Ramones, and a zillion other trends, adaptations and inventive people.

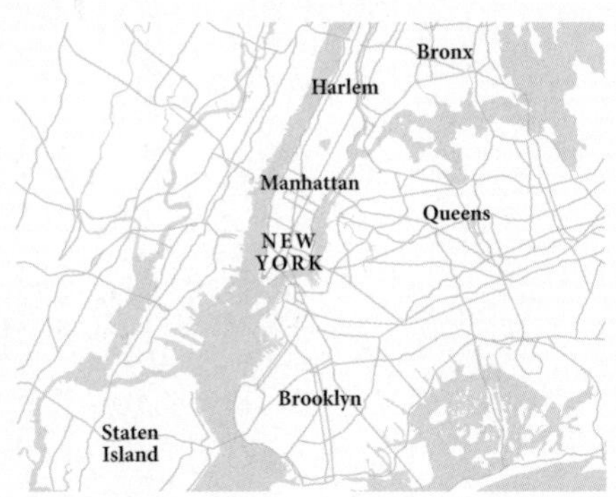

Whoever you are and wherever you're from, it's impossible not to be swept up by the beauty and romance of NYC. From Broadway to Central Park, to the Empire State Building, to the Brooklyn Bridge at sunset, everywhere seems to resound with a comforting familiarity, an eerie sense that you may have been here before, if not in person, then in a song, a movie, a play, or some other colorful apparition of the American Dream.

But, behind the glitzy trimmings, New York is more than just a city. It is a federation of neighborhoods, a beacon of tolerance, and a bastion of diversity sautéed over four centuries in a giant melting pot that stretches from the Bronx, through Manhattan, Brooklyn and Queens, to Staten Island. America's immigrant story was born and nurtured here, the dreams of millions made reality by their first glimpse of the Statue of Liberty or the bustling intensity of Ellis Island.

NYC's early immigrants went on to found their own neighborhoods and cement their individual legacies in Chinatown, Little Italy and Spanish Harlem. And thus began an ongoing story of assimilation and reinvention that still reflects New York's defining magic. Today the city is less a traditional metropolis and more a microcosm of world culture, a global map redrawn across five boroughs replete with dozens of subneighborhoods. There's Le Petit Senegal in Harlem, Little Guyana in Queens, Little Poland in Brooklyn, Little Puerto Rico in the Bronx, and many more.

By the early 21st century, 37% of New York City's population was foreign-born and the metropolis echoed to the sound of an estimated 800 languages, making it the most linguistically diverse city in the world. Annual parades evoke Irish, Chinese and Jewish traditions. Restaurants meld exotic foods into fusion cuisine. Yet bubbling underneath it all is a unifying force which sooner or later all new arrivals feel bound to embrace. That dynamic blend of fast-talking, ambitious, energetic, sometimes abrasive New Yorkness captured, sculpted and refined in the USA's self-proclaimed 'Big Apple.'

IMES SQUARE
FOX UFC
SAT. DEC. 14
XINHUA NEWS AGENCY
SAMSUNG
VISIT US INSIDE ON THE 3RD LEVEL
aerie
NYPD POLICE

TWO SIDES OF NEW YORK CITY

NEW YORK CITY / PEOPLE

New Yorkers divide into tribes delineated by a shared outlook on life, their group identities reinforced by the places they hang out, eat and party. Smart Upper East Siders are preoccupied by the next big society gala while nearby Harlem hums to a jazzier vibe. To understand its tribes is to know New York like a true local.

Right **Ginny's Supper Club,** Harlem, New York City

The Entertainers of Harlem

Making it in New York City is an increasingly unrealistic aim for New York musicians, with so many priced out by gentrification or creatively stifled by their need to make the rent. But Harlem still nourishes much of the city's talent. Harlem's tribe of musicians move to the rhythm of the open-mike night. Clothing is understated, but jazz musicians of a certain age exude the classiness of the era of their craft's birth. Their shined shoes and dark suits stand out in a city where torn jeans rule. Fedoras are worn without a trace of hipster irony.

Keeping that legacy vital today is the Studio Museum, a unique institution dedicated to advancing artists of African descent. Many musicians hope to score one of its three coveted artist-in-residence slots. Visitors to the modern, angular building are drawn into the ever-changing exhibitions, often of kaleidoscopic, color-saturated art that draws its palate from tribal textiles and African heritage.

Jazz is often cited as the only true American art form, and its inventors were of African descent – a heritage celebrated at Malcolm Shabazz Harlem Market. Named after civil rights leader Malcolm X, this covered craft market sells handicrafts and textiles from across Africa; at other stalls women offer hair braiding, surrounded by bottles of aromatic oils. You won't find the exquisite saxophones, trumpets and upright basses of the Harlem music scene here, but there is a brisk trade in rawhide African drums, a far simpler instrument on which to tap out your own jazz beat.

The Upper East Side Society Set

There is a timelessness to the Upper East Side, and to the well-heeled New Yorkers who live there. They live in apartments atop venerable pre-war buildings, tended to by a battalion of top-hatted doormen. Chanel suits beneath pearl chokers may as well be a uniform for the women here, and their sport is the city's charity gala circuit. Sitting on a museum or charity board is particularly prestigious for members of this old-world community of old money.

The circuit's rhythms, tri-weekly fêtes and endless planning meetings are strictly adhered to – as are its costumes. Repeating a gown is a faux pas, but the moneyed set are not needlessly profligate. Michael's, a second-storey consignment shop on Madison Avenue, is an open secret. A buzzer admits patrons to a room of racks, unassuming beneath fluorescent bulbs. Tug at a splash of azure crushed between black gowns, and you might find a Carolina Hererra or Dolce & Gabbana dress straight from a red carpet, the city's couture cast-offs.

After nearly every gala, you'll see the set in their rumpled tuxes and gowns heading to the Carlyle Hotel to finish the night at Bemelmans Bar. Straight-backed waiters shake martinis, each drink served with a tiny carafe for refills, sitting on a bed of chipped ice. A house band plays standards (sometimes Woody Allen stops by with his clarinet) at the center of the room, and murals ensconce listening drinkers. Inside, the tinkling of piano cutting through the blue dark, it's as if time has stopped – just the way Upper East Siders like it.

To read about:
Luxury Shopping Experiences see page 50
African American Music see page 164

Above **The Frick Collection,** Upper East Side, New York City

CYCLING THE MANHATTAN WATERFRONT GREENWAY

NEW YORK CITY / CYCLING

An epic ride of America's most famed city that leaves behind the crowds to reveal waterside glimpses of hidden New York.

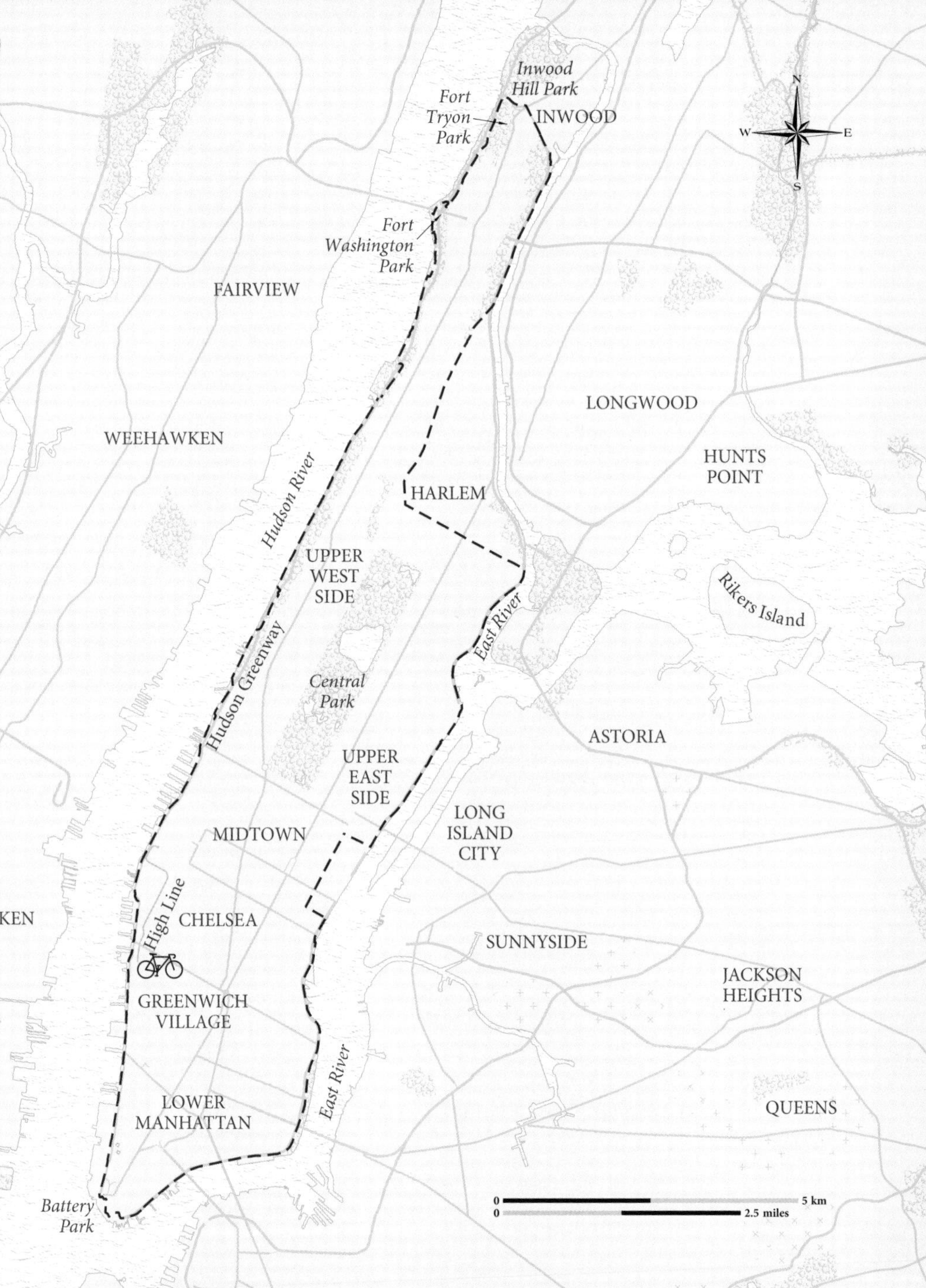

The bicycle renaissance is thriving in New York, a surprisingly rewarding cycling city. New York's bike friendliness extends from Central Park's wide-open boulevards, which are closed to cars for much of daylight hours, to an ever-increasing network of bike lanes crisscrossing iconic landmarks, to exhilarating bridge crossings. Few visitors to the city make their way beyond the far end of the Brooklyn Bridge, which is a shame because there is more fun to be had on two wheels by going further.

The jewel in the crown of New York cycling is the Manhattan Waterfront Greenway. This path snakes its way around almost the entirety of Manhattan Island, rolling for 31 glorious miles (50km), allowing cyclists to venture beyond the known city into places where tourists don't stray.

As with any circular ride, there's no 'right' way to go, but the prevailing view seems to be to head up the west side to the far north of the island, then back down the east side and complete the loop via the southern tip of the city.

Hit the Hudson bike path just south of the High Line, and your perception of the city might change. The endless blocks of busy streets stuffed with pedestrians, cars and honking taxis that make up the New York of the imagination are replaced by the broad Hudson River. A human scale emerges. Suddenly away from the noise of the city, you'll hear the grind of your wheels on the tarmac path, and the gentle yet firm calls to attention from runners overtaking pedestrians. These warnings became more shrill and direct as you approach the cruise terminal, with scores of bemused new arrivals blocking the recreational route of speeding locals – an instant reminder that you're still in boisterous New York.

This section is the Hudson Greenway. From here, landmarks of northward progression – in particular Central Park – roll past without notice but there are signs you are leaving Midtown: the drop in the height of buildings, the thinning out of fellow travelers. Fort Washington Park, marked by the Washington Bridge and the Little Red Lighthouse, are a signpost that you're leaving known areas behind. You might even experience feelings of solitude while moving around the world's most famous city.

Fort Tryon Park is home to one of the city's most marvelous oddities: The Cloisters. This annex of the Metropolitan Museum of Art is an ideal stop, as much for the remarkable merging of five medieval abbeys into one whole, as for the works of art inside. Beyond here, shortly before Manhattan stops, cyclists dip inland through Inwood Hill, emerging on the east side of Manhattan for the first time, on a path running along the Harlem Greenway. This was originally a horse-racing strip for weekending Manhattanites from which cyclists, ironically, were banned. Today a bike path follows it south until another detour takes you on a signed path through Harlem.

Beyond a small diversion around the United Nations complex between 54th and 37th Sts, the Greenway then trundles happily down to Battery Park. South of the Williamsburg Bridge it starts to pick up more cyclists. This is where you can add a few additional miles by crossing the Manhattan Bridge (racing subway trains crossing the water) and returning via the busy but exhilarating Brooklyn Bridge bike and pedestrian path.

Once you've cleared the crowds at Battery Park, it's a short pull back up the Hudson to complete the loop. Now you have a choice: return the bike or save it for another great ride that demonstrates the continued growth of cycling in New York. One such trail is the Brooklyn-Queens Greenway, a 40-mile (64km) route from Little Bay Park in Queens to Coney Island, linking such attractions as New York Aquarium, Brooklyn Museum and Brooklyn Botanic Garden.

The New York City Bike Map (www.nyc.gov/bikemaps) has details on cycle routes across Manhattan and beyond. A print copy is most useful and can be picked up in bike shops and tourist offices.

To read about:
Cycling in Vermont see page 264
Sausalito Cycling see page 270

Above **Brooklyn Bridge,** New York City

OPEN-MIKE SLAM POETRY

NEW YORK CITY / ARTS & ENTERTAINMENT

Now approaching 50 years in the Lower East Side, the cultural institution that is the Nuyorican Poets Café has been home to groundbreaking works of poetry, music, theater and visual arts for multiple generations.

Right **Nuyorican Poets Café,** New York City

Inhabiting an unassuming tenement in Manhattan's booming Lower East Side, the Nuyorican has been serving up slam poetry for nearly 30 years – almost since the format's creation in 1986. Joining the Wednesday-night queue snaking down 3rd St for its legendary open-mike slam events should be top of the list for any traveler spending a few days in NYC.

As you file into the cozy bar, your eyes are drawn to the solitary mike stand on the stage, naked in the spotlight's glare. If that makes you want to jump up and share your gift with the world, now's your chance – add your name to the list and prepare to be judged by your peers. The reward: a chance to take part in the following Friday night's invitational slam. Otherwise, take a seat in the shadows and settle in as the contestants each deliver their 3 minutes 20 seconds of dopeness.

The quality of performances on open-mike Wednesdays vary dramatically, from first-timers whose nerves might just get the better of them to accomplished lyricists with as much stage presence as you might expect to find a few blocks over on Broadway. If you want to avoid second-guessing each participant as they walk to the stage, choose the Friday night invitational slams instead. These events see 'Spotlight Poets,' invited by the SlamMaster, perform along with winners from Wednesday night's open-mike event, who face off for a chance, eventually, to join the Nuyo Slam Team and compete on the national stage.

The Nuyorican began life providing a home and outlet for marginalized poets in the early '70s, when it was founded by a group of writers and artists predominantly from minority backgrounds, struggling to find acceptance for their work in the mainstream publishing, academic and entertainment industries. Over the subsequent decades it has become part of the fabric of Alphabet City, and now as a nonprofit organization it plays a crucial role in supporting underprivileged artists, delivering educational programs and providing a performance space for just about anyone who's keen to take to the stage.

Although all manner of art forms are supported at the Nuyorican (its first showing of a full-length opera, *Carmen*, was staged in 2015), its most regular slots are still largely given to performances of jazz, hip-hop and, of course, poetry. Nowhere else in the world does spoken word performance quite like the US, and the Nuyorican's name has been synonymous with slam poetry since it hosted New York's first ever slam in the late 1980s. So get a ticket and treat yourself to a night of in-your-face, foot-tappin', finger-clickin' lyrical beats.

To read about:
Improv in Chicago see page 206
Mark Twain's USA see page 232

NEW YORK'S JEWISH CUISINE: NEW TAKES ON OLD COUNTRY

NEW YORK CITY / FOOD & CULTURE

Brought to the Big Apple by Eastern European Jews, what was once a cuisine for poor Lower East Side immigrants has been revitalized by a new generation of New York chefs.

A visit to New York's metropolitan melting pot is always epic, thanks to the more than 8 million diverse people who live, create and dine exceptionally here. When it comes to food, the city offers no shortage of adventures, but New Yorkers reserve a special place in their hearts for the soul-satisfying flavors of the city's Jewish cuisine.

Between 1880 and 1920, more than a million Eastern European Jews immigrated to New York's Lower East Side – a staggering addition to an already overcrowded neighborhood. Impoverished though they were, generations of Jewish mamas toiling in tenement kitchens turned out schmaltz-glistening staples while urging their children to *'esn, esn!'* ('eat, eat!'). On the streets, pushcarts peddled pickles, bagels and loaves of impossibly dark rye bread. And local Jewish butchers and fishmongers helped to introduce the joys of smoked meat and cured fish to the city.

Over the decades the community spread, leaving a trail of iconic delicatessens and bakeries in its wake, and mingled with other communities, resulting in some Jewish-hybrid celebrations likely impossible anywhere else in the world. The Egg Rolls, Egg Creams & Empanadas Festival brings the Lower East Side's Jewish, Chinese and Puerto Rican cultures together every June for a block party complete with live music and the festival's namesake foods. Meanwhile, the western hemisphere's only Jewish-Greek synagogue, Kehila Kedosha Janina, hosts the Greek Jewish Festival each May, with pastries, live music, dancing and crafts.

In recent years, a new crop of young Jewish restaurateurs (sometimes known as 'Heebsters') has taken up the reins. Inspired equally by their culinary heritage and the global food scene, they are revitalizing timeworn Jewish classics for a new generation. From their commitment to their craft and to sourcing quality ingredients to their whimsical remixing of flavors – for example, challah bread pudding and smoked-meat-topped eggs Benedict – their food exemplifies the reverential yet playful approach that makes 'eating Jewish' in New York so exciting.

For the best innovative Jewish cuisine, head to the following places.

Russ & Daughters: You can start the morning the traditional Jewish way, with a bagel topped with paper-thin slices of belly lox (salmon cured with salt) and a slick of cream cheese. Or take on the cheekily named 'Super Heebster' bagel, topped with whitefish and baked salmon salad, wasabi-infused fish roe and horseradish dill cream cheese.

Breads Bakery: Opened by Israel-born baker Uri Scheft in 2013, Breads Bakery is already an institution. Its pièce de résistance is babka made with laminated dough and swirled with a combination of Nutella and chocolate chips – a buttery revelation.

Brooklyn Farmacy: You'll find handcrafted sundaes and floats aplenty in this 1920s-era apothecary shop, but the menu's true highlight is the egg cream, a cocktail of milk, chocolate syrup and seltzer water first served on the Lower East Side in 1890.

To read about:
Greek Food in Tarpon Springs see page 172
Farm-to-Table Cooking see page 194

Innovation & Creation

World-Famous Arts, Music & Culture

The USA has long been a hotbed for inventive types. After all, this is the land that gave humanity the toilet paper roll (1871), electric guitar (1937) and high-five machine (1993) among the eight million patents it has issued since 1790.

Local visionaries come in many forms. Georgia O'Keeffe painted like no other. Her New Mexico landscapes of red hills, black mesas and white cow skulls are famed around the globe – as is the lesson she taught that women could equal men in the art world. Mark Twain wrote stories using humor and everyday language, peculiar traits that opened the door to modern literature. And all hail the bearded dudes in the Pacific Northwest who envisioned a more flavorful ale. They grew wild hops and brewed them into unorthodox, mouth-walloping suds, and thus launched the craft beer movement.

Architect Frank Lloyd Wright turned architecture on its head when he dismissed frilly ornamentation in favor of organic shapes and natural materials. He used the surrounding landscape as part of the design, and it was an international game changer. Rock music is a US creation whose influence has spread far and wide, especially when it comes to glittery festival culture. Plus who'd have thought artists with the bright idea to paint soup cans and comic-book scenes would become global sensations, like Andy Warhol and his fellow pop art pals?

Speaking of comic books, you can thank the USA for those, too. Superman, Batman and Wonder Woman morphed from cartoony pages starting from the 1930s and captivated legions of readers. The characters are still around, in movies and in person at events such as Comic-Con, where it's perfectly acceptable to dress in a superhero costume and hobnob with others doing the same.

You're welcome, world.

Farm-to-Table: A Taste of Place

USA-WIDE / FOOD & CULTURE

Once upon a time, dining out meant sitting politely in high-backed chairs through an assault of tiny yet intimidating dishes, smothered in mysterious foam and crowned with endangered fish eggs and meticulously tweezered gold leaf. Then farm-to-table foodies came along, and yanked the tablecloth right out from under the ostentatious fine-dining scene. These rebels have reminded us of a forgotten truth: some of our best meals are served family-style on picnic tables, made with sun-ripened ingredients fresh from our own backyards.

Right **Stone Barns Center for Food and Agriculture,** Pocantico Hills, New York

When you're passing around summer watermelon salad and grass-fed hangar steak still sizzling from the grill, farm-to-table seems like an obvious, tasty choice – hardly revolutionary. Yet as ubiquitous as the farm-to-table trend has become nationwide, many US diners still don't know where their food comes from. The correct answer? Very far away. Worldwatch Insitute reports that most ingredients travel 1500 miles to reach your plate. No wonder the wilted lettuce and sad tomato on your burger seem so jet-lagged.

California

Over the last few decades, pioneering farmers and farm-to-table chefs have been working together to make sure your date-night dinners don't taste like in-flight meals. The bright, fresh flavors of farm-to-table food first took root in the '60s, when farm workers took a stand against toxic pesticides and idealists headed back to the land to homestead. Organic farming and permaculture were radical notions captured in California's DIY bible *The Whole Earth Catalog*, and championed by chef Alice Waters with the 1971 launch of her landmark Berkeley restaurant Chez Panisse.

Farm-to-table food may seem like a natural pairing in upscale Berkeley bistros and Italian wine country – but it's also taken root between the cracks in LA sidewalks. LA may be better known for TV-chef-driven, flavor-of-the-month food trends, but it also has been home to renegade urban farming since 1965, when MudTown gardens were first planted over the site of the city's bloody Watts Riots. Now MudTown is expanding, claiming turf once fought over by rival Bloods and Crips gangs to grow vegetables. Meanwhile in South Central, self-titled 'gangsta gardener' Ron Finley earned his outlaw status by planting salad greens on street curbs in an area where fresh produce isn't sold for miles around. Finley doesn't call LA's nutrition-deprived south side a food desert – he calls it a 'food prison.'

Escaping fast-food chains isn't easy in south LA, but local food-truck superstar Roy Choi (whose story inspired the movie *Chef*) has teamed up with NorCal sustainable fine-dining icon Daniel Patterson to invent low-cost, farm-fresh takes on fast-food standbys at LocoL Watts. Here farm-to-table gets street smart with nourishing urban fusion soul food such as 'red beanzz and rice' bowls, lip-buzzing turkey chili, California apricot agua fresca, and sustainable-beef-and-whole-grain-patty 'cheeseburgs' topped with zesty scallion relish.

Detroit

Urban farm-to-table food isn't a new idea in Detroit, where the nation's longest-running city farmers market has operated since 1841. Eastern Market was founded at a waypoint on the Underground Railroad route to freedom, and today it's helping to revitalize downtown Detroit with farm-fresh Michigan produce. The decline of manufacturing and recession hit Detroit especially hard, but the city is making a virtue of necessity. Michigan's pioneering cottage industry laws allow residents to turn their family recipes into supplemental income, so Eastern Market also showcases local home-cooking – look for blueberry barbecue sauce, craft-brewed pumpkin ale, Mideastern flatbreads with local goat's cheese, and (oh yes) tart cherry pie.

Detroit proves that eating fresh local food doesn't require deep pockets – just a strong community. On purchases of locally grown produce, farmers markets citywide offer double the value of state food-assistance stipends. Finding food in depopulated areas of Detroit continues to be a challenge, so pioneering food security nonprofit organizations are converting vacant lots into organic community gardens and distributing low-cost and free produce to at-risk and underserved neighbors. Visitors can join the effort as volunteer gardeners at two of Detroit's landmark successes: Capuchin Soup Kitchen's Earthworks Urban Farm and Detroit Black Food Security Network's D-Town Farms.

Hawai'i

When it comes to farming, new Detroit has a lot in common with old Hawai'i, where caring for the land is a shared duty known as *malama'aina.* While a booming car industry left Detroit's soil oily and poor, Hawai'i's colonial pineapple and sugar-cane plantations left little room or topsoil for other food crops. The lush, fertile islands became dependent on imported staples, especially packaged foods like Spam that were easy to transport by plane or boat.

But today islanders are reviving Hawaiian foodways, and reinventing the native Hawaiian tradition of *ahupuaa* (self-sustaining smallhold farms). O'ahu's nonprofit Kahumana community farm

Above **Poke bowl**

has brought newfound independence to the island and its people since 1974, providing fresh organic food to local schools, housing for homeless families and care for disabled adults. The Kahumana farm cafe offers simple, local-flavor meals of field-green salads, macadamia nut pesto pasta, and the obligatory lilikoi cheesecake. On Maui, nonprofit community Hana Health Center has started its own Hana Fresh Farm to grow organic, traditional Hawaiian food and plants used in traditional medicine crops – stop by the farm stand for a restorative fruit smoothie and poke bowl, the Hawaiian staple of raw marinated local fish atop brown rice. Hawaii's Garden Isle of Kaua'i lives up to its name at Kauai Farmacy, which offers informative tours of its permaculture herb garden, including explanations of medicinal uses and tea tastings that let you drink in the scenery. She may be a latecomer to Maui's farm-to-table scene, but Oprah Winfrey's star power has already yielded bumper crops of kale on her recently established OW Ranch – and you may soon be able to sample it yourself at her farmstead B&B.

New Orleans

The restorative, feel-good powers of farm-to-table cooking were put to the test in New Orleans in 2005. Thousands of residents fled for their lives from the back-to-back catastrophes of Hurricanes Katrina and Rita, and those who returned had to start from scratch, with no homes, no electricity and almost no food. Fishing fleets were destroyed, and the Lower Ninth Ward's historic freehold farms were wiped out. Hope itself seemed lost in the hurricanes – but when the waters receded, a new sense of purpose emerged.

New Orleans began cooking to sustain itself, instead of catering to the tourist trade. Even with no guests to serve, landmark eateries reopened, to keep staff employed and offer a beacon of hope to returnees. Cut off from their usual supply chains, legendary local chefs Emerill Lagasse and John Besh sought out and supported local farmers and foragers, and began rebuilding culinary traditions from the ground up. Fresh, locally sourced ingredients added healthful counterpoints to hearty, slow-cooked New Orleans staples like red beans and rice, and locals began to crave 'New New Orleans cuisine' served at John Besh's upscale August, and Cody and Samantha Carroll's acclaimed Sac-a-Lait. Family recipes handed down for generations were lost forever, but New Orleans' Pulitzer Prize–winning *Times-Picayune* began reprinting recipes from its century-old archives to help nudge cooks' memories of the 'Old New Orleans Cuisine.'

Today New Orleans' culinary touchstone Commanders Palace proudly features 'new' and 'old' New Orleans dishes – including alarmingly healthy farm-to-table 'Eat Fit New Orleans' options alongside its reassuringly decadent 25-cent lunch martinis. For instant immersion in the city's resilient food and drink heritage without losing all sobriety, don't miss the new Southern Food and Beverage Museum. Here you'll find cooking demonstration lunches, Tuesday cocktail mixers and a car encrusted in red beans and rice permanently parked in the window.

New York

Southern chefs do have a distinct seasonal advantage over colder climates, where farm-to-table chefs have to learn to find the excitement in a winter's worth of root vegetables and cope with sudden gluts of summer squash. But at Stone Barns Center for Food and Agriculture in the New York hamlet of Pocantico Hills, chef-farmer Dan Barber has been showing how it's done since 2002. Instead of a menu, guests are presented with a glossary of the selected seasonal heirloom-varietal ingredients to be grilled over an open fire stoked with local lumber. His Manhattan Blue Hill bistro has given New Yorkers a taste of what they've been missing down on the farm: outsized flavor with a smaller carbon footprint than industrially processed food of dubious origins and nutritional value. Barber has challenged New York chefs to try style over substance, and build honest dishes around a humble tomato, instead of relying on gimmicks like edible strawberry-guava paper concocted at New Jersey's behemoth International Flavors and Fragrances factory.

North Carolina & Beyond

Perfectly grilled heirloom tomatoes may not be to everyone's tastes – and in less-skilled hands than Dan Barber's, could get a tad boring. In multicultural USA, even staunch locavores who prefer foods grown within a 100-mile (160km) radius crave international flavors – so farm-to-table chefs are increasingly drawing on diverse local and global influences. Beyond its established farm-to-table menu staples of barbecued heritage pork, native bison burgers and craft beer straight from the barrel, North Carolina's Asheville offers organic farm-to-table Indian street food at Chai Pani. In partnership with the Appalachian Sustainable Agriculture Project, Chef Meherwan Irani adds a southern drawl to South Asian classics, creating new American heritage foods like kale pakora and organic Carolina chicken tikka with coleslaw.

No matter where you go across the USA today, the farm-to-table vanguard is easy to find: just follow your taste buds. A tantalizing aroma wafting from sizzling street-food joints, sun-warmed farm-stands and breezy bistro patios carries with it a promise of bright flavors and satisfying nourishment. Joining the farm-to-table movement is simple: have a bite. Every time you enjoy locally grown food, you honor your hosts, their work and the place they call home – and everyone gets to leave the table satisfied.

To read about:

New York see page 182
Urban Farming see page 306

Alice Waters' Influence Runs Deep

At Chez Panisse, chef Alice Waters celebrates local, organic, seasonal flavors and rustic preparations over imported frozen ingredients disguised with fancy French technique – and has cultivated a network of 90 sustainable local food suppliers and a dedicated foodie following rock stars might envy. Chez Panisse's revolutionary menu crediting local farmers wasn't idle name-dropping, but a way of acknowledging the work that goes into growing food, and honoring it with careful preparation.

Today queues form at farm stands for produce featured at Chez Panisse, and so many star chefs have taken turns churning organic butter in Waters' kitchens that James Beard Food Award banquets resemble Chez Panisse alumni reunions. Beyond the table, Waters has leveraged her influence to install organic edible gardens at the Obama White House and revolutionize school lunches with her nonprofit Edible Schoolyard Project, teaching nine million budding farmers in 5500 schools globally to prefer their own homegrown vegetables to packaged snacks.

Brewphoria: The Rise of Craft Beer

USA-WIDE / DRINKS

Back in the days of bell-bottoms, US beer had a reputation for being insipid and boring. Hampered by the legacy of Prohibition, the market was dominated by a consortium of six big brewers who controlled over 90% of national production. Then in 1978, the Carter Administration, in one of its more revolutionary enactments, legalized home-brewing. It was a pivotal moment. Half a century of pent-up creativity and entrepreneurship was suddenly let loose.

The nation's first microbrewery was inaugurated – like so many new trends – in California, but the real driving force in the shift from macro-brewed to micro-brewed beer was the Pacific Northwest.

The trick lay in the hops. The climbing herbaceous plants that provide a bitter bite to America's best brews grow abundantly in Eastern Washington, a sunny but superbly irrigated region of deep coulees and grassy hills which produces three-quarters of the US crop. Add in a strong culinary culture, a Northwest penchant for innovation, and an abundance of iconoclastic entrepreneurs itching to get their creative hands on a much maligned beverage, and you had the perfect conditions for cities like Seattle and Portland to become the engine-rooms for the newly christened craft beer movement.

The aim was to produce small but think big. By playing around with flavors and production methods, craft brewers sought to put a bit of zing back into mass-produced beer which, by the 1970s, had become more about quantity than quality. From a handful of establishments in the late 1980s, the total number of US microbreweries had grown to more than 2500 by 2012. Five years later and the number had doubled again to more than 5000, with tasting rooms and brewpubs spreading like wildfire around the country. Today, California alone supports more than 600 breweries, while tiny Vermont has the highest number of craft breweries per capita. The only region where microbrewing hasn't (yet) gone ballistic is the South, where corporate interests and a history of religious temperance seem to have stymied progress.

Growth meant innovation. American micro-brewers have embraced many different drink styles since the 1990s, from light and malty blonde ales to heavier, darker porters and stouts. But, the star drink in the USA's ever-expanding craft beer universe is IPA, aka India Pale Ale, a hop-heavy beer invented in Olde England in the late 18th century for easy shipment to the Indian colonies. Sometime in the 1990s, the Americans took IPA and started to subtly reinvent it, adding more alcohol and loading up on their own New World hops. Classic American IPAs from the Northwest are strong, bitter and tinged with the fruity, citrusy, pine-infused nuances of locally grown hops. Meanwhile, East Coast IPAs, especially those from Vermont, are lighter and less bitter, maintaining a finer balance between the hops and malt.

In the early 2000s, the Californians, milking America's new love affair with hops, invented the vindaloo of beers: Imperial IPA, an intense, powerful brewing style loaded with a double whammy of hops and bitterness. As potent as they were tasty, Imperials quickly established themselves as potentially embarrassing tongue looseners for those not familiar with their strength (between 7.6% and 10.6% alcohol by volume).

By the 2010s, beer appreciation had moved full circle with countries like the UK and Germany, who had once derided American beer for being one step up from water, sticking super-potent 'American-style' IPAs on their bar menus. It was a long way from the sobriety of Prohibition.

To read about:

The World's Largest Six-Pack see page 58
Maine Breweries see page 260

For Your Amusement: Pop Art

When Andy Warhol and pals made US pop culture – Elvis, Coke bottles, comic books – the subject of their bright, cartoony paintings, they upended the art world. Critics snarled. Viewers were beguiled. Collectors got rich, because today those zippy canvases of soup cans and 'Varoom!' images sell for $100 million or so.

USA-WIDE / ART

The New Rebellion

Pop art started as a revolt against Abstract Expressionism. It was the early 1960s, and the USA's new generation of artists pooh-poohed the style of Jackson Pollock and his fellow splatterers as pretentious and extreme. Instead of 'high' art, the new artists dove into popular culture. They drew inspiration from television, Hollywood movies, comic strips, pulp magazines and consumer goods – ie, images from everyday life – and painted them using fun, bold colors.

The result was whimsical and easy on the eyes. But there was still much to consider. Was pop art critiquing or celebrating consumerism and celebrity culture? Was it a joke? Or was it a democratic style meant for the masses to appreciate? Turns out it was all of the above, with a big dose of irony.

Warhol's Soup Cans

Andy Warhol (1928–87) reigns as pop art's most renowned practitioner. Born into a working-class family in Pittsburgh, Pennsylvania, where he went to art school, Warhol soon fled to New York City, got a nose job and made himself famous.

Think 'Warhol' and the first thing that springs to mind is probably Campbell's soup cans. His rendering of 32 red-and-white cans, each a different flavor on a different canvas, was part of his first big exhibition. When Warhol was deciding what to create for the show, a friend suggested he paint something he saw each day. He chose Campbell's soup, which he claimed to eat daily.

Warhol also loved using celebrities as subjects. His neon-hued portraits of Marilyn Monroe, Elizabeth Taylor and Jacqueline Kennedy are among the most recognizable works of the 20th century. For these he often used a silkscreen process, a commercial technique that allowed him to make multiple images. He applied it to prints of everything from dollar bills to mushroom clouds to Coke bottles. Mickey Mouse, Mao and Mona Lisa got the treatment, too.

Lichtenstein's Comics

Roy Lichtenstein (1923–97) is pop art's other leading man. His claim to fame is his comic book style, which includes the use of Ben-Day dots (to look like newsprint), black outlines for figures, speech bubbles and text exclamations.

For his source material, Lichtenstein perused pulpy comics and then riffed off images that grabbed his interest. He re-imagined the composition and form, and changed the color and words so the painting tells its own story.

Drowning Girl (1963) is one of his best-known works. It shows a woman crying while being swept up in a turbulent sea: a speech bubble has her declaring she'd rather sink than call Brad for help. He produced *Whaam!* (1963) around the same time. It shows a fighter plane shooting another plane, which explodes into a ball of fire under a big yellow text 'Whaam!' Both pieces are bizarre, melodramatic and gripping. The style launched Lichtenstein to widespread commercial success.

Right *In The Car* by Roy Lichtenstein, 1963

Other Pop Stars

Claes Oldenburg (1929–) is known for taking everyday objects like hamburgers and light switches and re-creating them as jumbo sculptures. Many of his early pop art pieces are soft sculptures, say a giant ice-cream cone made of foam-rubber-stuffed canvas, or a mega bacon, lettuce and tomato sandwich made of kapok-plumped vinyl. In later years, he worked mostly on large-scale public commissions. *Spoonbridge and Cherry* (1988), a 7000lb (3175kg) steel colossus that depicts a spoon holding a – yes – cherry, remains one of Oldenburg's most popular works; it's located in Minneapolis, Minnesota.

Ed Ruscha (1937–) began his career painting signs. The text-and-image relationship continued to intrigue him as his work progressed. He often focused on showcasing words, like his canvas that simply says 'OOF' in bright yellow letters on a midnight-blue background. *Actual Size* (1962) looks similar, only the text says 'SPAM' and mimics the logo of the popular blue-tinned meat, while adding a cartoony image of the product blasting through space. Ruscha's word paintings continue to be his most recognized works, though he is also a prolific photographer and printmaker.

Wayne Thiebaud (1920–) is the painter who makes you hungry. His renderings of multiple pie slices, frosted cakes and gumball machines resemble Warhol's soup cans, but they're warm and evocative instead of cool and ironic. Thiebaud went on to portray lipsticks, paint cans, hammers and other items of mass culture, all pop art classics thanks to their vivid colors and flat, ad-like look.

Though the genre's heyday was the 1960s, its influence lingers. Many artists still turn to US popular culture for inspiration, and their bright, animated images still sell big time.

Pop Art Museums

New York's Museum of Modern Art hangs masterpieces aplenty. The best of the best by Warhol, Lichtenstein and Ruscha are here.

The Andy Warhol Museum in Pittsburgh, Pennsylvania, provides a six-story dive into the work of the city's premier native son. Exhibits include a simulated Velvet Underground happening and pieces

Top Pop Art Works

Campbell's Soup Cans (1962), Andy Warhol, Museum of Modern Art, New York

Drowning Girl (1963), Roy Lichtenstein, Museum of Modern Art, New York

Lipstick (Ascending) on Caterpillar Tracks (1969), Claes Oldenburg, Yale University Art Gallery, New Haven, Connecticut

OOF (1962), Ed Ruscha, Museum of Modern Art, New York

Cakes (1963), Wayne Thiebaud, National Gallery of Art, Washington, DC

of Warhol's extensive knickknack collection, plus heaps of paintings and drawings.

Washington, DC's National Gallery of Art holds the largest collection of works by Roy Lichtenstein, while the nearby Smithsonian American Art Museum provides a hearty dose of Wayne Thiebaud's paintings.

In the Midwest, Minneapolis' Walker Art Center shows a terrific Warhol collection, heavy on the soup cans and Mao prints. And Claes Oldenburg's *Spoonbridge and Cherry* rises in the museum's sculpture garden.

To read about:
Sculptures in Seattle see page 210
Street Art in San Francisco see page 242

Improv in Chicago: Learning to Play

CHICAGO / COMEDY & ENTERTAINMENT

Bill Murray. Tina Fey. The 'Key' in Key and Peele. Stephen Colbert. If a person learned to be funny in the United States, there's a good chance it was at Chicago's famed Second City. The ground-breaking improv theater has been performing and teaching funny since 1959. Come watch a show, or stay a week and learn a thing or two.

Right **Matt Baram,** Second City

Chicago winters are bitterly cold, adulthood is hard, and neither offer enough opportunities for play. Back in the 1940s and '50s, a theater teacher and academic in Chicago named Viola Spolin had watched her acting students lose that sense of creative magic and freedom as they got slowly hijacked by the rigors of adulthood. She wanted to give her students a way to tap into the type of play that came so easily to children.

Improvisational theater had been around since Roman times, when actors would make up their lines on the spot, and was reinvented as Commedia dell' Arte street theater in Renaissance Italy. But leave it to the Windy City to re-invent an Italian classic (exhibit B: Chicago-style, extra-thick pizza) – Spolin's Chicago-style improv has a different structure than improvisational theater. The performers on stage will often take a suggestion from the audience and then run with that in improv-specific games and scenes.

Most people think of improv as actors trying hard to be really funny, but the truth is often far more funny than comedy. Which is why regular people (that is, non-actors) often end up surprising themselves when they find that they, too, can do improv. Improv students come from all different backgrounds – barbers and bartenders, teachers and travel agents.

Spolin's son Paul Sills helped found Second City Theatre in 1959, and soon thereafter, the training school. The school teaches improv, sketch writing, acting, stand-up comedy, even writing for the Onion humor website.

Second City helped Chicago become the staging grounds of funny in the United States, and comedy now blankets Chicago. Every day there are dozens of improv or comedy performances and classes at Second City, or improv theaters like iO or the Annoyance. Every year or so, a Chicago improviser makes it big, so catch them before they end up on *Saturday Night Live* or on tour.

Do you have to be a professional actor or comedian-in-training to take a class at Second City? Not according to the vast majority of current students. The rules of Chicago-style improv are simple: listen; pay attention; say 'yes, and.' When improvising a scene, focus on making your partners look good and on adding rather than blocking. Don't think about being funny. In fact, don't think at all. Focus on these rules, let your creative intuition trump your inner critic, and the creative magic will happen.

If you don't live in Chicago but want to take a class, don't fret; buy a plane ticket. Second City offers weeklong intensive courses for people visiting from around the world. Bring your kids; summer kids' camps are timed with adult intensives.

Second City also has branches in Toronto and Los Angeles, and improv theater schools have opened around the US and the world – BATS in San Francisco, Upright Citizen's Brigade in New York City, the aptly named Boom! Chicago in Amsterdam. But for improv served with deep-dish pizza in sub-freezing temperatures, you'll have to come to Chicago.

To read about:
Chicago on Route 66 see page 104
Chicago's Chinatown see page 176

O'Keeffe Country, New Mexico

NEW MEXICO / ART & LANDSCAPES

New Mexico's charm is best expressed in the iconic paintings of Georgia O'Keeffe. The artist herself exclaimed, on her very first visit: 'Well! Well! Well!… This is wonderful! No one told me it was like this.' It was no wonder O'Keeffe loved New Mexico's expansive skies, so similar to her paintings' negative spaces. As she spent more time here, landscapes and fields of blue permeated her work.

Right **Ghost Ranch**

Love of the Land

Although classically trained as a painter at art institutes in Chicago and New York, Georgia O'Keeffe was always uncomfortable with traditional European style. For four years after finishing school, she did not paint, and instead taught drawing and did graphic design.

After studying with Arthur Wesley Dow, who shared her distaste for the provincial, O'Keeffe began to develop her own style. She drew abstract shapes with charcoal, representing dreams and visions, and eventually returned to oils and watercolors. These first works caught the eye of her future husband and patron, photographer Alfred Stieglitz, in 1916.

In 1929 O'Keeffe visited Taos' Mabel Dodge Luhan Ranch and returned to the area to paint *The Lawrence Tree;* the tree still presides over the DH Lawrence Ranch in northern New Mexico. She then tackled the San Francisco de Asís Church in Ranchos de Taos – though the church had been painted by many artists before her, she considered it in a new way, presenting only a fragment of the mission wall, contrasted against the blue of the sky.

Over the next couple of decades, O'Keeffe lived on and off in New Mexico, before moving there permanently in 1949. From 1934 onwards, she lived and worked for extended periods at Ghost Ranch, a dude ranch set amid the colorful bluffs 15 miles (24km) northwest of the tiny adobe village of Abiquiú (it rhymes with 'barbecue'). With the Rio Chama flowing through farmland, spectacular red rock formations and distant mesas that glow purple in the sunset, the ethereal landscapes around Abiquiú continue to lure artists.

Telltale scrub marks and bristle impressions reveal how O'Keeffe blended and mixed her vibrant colors on the canvas – an effect that is not visible in photographs of her works, which convey a false, airbrush-like smoothness. During desert treks, she collected the smooth white bones of animals, subjects she placed against that sky in some of her most identifiable New Mexico pieces.

Georgia O'Keeffe died in 1986, at age 98.

The O'Keeffe Experience

Georgia O'Keeffe Home The Spanish Colonial adobe house she restored is open for guided visits, run by the Georgia O'Keeffe Museum in Santa Fe. Tours tend to be booked months in advance, so plan way ahead.

Georgia O'Keeffe Museum With 10 beautifully lit galleries in a rambling 20th-century adobe, this museum boasts the world's largest collection of O'Keeffe's work. The changing exhibitions feature not only her luminous New Mexican landscapes but range through her entire career, from the early years through her time at Ghost Ranch. Major museums worldwide own her most famous canvases, so you may not see familiar paintings, but you're sure to be bowled over by the thick brushwork and transcendent colors on show.

Jackalope Essential pieces of Southwest decor can all be yours at this sprawling shop. Start with a cow skull like the ones O'Keeffe made famous, snap up a kiva ladder, add some colorful pottery and Navajo pot holders, and you'll be set.

San Francisco de Asís Church Just off Hwy 68 in Ranchos de Taos, this iconic church was completed in 1815. Famed for the rounded curves and stark angles of its sturdy adobe walls, it was repeatedly memorialized by O'Keeffe in paint, and by Ansel Adams with his camera.

DH Lawrence Ranch & Memorial In 1924, Mabel Dodge Luhan gave DH Lawrence's wife, Frieda, this 160-acre (65-hectare) ranch, where the Lawrence-obsessed can pay their respects to the famed author of such classics as *Lady Chatterley's Lover.* Relax beneath the Lawrence Tree, which brings in the O'Keeffe fans (yep, it looks just like her painting) and contemplate what Lawrence called 'the greatest experience I ever had from the outside world.'

Ghost Ranch Now a retreat center run by the Presbyterian Church, Ghost Ranch welcomes visitors and overnight guests. This distinctive landmark is visible from the highway, but the steep hike up to reach it, which takes around 40 minutes each way, is truly superb. Stupendous views unfold the higher you climb, while Chimney Rock itself, an enormous pillar breaking off from the mesa-top, is breathtaking. Other activities at Ghost Ranch include guided tours about Georgia O'Keeffe and covering the various movies (such as *City Slickers)* that have been filmed here.

To read about:
The Grand Canyon see page 34
Museums & Art Galleries see page 46

Seattle's Peculiar Sculptures

A 16ft-tall bronze Bolshevik, a giant troll hidden beneath a bridge, a Cold War rocket that didn't make lift-off, and a row of cement commuters waiting for a train that never comes.

SEATTLE / ART

Welcome to the weird and wonderful neighbourhood of Fremont in Seattle, where the community motto is *de libertas quirkas* (freedom to be peculiar) and the streets are decorated with outlandish public art.

Located 3 miles (5km) north of downtown Seattle, Fremont is an irreverent quarter in a city well known for its free spirits. Abutting Lake Union, the treelined streets regularly fall victim to 'art attacks': spontaneous sculptures and exhibits that spring up anonymously overnight before disappearing again just as quickly. More permanent are the half-dozen pieces of public sculpture.

Close to Fremont Bridge and testimony to Fremont's love of wit and humor is *Waiting for the Interurban*, a study in cement of five commuters and a dog standing forlornly at an imaginary tram stop. It is Fremont tradition to dress the quintet up in clothes or other paraphernalia to celebrate a sporting victory, satirise a political event, or simply make an artistic statement. Needless to say, the statue is rarely naked.

A few blocks away is another notorious creation – the *Fremont Troll*, a one-eyed monster crushing a Volkswagen Beetle in its fist. Winner of first prize in a local arts council competition in 1990, the statue (created by artists Steve Badanes, Will Martin, Donna Walter and Ross Whitehead) was an early example of Fremont's wry contrarianism and has been prowling under the George Washington Memorial Bridge ever since.

To regain your sense of direction, gravitate towards the Guidepost, Fremont's community totem that points in multiple directions and announces itself as the 'center of the known universe' (an unsubstantiated Fremont claim). The guidepost will direct you towards the next head-scratching oddity, the Lenin statue, a fierce-looking study of the Soviet strongman that was rescued by a Seattle teacher from a junkyard in the former Czechoslovakia soon after the Velvet Revolution. It's technically for sale, should you fall in love with it.

Lenin seems to be striding hurriedly towards the *Fremont Rocket*, an unused piece of Cold War hardware now grafted on to the side of a shoe shop that once playfully emitted steam if you pushed a coin into a slot and waited. These days the most supersonic it gets is when it is lit up at night.

Slightly more down to earth are Fremont's Apatosaurs down by the ship canal, two life-size topiaries made out of creeping ivy. Like most of Fremont's sculptures, the dinos were salvaged – a community group bought them for $1 from the Pacific Science Center in 1999. Sit for a moment and contemplate their pleasant greenness (and their weirdness) and then be on your merry way.

To read about:

Street Art in San Francisco see page 242
Sand Sculpture see page 262

Right **Fremont Troll,** by artists Steve Badanes, Will Martin, Donna Walter and Ross Whitehead

Music Festival Magic

The uninitiated may write them off as chaotic outdoor concerts, or fret about the hassles of parking and pricey beers. But anyone who's journeyed far to hear the music they love mingle with the roar of a crowd knows that a great music festival isn't merely a good time – it can change your life.

USA-WIDE / FESTIVALS

No US festival is shrouded in lore and legend quite as much as Woodstock – 'three days of peace and music' that unfolded in August of 1969 and became a symbol of a generation. Held in a natural amphitheater in Bethel (not Woodstock), New York, the event drew hundreds of thousands of fans during the so-called Summer of Love to see the most notorious rock acts of the era – including Jimi Hendrix, the Who, Janis Joplin and Jefferson Airplane. It was the ultimate, mind-expanding convergence of music, sexual liberation and free thinking. And no festival since can hold a candle to it (not even the muddy sequel on the event's 25th anniversary). Today, the site of the festival has earned a place on the National Register of Historic Places.

Though Woodstock has few equivalents, one of the contemporary contenders is the Coachella Valley Music and Arts Festival. Held at the Empire Polo Club in Indio, California, over two weekends in April, Coachella has grown from a popular indie event to the star-stuffed kick-off of the US festival season, featuring big-time headliners and rising stars. A buzzing hive of fashionable, see-and-be-seen crowds from Los Angeles, and performances from the likes of Beyoncé and Radiohead define the event today. Critics deride Coachella for being too mainstream – *New York Times* writers Jon Pareles, Ben Ratliff and Jon Caramanica referred to it as 'a codified, consensual, safe and purchasable bohemia' – but the allure generated by its surprise reunions and buzz-worthy sets has made it one of the USA's premier live music events.

Another early season festival that grabs the nation's attention is Bonnaroo – the only large-scale 24/7 event in the country. Set on a 700-acre (284-hectare) farm, 60 miles (97km) southeast of Nashville, Bonnaroo combines camping, comedy, cinema, food, beverage and art, which lends it a communal feel. But it's the music that rules, spread out over four blissfully raging days.

Halfway across the country, Lollapalooza is a grittier, Midwestern cousin of Coachella and Bonnaroo. In the 1990s, the name was synonymous with a traveling playground for lovers of alternative music, but the festival found a permanent annual home in Chicago's Grant Park. Today it's major, with more than 100 bands spilling off eight stages, which have included the likes of Red Hot Chili Peppers, Florence + the Machine and Metallica. With booths featuring dance, comedy and crafts, Lollapalooza also provides a platform for political and nonprofit groups. And it's not just for arm-flailing, art-loving adults – Kidzapalooza is a festival within the giant rock festival. In addition to the stellar lineup of kid-favorite bands, budding rock stars can bang sticks in the Drum Zone and get a Mohawk in the kids' area.

The hipper, headier offspring of Lollapalooza in Chicago is the annual Pitchfork Music Festival, hosted by the taste-making indie blog. Catering to younger crowds and

Right **Coachella Festival,** California

Above Festival-goers, Pitchfork Music Festival, Chicago

more adventuresome tastes, Pitchfork is a genre-blurring melting pot of rock, hip-hop, electronic, jazz and punk – including recent performances from A Tribe Called Quest, Wilco, Chance the Rapper and all sorts of artists who you should have heard of. There's also a record fair and amazing food and beverages from local vendors.

Far from the skyscrapers of Chicago and deep in a relatively remote part of Washington, the Sasquatch Festival is another of the country's most popular indie events. Half the fun is the popular campsite, which turns into a wild after-hours party after the multi-stage event that features critically adored singer-songwriters and indie rockers. It takes place over Memorial Day weekend, in May, and tickets are often in high demand because many include this festival among their summertime must-attend events.

If jazz is your thing, one of the best fests in the nation is the Monterey Jazz Festival, held every September on the 20-acre (8-hectare) Monterey Fairgrounds in California. It's been around since 1958, making it the world's longest-running jazz festival. The three-day celebration brings together jazz luminaries from around the world, as well as panel discussions, workshops, exhibitions, clinics, and an international array of food, shopping and festivities. Another great jazz-focused festival unfolds annually in the birthplace of the genre: the New Orleans Jazz and Heritage Festival is held in the spring, and presents city natives (such as Harry Connick Jr and the One Love Brass Band) alongside classic and up-and-coming rock acts such as the Alabama Shakes.

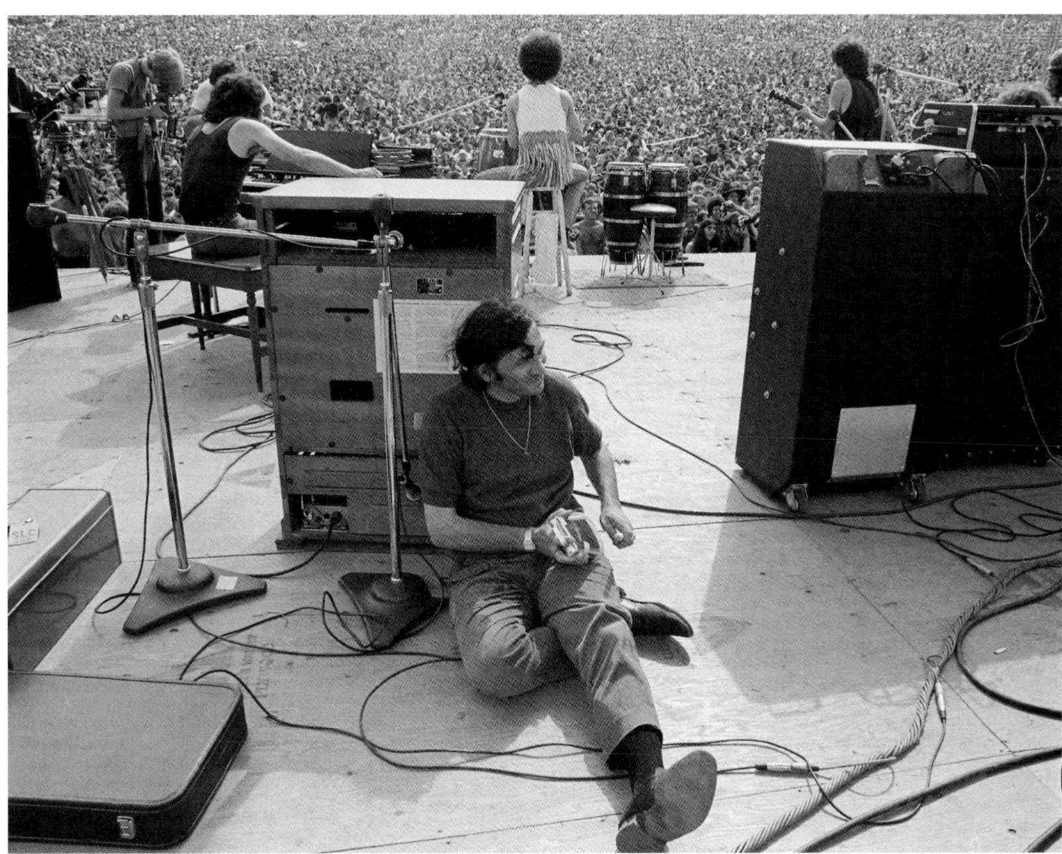

Above **Bill Graham,** Woodstock Festival, New York, 1969

Although every region in the country will have their own big-ticket event, San Francisco hosts one of the nation's best free festivals, the Hardly Strictly Bluegrass Festival. Although the festival has deep roots in Americana, country and bluegrass it has expanded its reach in recent years to include rock and soul acts. Spread over a handful of stages in San Francisco's iconic Golden Gate Park, Hardly Strictly is one of the city's most cherished annual events, held in early October.

But these are just the tip of the iceberg. Look to New York City and you'll find gems like the Governors Ball Music Festival, which recently featured Lorde, Kanye West and Drake. New York also boasts slightly more off-the-radar events like the Afro Punk Festival, which celebrates black communities within international alternative punk scenes with a wide range of genre-shifting artists from around the world. Among the nation's best electronic music events is Detroit's Movement, a gathering of taste-making artists that takes place each Memorial Day weekend and features the best DJs and producers on the planet.

No matter the destination, the diversity of music festivals in the US offers plenty of opportunities to build a traveler's itinerary. And it's not the weather or the price of beer that you'll remember when you leave an epic festival. It's the transformative moment that you'll take with you the rest of your life, one that, when it comes back to you, will make you realise, with a sense of wonder, 'I was there.'

To read about:

Live Music in Austin see page 144
San Francisco's Summer of Love see page 246

The Nation's Pastime

USA-WIDE / SPORTS

What really draws Americans together, sometimes slathered in blue body paint or with foam-rubber cheese wedges on their heads, is sports. In spring and summer there's baseball nearly every day; in fall and winter there's football. Head to a game and you can't help but get caught up in the fervor. So let the team spirit and high fives begin.

Baseball

Despite rumors to the contrary, baseball remains the USA's favorite pastime. Sure, it takes a knock for being too slow and boring to captivate modern fans. And its TV viewership does lag behind football's ratings. But that's because baseball has 162 games over a season versus 16 for football.

Besides, baseball isn't about seeing it on TV, it's all about the live version: being at the ballpark on a sunny day, sitting in the bleachers with a beer and hot dog, and indulging in the seventh-inning stretch, when the entire park erupts in a communal singalong of 'Take Me Out to the Ballgame.' The New York Yankees, Boston Red Sox, Chicago Cubs and Los Angeles Dodgers are the USA's most popular teams, drawing around 40,000 people per game. It's just a bonus if you attend on one of the souvenir giveaway days and score a player-lookalike garden gnome or bobble-head doll *for free*.

Minor-league baseball games are also a blast. They cost less and provide a more intimate setting, with lots of audience participation, stray chickens and dogs running across the field, and wild throws from the pitcher's mound. While there are 30 major league stadiums, more than 150 minor league ballparks offer action across the country.

Lest you still think baseball is losing its mojo, consider this: when the Chicago Cubs won the 2016 World Series championship after 108 years of futility – the longest dry spell in US sports history – the city threw the team a ticker-tape parade. An estimated five million fans attended.

Football

American football is another beloved diversion. With the shortest season and least number of games of any of the major sports, every match takes on the emotion of an epic battle, where the results matter and an injury can deal a lethal blow to a team's play-off chances.

Players are big, physical and gladiator-tough, and they compete in all manner of rain, sleet and snow. Some of history's most memorable matches have occurred at below-freezing temperatures. Green Bay Packers fans are in a class by themselves when it comes to severe weather. Their stadium in Wisconsin, known as Lambeau Field, was the site of the infamous Ice Bowl, a 1967 championship game against the Dallas Cowboys where the temperature plummeted to −13°F/−25°C (−48°F/−43°C with the wind chill). And 50,000 people still sat there and cheered on their team.

Going to a game where the body paint, profane chants and beers flow in abundance is awesome, though tickets to National Football League (NFL) matches can be tough to get. Not to worry: team bars are a fine place to feel the energy. Renowned squads such as Green Bay, Dallas, the New England Patriots and Pittsburgh Steelers have fans around the nation. Bars in many cities cater to them, offering a prime spot to don your jersey, yell at the TV and bond over a dramatic overtime finish. Or seek out the local tailgate scene. It takes place in the stadium parking lot before each game, when fans fire up portable grills and indulge in a communal beer-and-barbecue feast.

The rabidly popular Super Bowl is pro football's championship match, held in late January or early February. More than 110 million people tune in to watch. The cultural phenomenon is estimated to cost the USA $1 billion dollars in lost workplace productivity as employees gossip about the game, swap nacho recipes and place wagers in the office betting pool.

College Football

It is impossible to overstate the importance of college football to US culture. Epic rivalries, fabled traditions, historic games – it all goes down amid orange and yellow leaves on autumn Saturdays.

The first thing to know about the scene is that many college stadiums are bigger than their NFL counterparts. Capacity of 100,000 or more is common, while NFL venues max out around 80,000. Heck, some college arenas hold more people than the surrounding town holds.

So size matters. So does pageantry. Each team has its time-honored rituals that are as crucial to the game as the players snapping the ball. There's Auburn's war eagle soaring over the stadium before each game, and Ohio State's marching band forming a script 'Ohio' on the field at half-time. A pony-led pioneer wagon, aka the Sooner Schooner, charges onto the field whenever Oklahoma scores. Fans go wild.

They also lose their heads when certain adversaries come to town. Florida versus Georgia, Army versus Navy, Ohio State versus Michigan: these football rivalries

have been stoked for over a century. Their games are where you'll find sportsdom's most passionate fans, screaming, crying and cheering until the last whistle blows.

Basketball & Hockey

Basketball keeps the adrenaline going through the long days and nights of winter. On the pro side, teams bringing in the most fans include the Chicago Bulls (thanks to the lingering Michael Jordan effect), Cleveland Cavaliers (thanks to the LeBron James effect), Golden State Warriors and Los Angeles Lakers. Small-market teams such as Sacramento and Portland have true-blue fans, and such cities can be great places to see a game and experience the kiss cam (jumbotron images of smooching couples), T-shirt cannon (a bazooka-like device the team mascot uses to shoot shirts into the crowd) and booty-shaking dance squads.

College-level basketball also draws millions of fans, especially every spring when March Madness rolls around. This series of college play-off games culminates in the Final Four, when the four remaining teams compete for a spot in the championship game. The Cinderella stories and unexpected outcomes rival the pro league for excitement. The games are widely televised...and bet on. This is when Las Vegas bookies earn their keep.

Basketball teams often share their arenas with hockey teams. Once favored only in northern climes, ice hockey is now well attended nationwide, with five Stanley Cup winners since 2000 hailing from either California or the South. Attendance figures are similar for both sports, as are encounters with the kiss cam and T-shirt cannon.

Iconic Sporting Venues

Fenway Park, Boston Baseball's oldest park (1912); home of the 'Green Monster' (aka the tall left-field wall).

Wrigley Field, Chicago Another vintage ballpark (1914), with ivy walls, a classic neon sign and good-time neighborhood bars all around.

Lambeau Field, Green Bay, Wisconsin Stadium of the NFL's Packers; nicknamed 'the Frozen Tundra' for its insanely cold weather.

Yankee Stadium, NYC Home of baseball's most storied – and winning – team. It's not the Yanks' original field, but it's still steeped in history and the ghost of Babe Ruth.

Madison Square Garden, NYC Not only do the Knicks dribble at the 'mecca of basketball,' but Ali boxed here and Elvis rocked here.

To read about:
Beach Volleyball in Los Angeles see page 93
Cycling in New York City see page 186

Thanks-givoween: Ragamuffin Day

USA-WIDE / HISTORY & CULTURE

On the fourth Thursday of November, Americans gather with family and friends over day-long feasts – roast turkey, sweet potatoes, cranberry sauce, wine, pumpkin pie and loads of other dishes. But this wasn't always the extent of the festivities – back before trick or treating became a yearly ritual on Halloween, the young and old participated in a strikingly similar tradition, except this time on Thanksgiving.

Right **Ragamuffin dress,** New York City, 1910s

In New York City, where the tradition held out the longest, the *New York Times* reported, just before the turn of the 20th century on December 1, 1899, that 'Thanksgiving masquerading has never been more universal. Fantastically garbed youngsters and their elders were on every corner of the city.'

Masked children went door to door dressed as ragamuffins in parodies of beggars, asking, 'Anything for Thanksgiving?' Everyone 'was generous with pennies and nickels, and the candy stores did a land-office business.'

The tradition initially caught on after Abraham Lincoln proclaimed Thanksgiving a holiday in 1863, with towns across the USA holding masquerade balls. New York City started hosting an annual parade, with boys dressed in oversized women's clothes, and girls in men's frock coats. Papier-mâché mask makers cashed in on the celebrations, and by 1897 Thanksgiving was the busiest time of the year for the mask manufacturers.

The scores of children dressed in rags, parading the streets asking for pennies, become so common that the day was unofficially dubbed 'Ragamuffin Day.'

In 1911, the *Pittston Gazette* noted that New York children 'have no limit set on their hilarity short of the actual commission of crime.'

Not everyone was on board with the frivolity, and some New Yorkers threw stove-heated pennies, known as 'red pennies' to scorch the children who eagerly picked them up.

HalloweeNY

Around October 31, in the villages of Westchester County, New York, the last of the leaf-peeping season provides a colorful backdrop to Halloween celebrations. More than 7000 glowing jack o'lanterns can be seen at the Great Jack O'Lantern Blaze, held in the grounds of the 300-year-old Van Cortlandt Manor. Nearby is Sleepy Hollow, home to the Old Dutch Burying Ground, and the headless horseman of Washington Irving's 1820 tale, *The Legend of Sleepy Hollow.*

With the onset of the Great Depression in the 1930s, the pennies dried up and the tradition fell to the wayside, only to give way (a decade or so later) to the trick or treating tradition on Halloween we know today.

To read about:
Classic Candy see page 56
Fourth of July Fireworks see page 96

Albuquerque International Balloon Fiesta

NEW MEXICO / FESTIVALS

You simply haven't lived until you've seen a three-story-tall hot-air balloon land in your hotel courtyard, and that's exactly the sort of thing that happens during the largest balloon festival in the world. Held every October.

To read about:
Fireworks see page 96
New Mexico Landscapes see page 208

Superheroes Convene! Comic-Con International

It's official: superheroes dominate the world! Marvel Comics and DC Comics characters clash on the cinema screen as well as being splashed across the pages of more than a hundred comic titles every month. But where did it all begin, and where's the best place to immerse yourself in the best that comics, science-fiction and fantasy have to offer?

SAN DIEGO / FESTIVALS

Walking into a comic convention is a rapid immersion in a technicolor world found only in comic books and superhero movies, and Comic-Con International in San Diego is the exemplar of the con experience. Hold your breath, prepare your Sonic Screwdriver or Batarang, and dive right in. Excelsior!

Nowhere else can you meet a world-famous movie star or award-winning comic creator face-to-face, then turn to your left to take a selfie with a Jedi or Avenger, and then pivot right to test out Klingon or Dothraki pleasantries with a heavily armed warrior.

SDCC brings together the best that comic publishers and movie and television studios have to offer, and the exclusivity and camaraderie is an integral part of the experience. Every media company is in competition for your attention – that is, if you can tear your eyes away from the magnificently outfitted cosplayers gracing every corner of the convention center. Exclusive film and television previews, question-and-answer sessions with creators and actors, and convention-only editions of comics and toys are just some of the riches on offer. In addition, Artists Alley offers art commissions from famous artists, you can score those missing issues needed to complete your comic collection, and hundreds of exhibitors offer every geek- and genre-related treasure imaginable. If you still have energy left at the end of the day, San Diego nightlife takes on comic flair as creators and fans collide in parties (and after-parties) of all themes and sizes.

If San Diego isn't on your itinerary, or you missed out on securing tickets in the frenetic online clash for highly sought-after registration badges, then set your atomic batteries to speed and head to New York Comic Con or one of the many Wizard World Comic Cons. Or, for those who find the multimedia frenzy of the big convention scene too much, there's Baltimore Comic-Con, a more low-key, traditional event where the focus is fixed purely on comics, their creators and, of course, their heroic creations.

To read about:
Nevada's Extraterrestrial Highway see page 250
Salem 'Witch City' see page 274

Right **Comic-Con International,** San Diego

The Golden Age of Comic Books

The Golden Age of Superheroes (1938–50) began with Superman, created by Jerry Siegel and Joe Shuster, schoolboys from Cleveland, Ohio. Fawcett Comics' Captain Marvel followed, and soon a veritable society of heroes entertained American children every week: Wonder Woman, Batman, Captain America, the Flash, the Green Lantern, the Blue Beetle and more.

While increasingly patriotic primary-colored superheroes dominated the Golden Age during WWII, comic books eventually drifted towards other genres, and superheroes faded temporarily from prominence. However, the Silver Age, spurred by a new Flash in 1956 and the emergence of luminaries such as Stan Lee and Jack Kirby, saw a resurgence of superheroes, on their way to recapturing world domination.

Frank Lloyd Wright's Organic Architecture

USA-WIDE / ART & ARCHITECTURE

Much in sympathy with the turn-of-the-20th-century arts-and-crafts style, Wright's designs were anti-industrial, inspired by and aiming to exist harmoniously with nature. See the architect's influence writ large in locations across the USA, from Los Angeles to Arizona through the Midwest to New York.

Right & far right **Taliesin West,** Scottsdale, Arizona

Prairie School

Frank Lloyd Wright endowed Chicago with its most distinctive style, the Prairie School. Wright, a spottily educated ladies' man from a Wisconsin farm town, was the residential designer for Adler & Sullivan until 1893, when his architectural commissions outside the firm led to his dismissal. Forced into his own practice, he eventually set up a small studio in suburban Oak Park and by 1901 had built 50 public buildings and private homes around the Chicago metro area.

Over the next 15 years, Wright's 'Prairie Houses' contrasted the grand edifices of the First Chicago School with more modest charms. His unique residential buildings emphasized low-slung structures with dominant horizon lines, hipped (shallowly sloped) roofs, overhanging eaves and unadorned open-plan spaces that mirrored the flat Midwestern landscape. To blend visually, such natural, neutral materials as brick, limestone and stucco were often used.

Of all the Prairie Houses by Wright's hand, the Robie House is the most dramatic and successful. It's a measuring stick by which all other buildings in the style are often compared, and is alone worth the trip to Chicago's Hyde Park. The city is a treasure trove for Wright fans: two other notable sites are his only set of row houses, Bronzeville's Robert W Roloson Houses – which were designed in 1894 while Wright still worked for Adler & Sullivan – and the airy atrium of the Loop's landmark Rookery.

Above **Interior of the Solomon R Guggenheim Museum,** New York City

INTERIOR OF THE SOLOMON R. GUGGENHEIM MUSEUM, NEW YORK. USED WITH PERMISSION ©

Essential Wright Sights

Solomon R Guggenheim Museum, New York City A sculpture in its own right, Wright's building almost overshadows the collection of 20th-century art it houses from heavyweights including Kandinsky, Picasso, Pollock, Monet, Van Gogh, Degas and Mapplethorpe. Completed in 1959, the inverted ziggurat structure was derided by some critics but hailed by others, who welcomed it as a beloved architectural icon.

The Guggenheim came out of the collection of Solomon R Guggenheim, a New York mining magnate who began acquiring abstract art in his 60s at the behest of his art adviser, an eccentric German baroness named Hilla Rebay. Though Wright intended visitors to go to the top of the museum's ascending ramp and wind their way down past the artworks, the cramped single elevator doesn't allow for this. Exhibitions, therefore, are installed from bottom to top.

Charnley-Persky House, Chicago While he was still working for Louis Sullivan, Wright (who was 19 at the time) designed the 11-room Charnley-Persky House, which sparked a new era in architectural design. Why? Because it did away with Victorian gaudiness in favor of plain, abstract forms that went on to become the modern style. It was completed in 1892 and now houses the Society of Architectural Historians.

Taliesin, Spring Green, Wisconsin Taliesin was Wright's home for most of his life and is the site of his architectural school. It's now a major pilgrimage destination for fans – a wide range of guided tours cover various parts of the complex. The house was built in 1903, the Hillside Home School in 1932, and the visitor center in 1953.

Fallingwater, Laurel Highlands, Pennsylvania Among the Frank Lloyd Wright designs nominated for Unesco Heritage status, this masterpiece was completed in 1938 as a weekend retreat for the Kaufmanns, owners of a Pittsburgh department store. Built to bring the outside and inside together in harmony, it blends seamlessly with its natural setting, echoing its surroundings through terraces, ledges, cantilevering, circles and semi-circles. It's accessible only by guided tour, and the property also features 2000 acres (810 hectares) of attractive forested grounds.

At a total of $155,000, Wright's project was extremely over budget, although his commission was only $8000 (to give a sense of building costs at the time, master masons working on the home earned around 85¢ an hour). One of the home's most inventive features, which operates as a natural air conditioner, is the open stairway leading directly down to Bear Run stream. Photos can't do it justice – nor can they transmit the sounds of Fallingwater – and you'll likely need a return visit or two to really appreciate Wright's ingenuity and aesthetic vision.

Robie House, Chicago Of the numerous buildings that Wright designed around Chicago, none is more famous nor as influential as Robie House. Because its horizontal lines resembled the flat landscape of the Midwestern prairie, the style became known as the Prairie style. Inside are 174 stained-glass windows and doors, which you'll see on the hour-long tours.

After the Robies, the house passed from the Taylor family to the Wilber family. In 1926, the Wilbers sold it to the Chicago Theological Seminary for use as a dormitory. The seminary twice announced plans to raze the structure and build a bigger dorm: in 1941, a letter-writing campaign saved the house; and again in 1957, 90-year-old Frank Lloyd Wright himself showed up to ask that the home be preserved. That same year, Robie House became the first building declared a Chicago landmark.

Taliesin West, Scottsdale, Arizona Wright's winter home, school and studio is a prime example of organic architecture, with buildings incorporating elements and structures found in surrounding nature. Built between 1938 and 1940, it is still home to an architecture school. It's also a National Historical Monument, open to the public for informative guided tours.

Rookery, Chicago The famed firm of Burnham and Root built the Rookery in 1888 and Frank Lloyd Wright remodeled the atrium 19 years later. It's renowned because while it looks hulking and fortresslike outside, it's light and airy inside. You can walk in and look around for free, and tours are available on weekdays. The building is named after the pigeons that used to roost here.

Price Tower, Bartlesville, Oklahoma Tour the only Frank Lloyd Wright–designed skyscraper ever built, the 1956, 221ft (67m) Price Tower. Inside and out it is like *Architectural Digest* meets *The Jetsons*. Wright shopped the design around for 30 years before he found clients willing to build it here. All but abandoned in the 1990s, the building now houses an art gallery and hotel.

COURTESY OF FRANK LLOYD WRIGHT TRUST. PHOTOGRAPHER: JAMES CAULFIELD ©

Above **Robie House,** Chicago

Martin House Complex, Buffalo, New York This 15,000-sq-ft (1394-sq-meter) house, built between 1903 and 1905, was designed by Wright for his friend and patron Darwin D Martin. Representing Wright's Prairie House ideal, it consists of six interconnected buildings (some of which had to be rebuilt), each of which has been meticulously restored inside and out. A guided tour reveals the details that the Martin family fortune allowed Wright free rein to indulge, including a central fireplace with a wisteria-pattern mosaic.

Kentuck Knob, Laurel Highlands, Pennsylvania This home, designed in 1953 by Wright and completed in 1956, is built into the side of a rolling hill with stunning panoramic views. It's noted for its natural materials and obsessively designed interior – note the hexagons and honeycomb skylights. House tours include a jaunt through the on-site sculpture garden, with works by Andy Goldsworthy, Ray Smith and others.

The house was built at a cost of $82,000 for the Hagan family, friends of the Kaufmanns and owners of an ice-cream manufacturing company, who lived here full time for 28 years. It was purchased by Peter Palumbo (aka Lord Palumbo) in 1986 for $600,000 and opened to the public a decade later – Wright himself never saw the house in its finished state. In general, it's a cozier, more family-friendly and modest application

ROBERT P. RUSCHAK. COURTESY OF THE WESTERN PENNSYLVANIA CONSERVANCY ©

of Wright's genius than Fallingwater. Of a comparably small scale and with a fairly plain exterior, every nook and cranny of the 22,000-sq-ft (2044-sq-meter) home balances form and function, especially Wright's signature built-ins, such as the room-length couch and cabinets.

Gammage Auditorium, Phoenix, Arizona This fanciful colosseum-style auditorium is notable as Wright's last major public commission, and was based on unrealized designs for an opera house in Baghdad. A popular performance venue, it stages primarily Broadway-style musicals and shows.

Frank Lloyd Wright Home & Studio, Oak Park, Illinois Tours of the place where Wright lived and worked from 1889 to 1909 are filled with the details that made Wright's style distinctive.

To read about:

Museums & Art Galleries see page 46
Improv in Chicago see page 206

Left **Fallingwater,** Laurel Highlands, Pennsylvania

A Tour of Mark Twain's USA

MIDWEST, SOUTH & WEST / CLASSIC JOURNEYS

Hop aboard a Mississippi riverboat, bunk in the very room the one-time steamboat pilot patronized, navigate the western USA to experience the chill of a San Francisco summer fog, visit the house where he wrote his most famous works, witness the volcanoes of Hawai'i's Big Island...and get into the head of the oft-quoted genius Mark Twain.

BELLE OF LOUISVILLE

A Traveling Life

To follow in Twain's footsteps is to journey south, west and east from his native Missouri, with spurs floating down the Mississippi River into the Deep South, rambling across to San Francisco, resting in Connecticut and detouring to Hawai'i. Armed with the proper reading material, your mind will be opened and your point of view sharpened by the same land and waters that molded Twain's humor and insight, and inspired within him a literary mischief that bottled a still young and wild USA in the 19th century.

Whether he was writing about the small towns and thick wilderness along the Big Muddy from Missouri to New Orleans, hopping the first steamship to the Sandwich Islands or wandering the streets of San Francisco, Twain made his adventures, real and imagined, leap from the page and take anchor in a reader's mind and heart, as well as the USA's cultural zeitgeist, forever.

Born Samuel Clemens, in Florida, Missouri, in 1835, Twain moved the short distance to Hannibal when he was four. Missouri was a slave state and Hannibal's characters, scenery and politics would later inspire the fictional town of St Petersburg, home of Tom Sawyer and the mischievous orphan hero Huckleberry Finn.

After a stint as a printers' apprentice, Twain became a riverboat pilot and made dozens of trips up and down the Mississippi River before heading west into the Nevada Territory in 1861. He spent two weeks in a stagecoach rolling through the Great Plains and over the Rocky Mountains, before stopping briefly in the new Mormon community of Salt Lake City. After trying his hand at gold mining

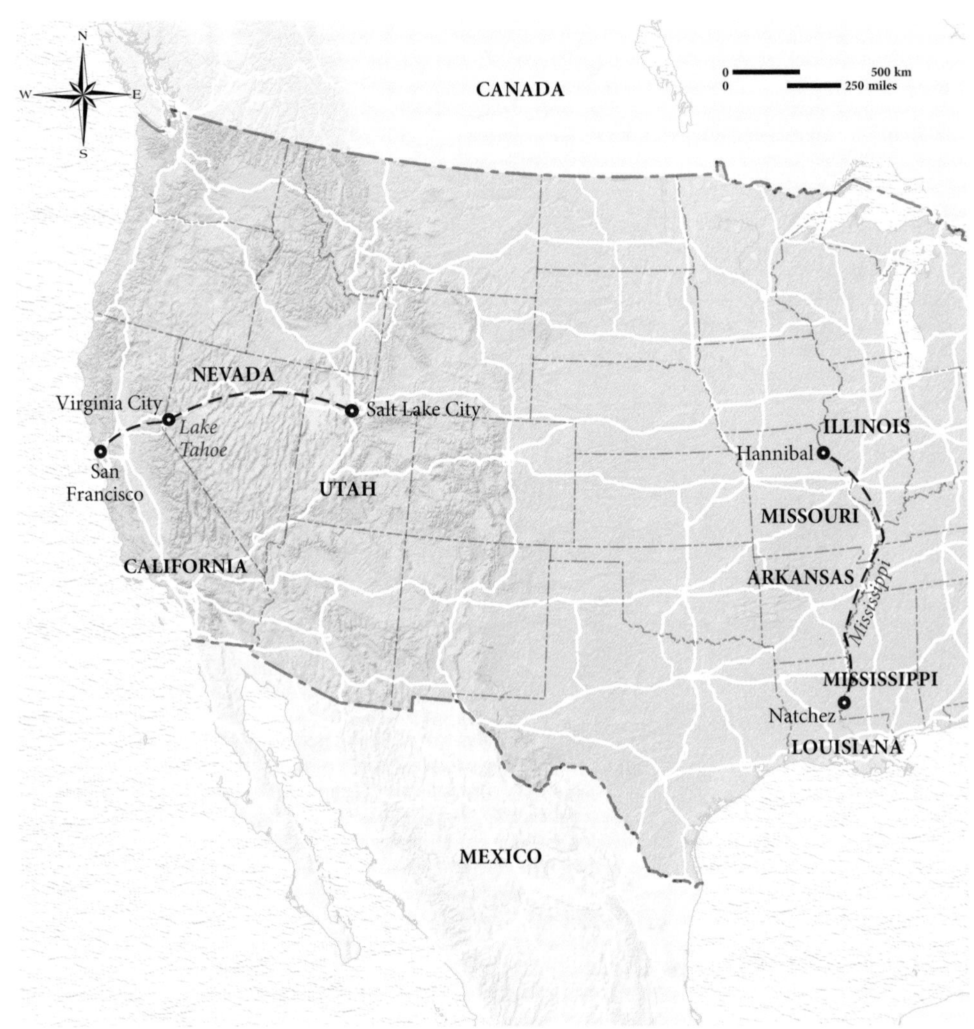

in Virginia City, Nevada, he became a journalist and moved to San Francisco in 1864. From here, local newspapers funded his sojourn to the Sandwich Islands (now Hawaii) and Europe. His most creative period was the 17 years he lived in Hartford, Connecticut, with his family.

The Journey

In Hannibal, the Mark Twain Boyhood Home & Museum is a complex of seven buildings including two houses Twain lived in and the home of Laura Hawkins, the inspiration for Tom's great love, Becky Thatcher. In his 20s, Twain was a commercial steamboat pilot on the Big Muddy, and he got to know all the bends and eddies, towns and outlaws, islands and sandbars that made Huck's grand escape with Jim, the runaway slave, so true to life. You don't have to pilot a driftwood raft to honor that legacy, just join a dinner cruise aboard the Mark Twain Riverboat.

Further downriver, historic antebellum mansions will greet you in Natchez, Mississippi. In the 1840s, there were more millionaires per capita here than anywhere in the world. When Twain passed through, he crashed in a room above the Under-the-Hill Saloon, which remains the best bar in town, with terrific live music on weekends. You can still sleep upstairs at what is now called Mark Twain Guest House. Reserve your bed at the bar.

It takes dedication to re-create the entire overland stagecoach journey he depicted in his 1872 tome, *Roughing It*, though the drive is worth it. You might instead pick up the Mark Twain trail in Salt Lake City. Once a Mormon camp and homestead, Utah's largest city remains one of the US West's best-kept secrets.

Essential Twain

The Celebrated Jumping Frog of Calaveras County (1865) Twain's first important work, originally published in the New York *Saturday Press*, is about a gold-rush gambler named Jim Smiley.

The Adventures of Tom Sawyer (1876) This US classic drew upon Twain's experience growing up along the Mississippi River.

Adventures of Huckleberry Finn (1884) Widely considered his greatest work. Huck Finn, a poor orphan teen, slips from the 'sivilizing' confines of St Petersburg, and escapes his violent, drunken father to float down the Mississippi with runaway slave Jim.

A Connecticut Yankee in King Arthur's Court (1889) In what is considered one of the original time-travel tales, a 19th-century Yankee mingles and meddles in the lives of King Arthur, Sir Lancelot and Guinevere.

Above **Mark Twain House,** Hartford, Connecticut

From here, drive I-80 to the foot of the Sierra Nevada and Virginia City, where you can tour the Mark Twain Museum, set in the offices of the Territorial Enterprise where Twain honed his skills as a journalist. Stay on I-80 and wind your way into the Sierra Nevada and Lake Tahoe. Tahoe trout was one of Twain's favorite foods, and you can still fish here in a deep cobalt lake ringed with jagged granite peaks, but it's all catch and release. San Francisco bay oysters were another favorite of Twain's. Bay pollution is far too severe to consider them a viable protein but you can slurp safely at Hog Island Oyster Bar in the Ferry Building.

Twain cut his teeth as a journeying writer on a nine-month sojourn through the Sandwich Islands in 1866 for the Sacramento Union. Twain-era Honolulu is long gone, but you can still taste wild 19th-century Hawaii on the Big Island, which the 31-year-old explored on horseback. He also paddled with local surfers and rode to the edge of the Kīlauea caldera, its lava flowing then and now.

The former Hartford, Connecticut , home of the legendary author, is now the Mark Twain House & Museum. It was here that Twain penned many of his greatest works, including *Tom Sawyer, Huckleberry Finn* and *A Connecticut Yankee in King Arthur's Court*. The house itself, a Victorian Gothic with fanciful turrets and gables, reflects Twain's quirky character. Inside you'll find 25 rooms including a glass conservatory, a grand library and a billiards room. The house was built in 1873–74, but financial issues demanded a move to Europe in 1891 and the Twain family never lived in the Hartford house, Twain's all-time favorite nest, ever again.

Essential Experiences

- → Visiting the Mark Twain Boyhood Home & Museum in Hannibal to bone up on your Huck Finn knowledge and find the places he transposed into his famous novel.
- → Listening to a banjo strumming, and the Big Muddy sloshing against the bow, on a real Mississippi riverboat.
- → Surveying the Mississippi River from the atmospheric Under-the-Hill Saloon, a glorious dive with bluegrass bands jamming on weekends.
- → Setting out on one of the most beautiful drives in the US West, following the route Twain took through the Utah high desert, up and over the Sierra Nevada, past Lake Tahoe to San Francisco Bay.

To read about:

Kīlauea Volcano see page 76
San Francisco see page 238

Left **Mark Twain,** New Hampshire, 1906

SAN FRANCISCO

City by the Bay

Way back in the olden days – before Google, YouTube, Netflix, Airbnb, Uber, Lyft, social media and personal computers were invented in the San Francisco Bay Area – Spanish novelist Garci Rodríguez de Montalvo imagined California as an island where gold-clad warrior queens paraded around on dragons. Five hundred years later, truth is stranger than fiction in San Francisco. It's got parades of dancing dragons, self-driving bubble cars and glitter-covered queens year-round, from Lunar New Year to Day of the Dead.

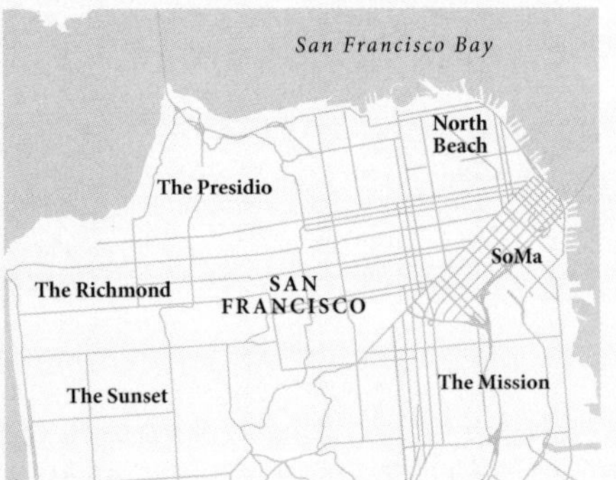

San Francisco has been a hot spot for innovation since WWII, when it served as a base for Allied Pacific operations – and served sass to sailors at drag-hostessed Sunday 'tea dances.' Women and African American technicians led the shipbuilding effort and painstakingly welded together the microchips that launched Silicon Valley. Meanwhile at the Veterans Administration Hospital, the CIA tested LSD on human subjects, intending to create the ultimate soldiers. Instead they kicked off the psychedelic era, with trippy hippie acts at Fillmore Auditorium and optical illusions at the Exploratorium, San Francisco's hands-on museum of human perception. In his pioneering *Whole Earth Catalog,* acid tester Stewart Brand shared his vision of military-grade computers in peaceful hands – and 40 years later, Steve Jobs called Brand to report that his hand-held-computer hallucination was becoming reality.

Today, workdays end in a flourish of smartphones, as people seek happy hours using search engines, killer apps and social platforms that started as cocktail-napkin sketches in Bay Area bars. Ever since biotech pioneer Genentech was founded in a SoMa neighborhood dive in 1976, bartenders have done a brisk trade in start-up launches. Yet this bar scene isn't all business: besides tech giants, SoMa is home to leather bars, art schools and Folsom St fetish fair – San Francisco hasn't blushed since the 1960s, when blue comic Lenny Bruce and burlesque diva Carol Doda defied censorship laws in North Beach bars.

San Francisco's signature blend of artists, techies and LGBT community could be the key to its innovation streak, according to economist Richard Florida's *Rise of the Creative Class.* Where people and ideas meet with acceptance, he argues, they thrive – but that didn't happen overnight. Generations of Bay Area activists have led pioneering civil rights efforts, from overturning the race-based Asian Exclusion Act and anti-gay Defense of Marriage Act to extending basic protections to refugees and immigrants with sanctuary ordinances. Today you can walk in the footsteps of civil rights giants at San Francisco's Chinese Historical Society of America, Japantown History Walk, Castro LGBT Rainbow Honor Walk, and the Mission's mural-lined Calle 24 Latino Cultural District. Walk away feeling braver and bolder, and take San Francisco's golden magic with you.

QUEENS OF SAN FRANCISCO

SAN FRANCISCO / CULTURE

Forget RuPaul's Drag Race. You haven't lived until you've seen a real, live drag show up close and in your face. San Francisco's drag scene dates back to the 1930s, and today the city is at the vanguard of the art form, with fierce, funny and fabulous performances that include everything from exquisite dancing and lip-synching to outrageous performance art.

Here's where to find San Francisco's reigning queens (and kings!) of drag. Prepare to feel underdressed – and to come home with mystery smudges of glitter on your face.

Oasis Topping many a San Francisco 'Best' list, this drag-stravaganza is hosted by beloved SF drag queen Heklina of Trannyshack fame. Their signature show Mother is the quintessential drag experience, and Daughter showcases outrageous up-and-comers.

Aunt Charlie's Located in the Tenderloin and advertising itself as 'sleazy downtown glamour,' old-school Charlie's prides itself on being a little raunchy, a little run-down. Check out a show by the Hot Boxx Girls, or join the fun at a drag dance party.

The Starlight Room Not a night owl? Sunday brunch and sequined drag make a delicious combination. Grab an omelet and watch the fabulous ladies of Sunday's a Drag at this famous venue at the top of the Sir Francis Drake Hotel.

Peaches Christ If you're lucky enough to find one of Peaches' live re-enactments of camp-movie classics on the schedule at the Castro Theater, jump on it immediately: it's one of San Francisco's most iconic shows.

Sisters of Perpetual Indulgence Since 1979, this community-service-oriented group of queer nuns has turned heads all over town with their outlandish habits and drag makeup.

AsiaSF It doesn't have the over-the-top entertainment value of a typical drag show, but watching your 'gender illusionist' server hop up on the bar for a lip-sync number can be titillating for tourists, bachelorette parties, and middle-aged aunts.

Edge Check out the fabulous Monster Drag Show, billed as a 'multi-queen, drag mash-up spectacular,' or Bootie SF, the monthly drag dance party.

Drag king shows Emerging female performers are claiming their place in SF drag history with the monthly show Kingdom and the San Francisco Drag King contest.

To read about:

Vegas Lights see page 40
Mardi Gras in New Orleans see page 178

ART ON THE STREETS OF SAN FRANCISCO

SAN FRANCISCO / ART

Art explodes from frames and jumps off the pedestal in San Francisco, where murals, street performances and impromptu sidewalk altars flow from galleries into alleyways. San Francisco has some unfair artistic advantages: it's a photogenic city with a colorful past. Homegrown traditions of '50s Beat collage, '60s psychedelia, '70s punk, '80s graffiti, '90s skater graphics and 2000s new-media art keep the city's scene vibrant.

Right **Generator mural,** by artists Aaron Noble and Andrew Schoultz

Mission School

With Balmy Alley murals as inspiration, skateboard decks and Clarion Alley garage doors were transformed in the 1990s with boldly outlined, oddly poignant graphics, dubbed 'Mission School' for their storytelling *muralista* sensibilities and graffiti-tag urgency. The Mission School's professor emeritus was the late Margaret Kilgallen, whose closely observed character studies blended hand-painted street signage, comic-book pathos and a miniaturist's attention to detail.

Clare Rojas expanded on these principles with urban folk-art wall paintings, featuring looming, clueless California grizzly bears and tiny, fierce girls in hoodies. Street-art star Barry McGee painted piles of found bottles with freckled, feckless characters, and still shows at the Luggage Store Gallery. Some Mission School art is derided as the faux-naive work of stoned art grads – but when its earnestness delivers, it hits you where it counts.

Sculpture

San Francisco owes its sculpture tradition to a nude sculptor's model: 'Big Alma' Spreckels. She came into a sugar-plantation fortune, which she donated to build the Legion of Honor and its Rodin sculpture court. The government-funded Aquatic Park Bathhouse commissions of the 1940s included the totemic seal by Beniamino Bufano and a sleek green-slate nautical frieze by pioneering African American artist Sargent Johnson.

Bufano also sculpted Chinese revolutionary Sun Yat-sen's statue in Chinatown and San Francisco City College's 1968 *St Francis of the Guns,* made of 1968 guns collected in a local gun-buyback scheme. St Francis' mosaic robe features four assassinated leaders: Abraham Lincoln, Dr Martin Luther King Jr, John F Kennedy and Robert Kennedy.

But the sculptor who made the biggest impact on the San Francisco landscape in terms of sheer scale is Richard Serra, whose contributions range from the lobby sculpture maze at SFMOMA to the University of California San Francisco's Mission Bay campus. Serra's massive, rusted-metal minimalist shapes have been favorably compared to ship's prows – and, less generously, to Soviet factory seconds.

The Less Beloved

Public sculptures have been favorite subjects of debate in the city since 1894, when vigilante art critics pulled down the statue of dentist Henry D Cogswell over a public drinking fountain he'd donated. And Claes Oldenburg and Coosje van Bruggen's 2002 *Cupid's Span* might represent the city's reputation for romance with a giant bow and arrow sunk into the Embarcadero, but the city wasn't smitten: a recent poll ranks it among San Francisco's most despised public artworks. Tony Bennett's musical anthem 'I Left My Heart in San Francisco' inspired the General Hospital's Hearts in San Francisco fundraising project, but the cartoon hearts are regularly graffitied, denounced as eyesores and marked by territorial canine critics.

To read about:
Museums & Art Galleries see page 46
Sand Sculptures see page 262

Best Murals

- → Balmy Alley (The Mission)
- → Clarion Alley (The Mission)
- → SF Art Institute's Diego Rivera Gallery (Russian Hill)
- → Coit Tower (North Beach)
- → WPA Murals at Rincon Annex (SoMa)
- → Women's Building (The Mission)

TOURING SAN FRANCISCO BY CABLE CAR

SAN FRANCISCO / CLASSIC JOURNEYS

Carnival rides pale in comparison with cable cars, San Francisco's vintage public transit. Novices slide into strangers' laps (cable cars were invented in 1873, long before seat belts) but regular commuters just grip leather hand straps, lean back and ride downhill slides like pro surfers.

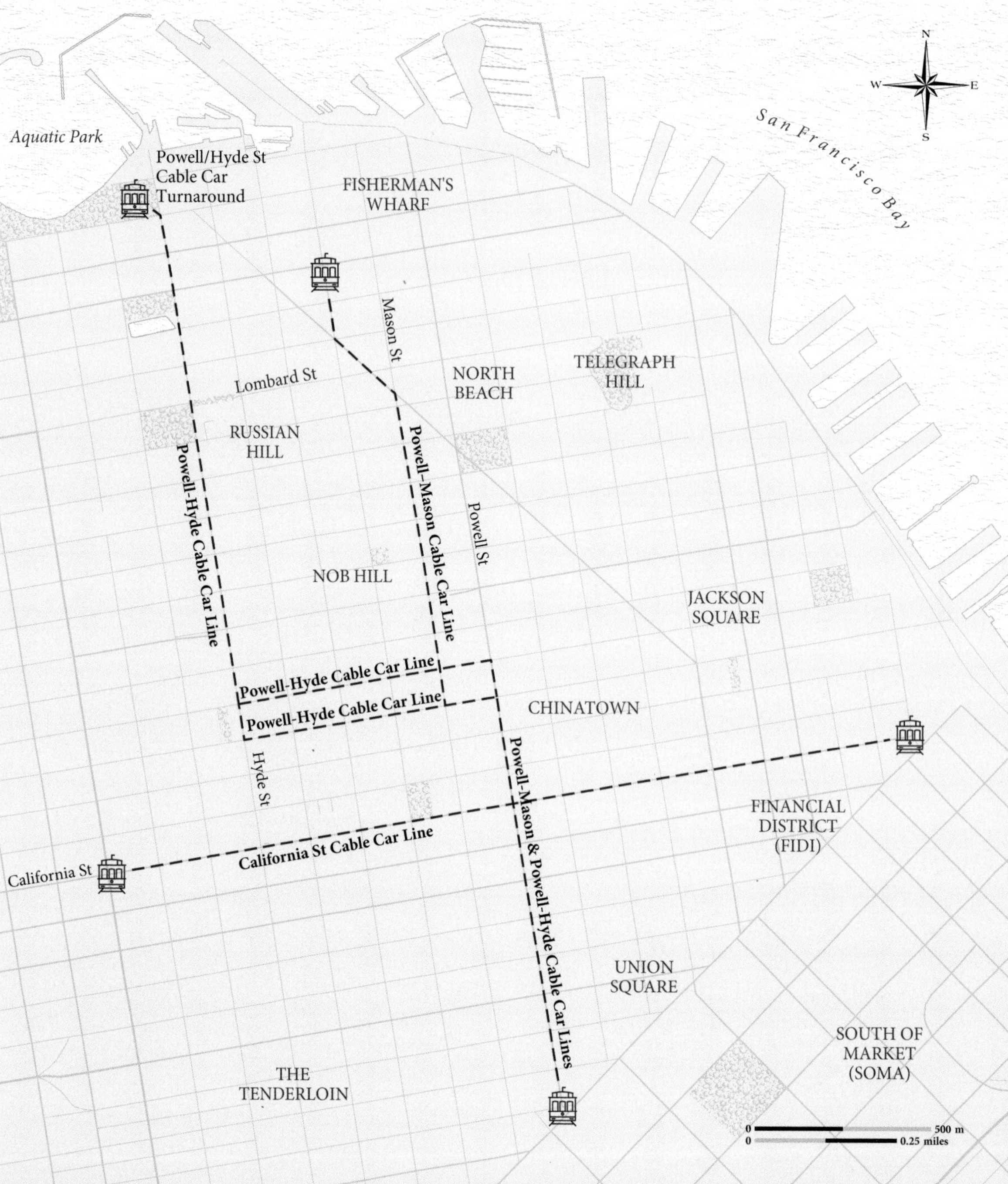

Head to the Powell St Cable Car Turnaround, where you'll see operators turn the car atop a revolving wooden platform. Boarding the red-signed Powell-Hyde cable car marks the beginning of your 338ft ascent of Nob Hill.

As your cable car lurches uphill, you can imagine horses struggling up this slippery crag. Nineteenth-century city planners were skeptical of inventor Andrew Hallidie's 'wire-rope railway' – but after more than a century of near-continuous operation, his wire-and-hemp cables have seldom broken. Hallidie's cable cars even survived the 1906 earthquake and fire that destroyed 'Snob Hill' mansions, returning the faithful to rebuilt Grace Cathedral. Hop off for a closer look at the cathedral, and to say hello to San Francisco's gentle patron, St Francis, carved by sculptor Beniamino Bufano.

Back on the Powell-Hyde car in the same direction, bay views are on offer as you careen past crooked, flower-lined Lombard St down toward Fisherman's Wharf. The waterfront terminus is named for Friedel Klussman, who saved cable cars from mayoral modernization plans in 1947. She did the math: cable cars brought in more tourism dollars than they cost in upkeep. The mayor demanded a vote – and lost to 'the Cable Car Lady' by a landslide. For Klussman's funeral, in 1986, cable cars citywide were draped in black.

Take a wander around the wharf, seeing San Francisco as sailors did, by descending into the submarine USS *Pampanito*. Then hitch the Powell-Mason cable car to North Beach.

Here's your chance to see Diego Rivera's 1934 cityscape at the San Francisco Art Institute, stroll through North Beach and Chinatown alleyways, or hop back on the Powell-Mason line to time-travel through the Chinese Historical Society of America. To top your journey off, catch a ride on the city's oldest line: the California St cable car. Its terminus is near the Ferry Building, where champagne-and-oyster happy hour awaits the weary cable-car traveler.

To read about:
The Pacific Coast Highway see page 42
California Zephyr Trains see page 70

REMEMBERING THE SUMMER OF LOVE

SAN FRANCISCO / HISTORY & FESTIVALS

In 1967, peace, love and psychedelia burst from the San Francisco underground into the mainstream, heralding the Summer of Love. Pop the Grateful Dead on your headphones, stick on your finest floral shirt and make for these must-see sights in the one-time heartland of the hippies.

To understand how the hippies took over San Francisco, you need to go back to the 1950s and explore that other Californian cultural phenomenon, the Beats. The Beat Museum in North Beach chronicles Jack Kerouac's pioneering journeys across America that led to his seminal novel *On the Road,* a huge influence on the teenagers who would pioneer the hippie movement and be at the forefront of the Summer of Love. The museum retains a chilled vibe very much in keeping with 1967, with old hippies selling tickets and sharing tales of the good old days.

Nearby City Lights bookstore, founded by Beat poet Lawrence Ferlinghetti, was and is a totem of San Francisco's countercultural movement. Its leftfield selections and readings by local authors made it the intellectual heart of the Summer of Love. These days the shelves are stacked with everything from surrealist treatises to green politics: a true reflection of the academic side of the hippie dream.

The unquestionable epicenter of the hippie movement that began in San Francisco in 1964 was the intersection of Haight and Ashbury. Known simply as the Haight, the area was home to some of the scene's biggest names, from Jefferson Airplane to Janis Joplin, as well as the first 'head' shop, helping the booming numbers of visiting teenagers 'turn on, tune in and drop out.' Having emerged from years as a seedy district, the Haight now trades on its hippie past with vintage clothes stores, bars and brunch spots.

San Francisco's vast Golden Gate Park was the go-to spot for the hordes piling into the city as 1967 got underway. The park's Polo Fields were the site of the Human Be-In in January 1967, with as many as 30,000 young people gathering to see Timothy Leary urge them to 'drop out,' and Big Brother and the Holding Company play their brand of bluesy psychedelic rock. Today it's seen as a defining counterculture event, which kicked off the Summer of Love.

The tripped-out tracks of 1967 define the Summer of Love to this day. And no venue was as important to this burgeoning scene as the Fillmore Auditorium. The focal point of the San Francisco music boom, the Fillmore was turned into the coolest auditorium in the world by the hottest bands, and you hadn't made it until you took to the stage there. Jimi Hendrix, the Byrds, the Doors and Pink Floyd all rocked out during that heady summer.

The Summer of Love might never have happened were it not for author Ken Kesey and his Merry Pranksters, a band of early hippies who rode a colorfully painted bus from San Francisco across the United States. To round off your '60s San Francisco flashback, do a local version with San Francisco Love Tours – it offers rides in a converted 1970s VW campervan, replete with beaded curtains, garish seats and a psychedelic paint job, taking in all the classic sights around the city with bonus flowers and blissed-out folk on the stereo.

To read about:
Fireworks see page 96
Marijuana Edibles see page 272

Surprising Experiences

The Underrated, Unexpected & Downright Mysterious

In the USA you expect cars and burgers, baseball and apple pie. But houseboat villages and firefly mating parties? These are less-heralded wonders – and there are many along the nation's byroads and back roads. Rest assured that even in this Google-mapped, Instagram-snapped era, you can still roll into places that have the power to astonish and turn assumptions upside down.

Take the Extraterrestrial Highway that runs through a forsaken patch of Nevada desert. You might think of Americans as a practical, no-nonsense bunch, but 45% of them believe aliens have visited the earth. The folks who live by the highway certainly do, and they have the UFO sightings to prove it. Here's another quirky statistic: 18% of Americans have seen a ghost, according to the Pew Research Center. Which may explain why haunted houses draw seekers nationwide, especially in paranormal hot spots like Salem, Massachusetts, where witches once roamed.

Michigan may be less enigmatic, but it still shocks with its 3288 miles (5292km) of coastline, prime for sunrise and sunset watching. Appalachia flies under the radar of typical tourist itineraries, though hip towns (and the aforementioned fireflies) dot the landscape. And who knew about America's caves? There are 5000 mapped miles (8047km) of them, which let you truly burrow into the country's underground scene.

The more offbeat and underestimated a site, the more it impresses. Americans have always embraced the underdog, stemming from the country's history as a wee colony that fought the power. Maybe that's why wildflowers blooming in California's bleak desert thrill, and why the city of Detroit's climb back from urban oblivion to urban innovator rouses so many cheers. You never know what you'll find out there.

Extraterrestrial Highway

NEVADA / ROAD TRIPS, WEIRD & WONDERFUL

Strange lights in the sky, top-secret government facilities and little green men – something strange is going on in Nevada. This desert-swept region of the southern part of the state has the highest concentration of UFO sightings in the US (the top-secret Area 51 base nearby is a likely source), and it's all along a single stretch of road.

Running 98 miles (158km) between the twin ghost towns of Crystal Springs and Warm Springs, Nevada State Road 375 cuts through a hard desert landscape of mountain peaks, cattle ranches and very few towns. But in this vast, empty land you might have your best chance of meeting someone from another world.

The highway has become a pilgrimage for sky-eyed travelers. Reports of aircraft flying at unimaginable speeds, alien technologies and an ultra-secret air-force base all add to the mysterious attraction of this otherwise barren desert. At just over two hours from Las Vegas, it's an easy road trip.

From Crystal Springs, travelers pass stops like ET Fresh Jerky, which sells myriad dried fruits and meats under a handpainted sign depicting a cow being lifted by the ray of a flying saucer's tractor beam. Stop here for snacks before hitting the road. It's also the last place to 'drop your toxic waste' until Area 51, according to the sign. A bit further reveals the 30ft-tall aluminum alien that marks the entrance to the Alien Research Center, a gift shop of sorts offering the latest Area 51 coffee mugs, T-shirts and books to channel your inner Fox Mulder.

Heading north, you'll find little save for the occasional cattle guard that rumbles beneath the tires or a dust devil in the distance. This close to Area 51, contrails and sonic booms become the norm. The base itself is off limits, and if you want a peek inside you'll have to stop for a hike up Mt Tikaboo, a summit nearly 26 miles (42km) away but the nearest one that hasn't been swallowed by the covert base. From this perch you can see the runways, hangars and industrial buildings of Area 51. It's also the perfect vantage point to spot UFOs.

The Black Mailbox

For years a solitary black mailbox stood at the side of the Extraterrestrial Highway. The only significant feature in the lone and level desert, the mailbox became the meeting point for hopeful UFO spotters. The mailbox acquired its own kind of lore, and people began filling it with messages to aliens. They also shot at it, painted it and eventually stole it. Steve Medlin, who owned the mailbox, replaced it with a padlocked bulletproof box listing his name, and a second one labeled 'ALIEN,' specifically for messages to extraterrestrial life. In 2014, though, both mailboxes were stolen. The stand-in box that replaced them has become a sort of alien shrine.

Rumors of strange encounters began just after WWII, when commercial pilots started seeing aircraft flying at never-before-seen altitudes, and odd, wedge-shaped flying objects began tearing across the skies. A secretive base known as Groom Lake, also known as its map designation Area 51, became the epicenter of these strange sightings.

The official story is that the UFOs were simply top-secret aircraft tests. As the Iron Curtain descended over the Soviet Union, the US military began testing methods to peep inside. Contemporary military aircraft, which flew at a maximum of 40,000ft (12,192m), were deemed too risky to penetrate Soviet borders, so Eisenhower approved the development of new aircraft that could fly at much higher altitudes.

Soon, the U-2 reconnaissance aircraft was born, topping out at 60,000ft (18,288m) on snooping missions. Further developments, including foreign jet fighters like the MiG-21 and the angular F-117 added to the stories of strange sightings. But maybe that's just what they want you to believe.

In 1989, reporter George Knapp interviewed a man on a Las Vegas TV station who said he was an employee at a facility near Area 51. Among several claims were that the man (named 'Dennis' to hide his identity) participated in the reverse engineering of alien technology and that aliens had been interacting with humans for over 10,000 years. 'Dennis' was unmasked for a second interview, and Bob Lazar was identified by name. The interviews were a mega hit, and news about the secretive facility went worldwide. Other stories of strange encounters at Area 51 became mainstream. Soon, curious alien-seekers began coming to the area to see for themselves.

They found a mostly quiet area in the Nevada desert that has the highest concentration of UFO sightings in the United States. In 1996, the Nevada Commission on Tourism capitalized on the interest, officially naming the SR 375 the Extraterrestrial Highway.

Today the Extraterrestrial Highway remains a spiritual journey for believers, but it's a lonely pilgrimage: fewer than 200 people make the trip down the highway each year. The route crosses no major roads, there are no stops for gas, and static rules the radio. In this strange, barren void, the eye is hungry for some signs of life – a flash on the horizon, movement against a distant mountain or lights dancing in a night sky are all welcome signs that we are not alone.

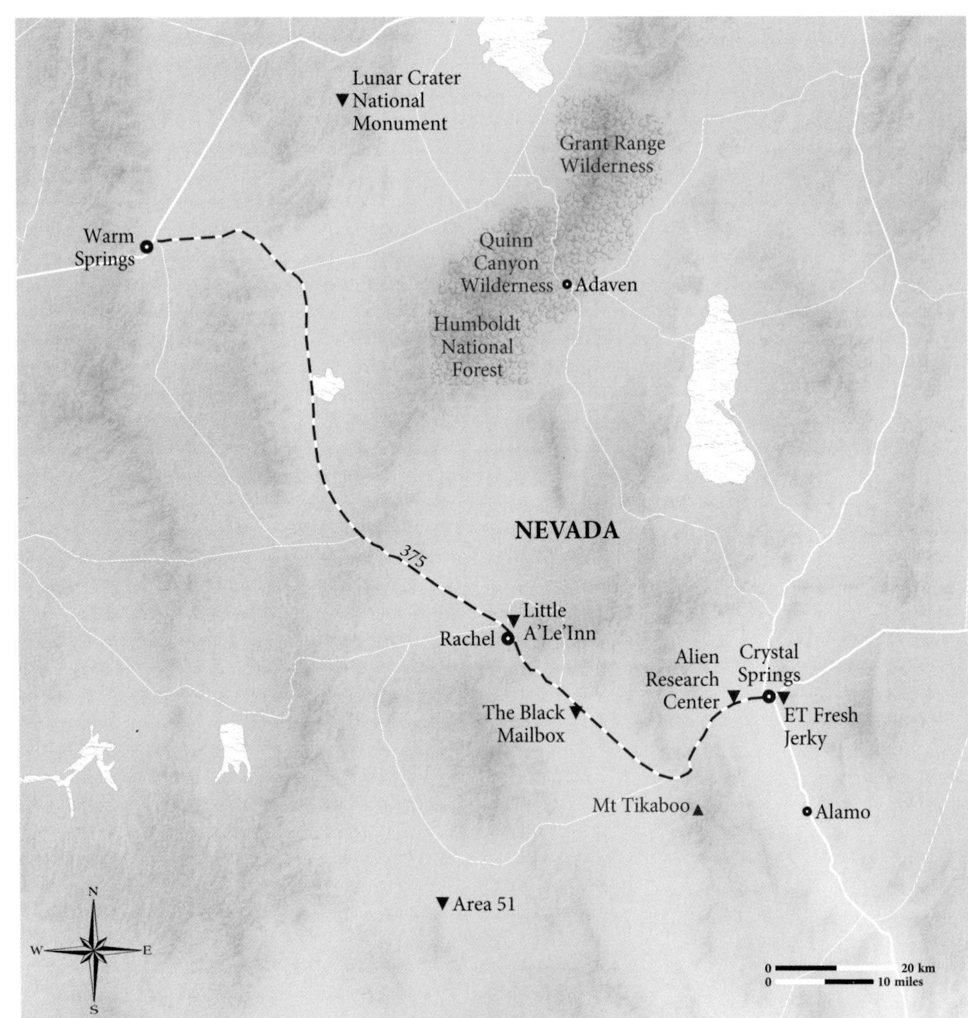

It's not until you hit Rachel, Nevada, that anything resembling civilization returns to the horizon. The nearest town to Area 51, Rachel is the best place to swap stories with folks who've had run-ins with mysterious government agents or seen strange lights in the sky. Most travelers make a pit stop at the Little A'Le'Inn (pronounced Little Alien), a diner and motel that serves up stories of strange encounters between hot cups of coffee. Spend the night to increase your chances of seeing mysterious lights dance in the sky. Ask nicely and you might just get directions to the dirt road that leads right up to the gates of Area 51.

But there's one last stop: just beyond the northern end of the Extraterrestrial Highway near Warm Springs, an alien world seems etched into the landscape. But in spite of its name, the Lunar Crater National Monument was created by a wholly terrestrial force. A deep 400-acre (162-hectare) and 430ft (131m) crater is the centerpiece of a 100-sq-mile (259-sq-km) volcanic field. Looking out over the crater rim, you might wonder why on earth visitors from another world would want to come to a desert wasteland in the middle of Nevada. But perhaps it's because it looks like home – the unusual, pock-marked landscape was used by NASA to prepare astronauts for the Apollo missions to the moon.

To read about:
Salem Witch Trials see page 274
Spooky Houses & Multiverses see page 296

Above **Little A'Le'Inn,** Rachel

California's Desert in Bloom

CALIFORNIA / LANDSCAPES

After the winter rains the wildflowers bloom, and California's national parks are the place to kickstart spring and see hundreds of flowering species such as desert lilies, sunflowers and lavender. Swaths of vibrant yellow, purple and orange buds cover central and southern California and, during the peak of the season from March to May, parks post updates on which flowers are in bloom and where to find them. The Anza-Borrego Desert State Park, the largest US state park outside of Alaska and home to more than 92 plant families, even provides a wildflower hotline for visitors to phone.

To read about:
The Grand Canyon see page 34
New Mexico Landscapes see page 208

Cruising the Lobster Shacks of Maine's Atlantic Way

MAINE / FOOD & DRINK

Lobster shacks, seafood baskets and warming chowders are a way of life in coastal Maine, where lobster is so ubiquitous it was once the preserve of the poor.

Right **Lobster boats,**
Camp Ellis, Maine

The southern coast of Maine wears its maritime heart on its windblown sleeve. Fog-draped lighthouses dot the coast. Fishing boats cruise island-speckled bays. Lobster pounds and clam shacks jostle for attention along the US 1 highway: lobster alone comprises 13.5% of the value of state exports. Once so common it was considered suitable only for the poor or prisoners, lobster today is a global delicacy.

Why do lobsters thrive here? Thank the rocky coastline, which offers hiding places for young lobsters, and effective protection measures that have been implemented to prevent over-harvesting. In this area of the USA, fish, oysters and clams are often fried, arriving with a simple side of French fries, coleslaw and tartar sauce. Lobsters are steamed or broiled and typically served with a side of drawn (melted), butter.

Every self-respecting coastal town from Kittery north to Calais has a scruffy lobster shack near the local dock – they're great places to slurp thick seafood chowders and savor warm lobster rolls. In the past decade, innovative chefs in Portland – southern Maine's urban anchor – have embraced all that is fresh and local while adding global kick, making it a highly respected center of gastronomy for a town of such a small size (population 66,000). The buzziest restaurants cluster in and around the Old Port district downtown. Allagash Brewing Co jump-started the craft beer scene when it began operations in 1995 and today the town is heaving with microbreweries. For road-trippers, travel in Maine is best enjoyed from late May through to October – many businesses close in colder months.

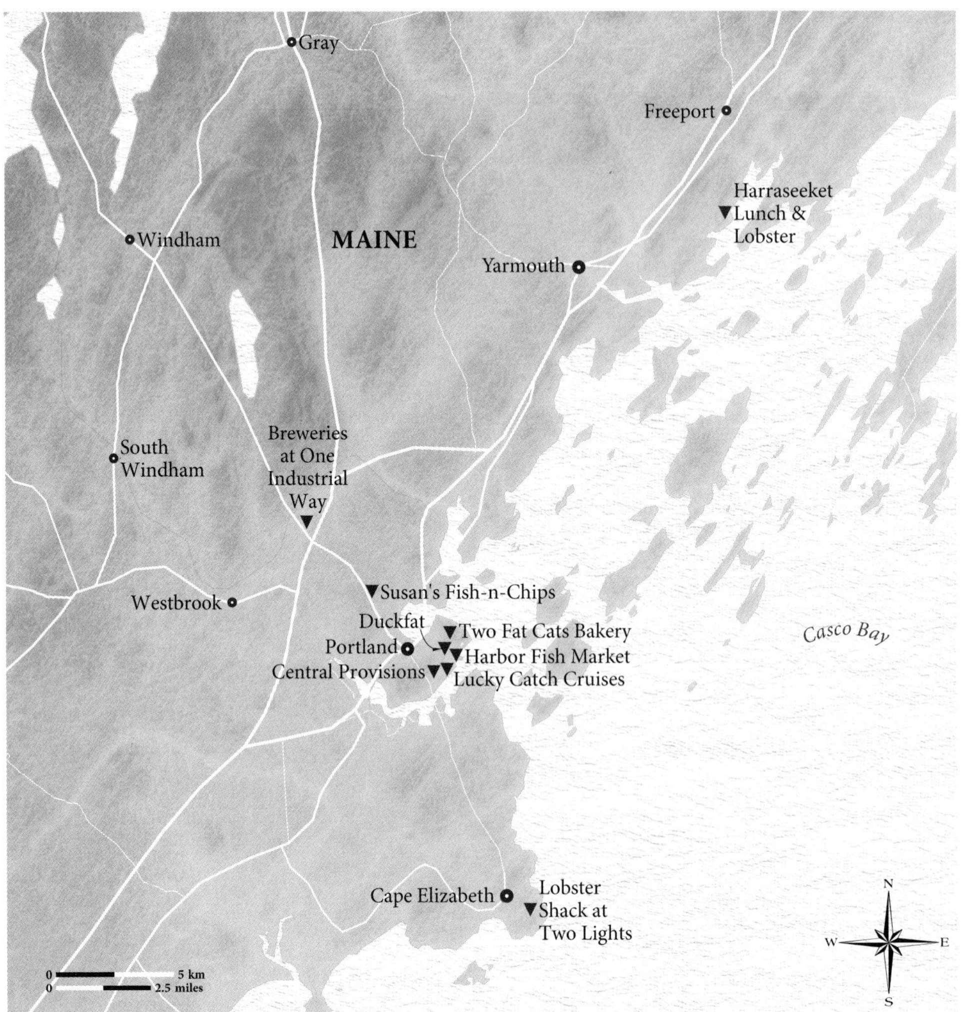

Lobster Shack at Two Lights

Red picnic tables overlook a craggy coast. A majestic lighthouse breaks the skyline. And a brigade of red food trays overflows with lobster rolls, clam chowders and crinkle-cut fries. Yep, you're stepping into a postcard at the Lobster Shack at Two Lights, perched beside the Atlantic Ocean in Cape Elizabeth, 8 miles (13km) south of Portland.

It's a scenic spot where you will bump elbows with other diners, but the crowds add to the sense of fun at this third-generation lobster shack. Lobster rolls here are simple and traditional: a hot-dog bun lined with lettuce, stuffed with fresh lobster meat and topped with mayo and a pickle slice. Drizzle some drawn butter for a whoosh of extra flavor.

Lucky Catch Cruises

You can live the life of a lobster-catcher – if only for 90 minutes – as a passenger aboard the *Lucky Catch,* a commercial lobster boat. Cruises depart throughout the day from Long Wharf in downtown Portland's Old Port district and head into Casco Bay to pull up lobster traps. During the trip, crew members show passengers how to bait and set traps and how to rubber-band lobster claws.

Captain and owner Tom Martin calls these excursions 'trap-to-table' experiences because guests can eat the day's lobster catch at Portland Lobster Company. After paying the wholesale price for the lobster, carry your precious cargo in and hand over to the restaurant: a meal for $10.

Duckfat

As you cozy into your seat at the bar, pause to appreciate the view into Duckfat's kitchen. The restaurant is tiny, but the food packs a punch: everything that can be fried is done so in delicious duck fat.

First up? Handcut Belgian fries. These wickedly good potatoes arrive in a paper cone along with the dipping sauce of your choice. The *poutine* French fries beckon with duck-juice gravy, cheese curd and a sunny-side-up egg if you want it (and you do).

Duckfat opened in 2005, kick-starting Portland's swift rise as one of Northeast USA's top food destinations. Award-winning chef Rob Evans and wife and co-owner Nancy Pugh source locally, from the bread to the produce to the duck eggs to the beer.

Two Fat Cats Bakery

Don't believe in love at first sight? Then you've never gazed at a whoopie pie inside the cozy confines of Two Fat Cats Bakery. Boasting a fluffy layer of marshmallow buttercream sandwiched between chocolate snack cakes, this Maine specialty is a flirt.

Made fresh each morning, whoopie pies and other classic American desserts are the focus at this 10-year-old bakery two blocks east of the Old Port district. Think red velvet cupcakes, mixed berry pie and three-level vanilla cake with lemon custard, all of it made from scratch. As for whoopie pies, they became Maine's official state treat in 2011. Popular in Maine as well as the Pennsylvania Amish Country, the treat earned its name, we hear, because Amish farmers yelled 'whoopie!' when finding one in their lunch pail.

Maine Festivals

Just to the north, Yarmouth sees 6000lb (2722kg) of clams served at the Clam Festival in mid-July. In mid-October, watch lobster chefs in action, join a beer-and-whiskey crawl and sample Maine's finest foods at Harvest on the Harbor in Portland.

Harbor Fish Market

Entering Harbor Fish Market is an adventure for the senses. There's the chatter of people and the action of traders steaking fish with sharp knives. You'll hear the sounds of the skinning machine and confront four large, bubbling lobster tanks as you enter. And did we mention the smell? Wrap up warm, because the sheer volume of ice can make the place quite damp. Co-owner Mike Alfiero has been running the market with his family for 50 years and says the location is unique – like going back in time. The variety of seafood for sale is impressive: if it lives in the sea, you'll probably find it here. For meals to go, staff can pack a cooler for a road trip or cook a lobster for you to take away.

Ready to tackle your first boiled lobster? Then bib up and follow these instructions: twist the skinny legs then slurp out the meat. Next, twist off the claws. After breaking the claws with the cracker, dip their meat in drawn butter. Savor the exquisite flavor. Next, twist the tail until you break it. Remove each flipper, extract the meat. And yes, you made a mess, but it's totally expected.

Susan's Fish-n-Chips

Mmm, chowder. Or *chowdah* as they say in New England. The best of these milk- or cream-based soups burst with local seafood. Chowders trace back to 16th- and 17th-century English and French coastal villages. New World settlers created their own variations based on local bounty and today, most are prepared with potatoes and onions.

What you won't taste in New England clam chowder? Tomatoes. Tomatoes are found in Manhattan clam chowder, a soup created in New York City and deemed inferior by self-respecting New Englanders. For her seafood chowder, Susan Eklund of Susan's Fish-n-Chips combines her thick and creamy fish and clam chowders with shrimp, scallops and lobsters – all fresh and local. Slurp it from a bread bowl or sprinkle it with crackers.

At this locals' joint just outside downtown Portland, you can also enjoy free coffee with your meal, scoop tartar sauce from a mason jar and, in summer, bite into fried lobster on a stick.

Central Provisions

The redbrick Central Provisions is Portland's latest It Girl. The critics love it and so should you – as locals will attest, this ingenue earns the kudos. The menu changes daily, spotlighting seasonal fare, while a thoughtful wine list and craft cocktails keep diners well watered. Small plates embrace the salt of the earth and the sea, such as local caviar, Otter Cove oysters and sea urchin.

This Old Port restaurant sits inside one of the city's oldest buildings, built in 1828. Angle for a seat overlooking the line chefs in action. In warmer months, look for locally sourced blueberry desserts. Local oysters are on the menu year-round.

Harraseeket Lunch & Lobster

The red-and-white icon that is Harraseeket Lunch & Lobster is hard to miss. A classic Maine lobster pound, it's more formal than a lobster shack but certainly not fancy. Lobster pounds traditionally hold lobsters in tanks with circulating water and sell the crustaceans by weight. Take a moment to enjoy the picturesque collection of yachts on the water before placing your order for a seafood basket and fried onion 'middles' at the front window.

For steamed clams or live or boiled lobsters, walk around the corner of the building to the lobster pound. If the picnic tables are full, dine off the hood of your car like a local. Harraseeket is BYOB so bring your favorite Maine beer for the meal.

Breweries at One Industrial Way

You'll hear the rumors about Epiphany well before your arrival at Foundation Brewing Company, an innovative microbrewery producing brown ales, IPAs and farmhouse brews. The golden-orange Epiphany, a double IPA, wins acolytes with its juicy blend of citrus, tropical fruit and pine. Co-owner John Bonney explains that it's all about the hops. You might taste pineapple and mango on the nose, then get a little bit of pine in the back. The bad news? It sells out.

Fortunately, several other craft beers are on tap at the thriving collection of breweries bordering Industrial Way, a strip of warehouses 20 minutes from downtown Portland. Foundation shares space with Austin Street Brewing and it can be a convivial scene, with food trucks (typically Thursday to Saturday) and patio lounging.

For your last afternoon, start at Foundation, hit Austin St then cross the street to Belgian-style powerhouse Allagash Brewing. From here, it's half a mile to DL Geary Brewing Company, which kick-started the Portland microbrewery scene.

Right **Bass Harbor Head Light,**
Acadia National Park, Maine

Driving Tour: Stephen King's Maine

Stephen King has two homes in Maine, and many of his gritty horror stories are set in the state. For this 300-mile (482km) road trip, take maritime US Rte 1 'downeast' from Portland to Ellsworth, then detour south and loop around the Acadia Scenic Byway, one of 31 All-American Roads.

The coastal route brings you past icons (the LL Bean store, the Bath Iron Works), natural wonders (the entire coastline), marvels of construction (the 1827 Pemaquid lighthouse, Bucksport's Penobscot Narrows Bridge), picturesque harbors (Camden, Bar Harbor) and unexpected artist havens (Portland, Belfast, Rockland). Get out of the car and hike in the Camden Hills or Acadia National Park. Or take a car ferry to explore the Fox Islands or Deer Isle. End up in pleasant Bangor, King's part-time residence and gateway to Maine's wild north. Crowds thin and the foliage is spectacular in the autumn; be ready for inclement weather at any time of year.

To read about:
World Food see page 88
American Diners see page 130

Sensational Sand-Sculpting

USA-WIDE / FESTIVALS

Sand-sculpting might be one of the world's most ephemeral art forms, but it's also one of its fastest-growing. Over the last decade, festivals and competitions have transformed US beaches into al-fresco museums, pushing the boundaries of sand-sculpture way beyond standard bucket-and-spade creations and into the realms of serious art.

Right **Texas SandFest**

Texas SandFest
Said to be the best-attended sand-sculpting extravaganza in the US, Texas SandFest attracts around 100,000 people to tiny Port Aransas (population 3400) in Texas for a three-day festival every April. Despite its size, the event prides itself on being a nonprofit, community-driven affair where the Michelangelos of the sand-sculpting world rub shoulders with neophytes taking their first lesson. This might just be one of the best small-town festivals in the US.

American Sandsculpting Championships
Not surprisingly, Florida hosts more sand-sculpting events than any other state. The pinnacle is the Fort Myers 'championships' that takes place every year in late November and is one of the largest sand art spectacles in the world, attended by masters and amateurs alike.

Master Sandsculpting Competition
New Hampshire has the shortest coastline of any US state (just 18 miles/29km), but this hasn't stopped master sand-sculptors descending on Hampton Beach every June to compete in this relatively new but hugely prestigious competition – with $15,000 in prize money up for grabs. At the competition's conclusion, the masterpieces are sprayed with a special glue to allow them to stand on show several weeks longer.

Neptune Festival
Part of a 44-year-old event encompassing wine, surfing and triathlon in Virginia Beach, Virginia, the Neptune has an international flavor with 300 sand molders from a dozen countries battling it out for a sizeable purse of prizes. The centerpiece is 'Land of Sand,' a huge tent full of accomplished sculptures that sit alongside rapid 'quicksand' creations fashioned by talented speed merchants. Many of the exhibits are lit up at night and left on show for 10 days.

Sandcastle Day
One of Oregon's most spectacular strips of sand gets to look even more magnificent during this 54-year-old festival in Cannon Beach that is now recognized as a 'heritage tradition.' Bonfires blaze, locals march in parades, and master sandbuilders race against the tide.

Blue Water SandFest
A relatively new event held in Port Huron, Michigan, in July that emphasizes fun and audience interaction with lessons, demonstrations, 10-minute head-to-heads and lots of family-friendly activities.

American Institute of Architects SandCastle Competition
Imagine! A sand-sculpting competition organized by architects. This sand-building bonanza held every June in Galveston, Texas, has 60 teams competing against each other in various categories, including technicality, creativity, carving, concept and execution. Not surprisingly, it inspires some unusually modern and avant-garde creations, with the winner taking home the distinguished Golden Bucket award.

To read about:
LA Beaches see page 92
Albuquerque Balloon Festival see page 222

A Leaf-Peeping Cycling Tour

VERMONT / CYCLING

Drink in the fall foliage – and gallons of maple syrup – on a cycling circuit between some of the Northeast's most winsome towns.

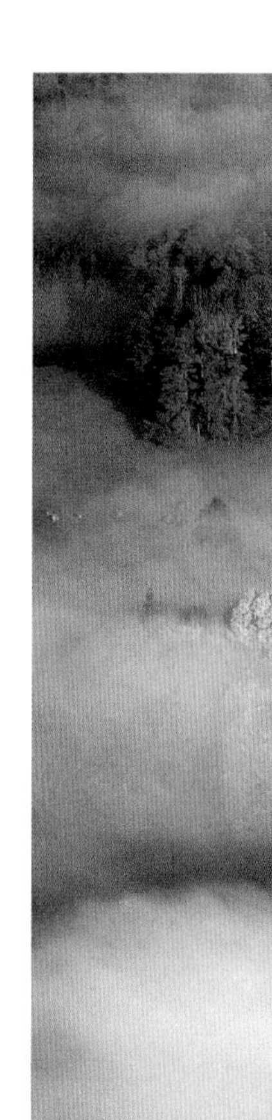

The flaming fall foliage in Vermont is a knockout. Cycling along the leafy back lanes of Addison County, you'll savor the gentle burn in your calves on the short ascents, then the whispered kiss of the September breeze on your face as you freewheel down. Alternately puffing and purring, you'll happily drink in the ubiquitous woodscapes of crimson and incandescent amber.

Riding through central Vermont in fall is like cycling through a succession of mesmerizing screensavers. Forested hillsides glow with traffic-light hues: red and amber and vibrant green. Red Dutch-gabled barns rise from cornfields, wooden covered bridges span serene waterways and pumpkins are piled at roadsides. It's idealized New England turned up to 11 – and biking heaven. Savor it all on this 100-mile (161km) triangular ride between three of the most charming burgs in the Champlain Valley, which lies midway from Massachusetts to Montreal. The broad, undulating dale, bounded by the Green Mountains to the east and New York State's Adirondacks to the west, is becoming renowned for inn-to-inn cycling tours, as is Vermont in general – with good reason.

For starters, it's predominantly rural – only Wyoming has a smaller population than Vermont; the state's tallest building is only 11 stories; and most of its roads are wide, quiet and eminently bike-friendly. The food's terrific, all artisan this and that, craft beers and, well, oceans of maple syrup. And it's breathtakingly beautiful.

Your three-day jaunt begins in Brandon, an artsy little settlement of clapboard houses where wicker chairs rock on shady verandas. Time your trip well and a handful of chilly nights will have kick-started the leaf-peeping season, so when you saddle up

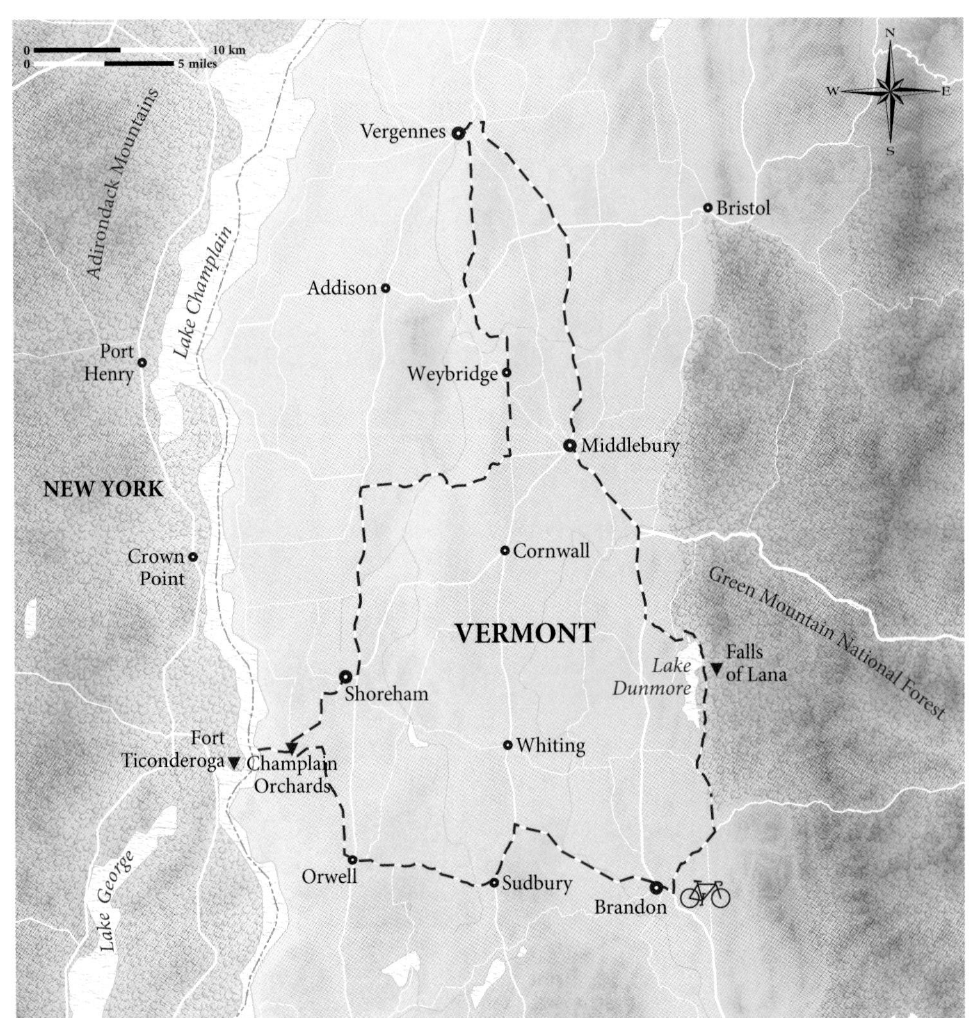

on a crisp September morning, the hilltops will already be smoldering with fall colors.

Toot languidly along Park St and out past traditional farmsteads, not forgetting to glance at the map to confirm your deliberately tortuous path. The plan is to pedal about four hours each day, covering 30 or 40 miles (48 to 64km) – but the line marking your route staggers around the map like a drunken spider, partly to avoid busy roads, partly to take in the most scenic patches.

A speedy pace is impossible anyway, because photo calls came thick and fast. You'll no sooner pack away the camera after one viewpoint than another materializes. First up is the Falls of Lana, cascading 66ft (20m) or so down the forested hillside. Then you'll skirt Lake Dunmore, wooden jetties jutting into placid waters. You might manage half a mile before being waylaid for 10 minutes snapping grazing cows, hayfields and grain silos, or a barn-cum-antiques-store from which spill toy cars, rusty signs, vintage hoes and whirligigs.

With these detours, it'll likely be mid-afternoon when you meander into the night's halt, Middlebury. The archetypal Vermont college town (Robert Frost lectured here) is blessed with white-spired churches, galleries, cafes and views over the burbling Otter River. Stroll along its brick-built main street and explore the Henry Sheldon Museum – 'Bringing Vermont History to Life Since 1882' – and Vermont Folklore Center, showcasing local arts and crafts.

Next morning, fuel up at the farmers market, its stalls laden with breads, cheeses, goat's milk soap, and mountains of pumpkins the glowing ochre of late afternoon sun. Not to mention maple syrup. Bottles and jugs and flasks and flagons of maple syrup.

Fall Cycle on the West Coast

Sonoma County is where California's velo and vino cultures collide in a happy claret splatter every autumn. For a classic Wine Country ride, leave the hub town of Healdsburg, ride along Westside and turn right onto West Dry Creek Rd, an undulating 9-mile (14km) avenue that's one of California's most popular cycling roads. At Yoakim Bridge Rd, cross the valley to Dry Creek Rd, hang a left and climb Canyon Rd before enjoying the descent into Alexander Valley. Turn right, roll through Geyserville, cross Russian River and take Hwy 128, Red Winery and Pine Flat roads back towards Healdsburg, via Jimtown, with valley-hugging vineyards to the right and hills ablaze with autumnal colors on your left.

Loaded with portable calories, pedal back into the countryside en route to Shoreham, 10 miles (16km) or so from Middlebury. But why go direct when you can enjoy the ever-more-scenic route? Instead of heading directly west, make a circuitous loop north via Vergennes, getting waylaid periodically by whimsical road names demanding to be checked out: Lemon Fair Rd, Bittersweet Falls Rd, Snake Mountain Rd. The latter traces a ridge providing panoramic views across the broad sweep of the Champlain Valley, Middlebury's college and steeples rising from a sea of autumn colors to your left.

Bolstered by a hearty breakfast in Shoreham – maybe, for instance, a mountain of blueberry pancakes – you might be in the mood for a final-day detour. Pedal for the turn-off to Larrabee Pt, where a ferry crosses Lake Champlain to New York State and historic Fort Ticonderoga. And if you pass a roadside army of painted wooden creatures, stop to investigate. In the adjacent barn is the gallery of sculptor Norton Latourelle, who has carved a Noah's ark of dogs, birds and rabbits – plus a curious long-necked beast labelled 'Champ' which, Latourelle claims, predates the Loch Ness Monster. Champ was described by the early French explorer Samuel de Champlain as a '20-ft serpent, thick as a barrel and with the head of a horse.' A tall tale, to be sure. But a search for a mysterious water creature might provide just the excuse to return and pedal some more of Vermont's snaking, sensational byways.

To read about:
South Bay Bicycle Trail in LA see page 93
Farm-to-Table Food see page 194

Apple Picking in Vermont

The century-old Champlain Orchards, 16 miles (26km) southwest of Middlebury, sells sweet and hard cider year-round, with pick-your-own cherries, peaches, plums and berries starting in June. Its busiest season is late summer, when more than 100 varieties of apples are ripe for the picking, and seasonal festivals fill the air with fiddle tunes and family fun.

Floating Houses in Sausalito

CALIFORNIA / ARCHITECTURE

With uninterrupted views across the bay to San Francisco and Angel Island, and perfectly arranged on a secure little harbor in Richardson Bay on the north side of the Golden Gate Bridge, the delightful community of Sausalito is justifiably famous for its colorful houseboats.

Originally named after the tiny willows that once populated the banks of its creeks, Sausalito started out as a 19,500-acre (7891-hectare) land grant to an army captain in 1838. When it became the terminus of the train line down the Pacific Coast, it entered a new stage as a busy lumber port with a racy waterfront, before dramatic changes during WWII when it became the site of Marinship, a huge shipbuilding yard. After the war a new bohemian period began, with a resident artists' colony living in 'arks,' or houseboats, moored along the bay. Hundreds of these floating abodes remain today, with the diverse structures ranging from psychedelic, mural-splashed castles to dilapidated salt-sprayed shacks to immaculate three-story floating mansions.

While Sausalito is a tight-knit community of around 7000 people, many of whom live on one of the 400 or so floating homes, it's easy to poke around the docks located off Bridgeway Blvd between Gate 5 and Gate 6½ Rds. A number of the gates remain unlocked for easy access to the houseboat docks, and you're sure to be warmly welcomed by residents if you stop and chat while they tend to their sprawling dockside gardens or while they wheel their groceries home across creaky wooden boardwalks.

Walking Tours

For one day each September a selection of 15 to 20 historically and architecturally significant houseboats are open to the public on a tour. The rest of the year, do a self-guided walking tour of the houseboat community.

Getting to Sausalito can be half the fun, too – two ferry services operate 30-minute ferry rides from downtown San Francisco several times a day, throughout the year, even passing by Alcatraz on the way – and many visitors opt to bring a bicycle across on the ferry (for no additional charge) or cycle over the Golden Gate Bridge. Once in Sausalito, you can hire a bicycle to get around or consider joining a kayak tour and paddling about on a full-moon evening.

To read about:
Frank Lloyd Wright Architecture see page 226
San Francisco see page 238

Beyond Brownies: Sophisticated Edibles

Until less than a decade ago, marijuana was something you 'scored' surreptitiously on the street from a drug dealer or smoked discreetly at hippie house parties. Then, quietly and unexpectedly, the drug grew up and became more sophisticated. By 2016, recreational marijuana was legal in eight US states and good for medical use in another 21. Even more surprising, eating it had become just as popular as smoking it.

USA-WIDE / FOOD & DRINK

Today's pot shops are a revelation to anyone who last imbibed weed illegally in the 1990s. Resembling civilized jewelry stores, marijuana-selling establishments are filled with polished glass cases displaying a wide array of cannabis-related products and paraphernalia. The servers are equally professional. Gone are the wild-eyed drug dealers of yore; instead you'll be greeted by an eloquent, well-informed 'budtender' who'll expertly talk you through the pros and cons of vapes, concentrates and a considerable assortment of stuff you can eat.

These days, the marijuana edibles industry includes far more than just 'space cakes' and hash brownies. Thanks to a combination of looser marijuana laws and creative entrepreneurs stealing tips from the craft-beer and slow-food movements, suppliers have developed all kinds of inventive new foods to savor. A quick tour of the pot shops of Colorado or California will reveal marijuana-infused beef jerky, macarons, root beer, glazed nuts, gummies, pizza sauce and even breath sprays. Cannabis Creamery, a business in Sausalito, California, has even experimented with weed-infused ice cream after making a 'special' blend for a Grateful Dead party in the 1980s. They are now regular suppliers for medicinal dispensaries in the Bay Area.

In the drinks field, specialist companies such as Ganja Grindz and Brewbudz have developed weed-infused coffee, better known as 'hippie highballs' or 'canna-coffee,' a seemingly contradictory mix of stimulant and relaxant that, purportedly, promotes a satisfying synergy. You can buy the stuff in pods and bottles or, alternatively, add cannabis-laced sugar, honey sticks or chocolates to your daily Starbucks for a similar effect.

For those more into DIY, home cooking is an increasingly popular field. In 2012, long-standing stoner magazine *High Times* published its first cannabis cookbook, providing recipes for such appetite-quenching munchies as 'time warp tamales' and 'hookah lounge hummus.' By the mid-2010s, sophisticated marijuana consumers were being dubbed 'cannassueurs' and the state of Oregon had more marijuana dispensaries than McDonald's restaurants.

Colorado has established itself as the nation's most pot-friendly state. In 2014, a sushi restaurant in Denver listed marijuana pairings on its food menu. Since then, the state has flirted with marijuana-themed cooking classes and private fine-dining banquets that offer marijuana-matching alongside the food. As more states succumb to '420 culture,' things are changing fast. Weed restaurants and food trucks could be just around the corner. After that, who knows? By the 2020s, we could be contemplating marijuana sommeliers and gourmet ganja bistros.

To read about:
Iconic Sweet Treats see page 56
Burning Man Festival see page 78

Right **Vegetable tarts made with medicated ricotta cheese,** Tacoma, Washington

Poignancy & the Paranormal: Salem Past & Present

MASSACHUSETTS / WEIRD & WONDERFUL

Once upon a time, Salem was known as a seaport. Then came the witch trials of 1692, which changed the fate of the town forever. After more than 300 years, Salem has finally found peace with the past: it still serves as a cautionary tale against religious extremism and false accusations – but it has fully embraced its reputation as 'Witch City.'

Right **The trial of George Jacobs for witchcraft,** Salem, c 1692

The Witch Trials

When two little girls began to behave oddly in the summer of 1692, the head of the household – a Puritan minister – called in a local doctor. The doctor couldn't find any physical reason why the girls would hide under furniture, convulse, cry out in pain, or even bark like dogs. So he drew the only logical conclusion a God-fearing man could: the girls had been afflicted by the 'Evil Hand' of witchcraft.

Theories abound as to whether the girls suffered some obscure 17th-century malady, believed themselves to be possessed, were acting out of their own guilt (they were Puritans after all), or were just seeking attention. But when asked who had cursed them, they didn't hesitate to point fingers, seemingly at random. Soon, other little girls became similarly afflicted, more accusations were made, and in the fervor that followed, more than 200 men and women were charged with witchcraft.

The smart thing to do was confess, because then the Puritans left it to God to decide your fate. Worse off were those who stood by their principles – a crime punishable by death. By the time it was over, 19 innocent men and women had been killed and another five had died in jail. All because of the accusations of a handful of young girls one summer – and the mass hysteria of the religious extremists who were all too willing to believe them.

Witch City Today

Nowadays, Salem has to walk a fine line. On the one hand, there's a lot of reverence for the history of the witch trials and the wrongly executed victims. On the other hand – witches!

Life in Salem

It's not just the downtown tourist area that gets in on the witchy shtick: even the suburbs have gone all-in with the Witch Town concept. The town water tower on Gallows Hill is painted with a witch riding a broomstick, and the streets have names like Cauldron Ct and Witch Way. Police uniforms include the witch motif in the form of an arm patch, and Salem High School's football and hockey teams have a pointy-hatted hag as their mascot.

Let's face it, embracing the moniker of Witch City and shamelessly emblazoning the entire town with images of stereotypical Halloween witches is good for business. People flock to Salem for the campy fun, the spiritualist vibe, the Halloween hijinks, the fortune-telling, and the chance to have their picture taken in front of the statue of Samantha Stephens, the nose-twitching head witch from TV's *Bewitched*.

There are not one but three witch museums, all offering their own take on Salem's past. The biggest is the Salem Witch Museum, housed inside an atmospheric Romanesque church. There's also the Witch History Museum, with re-created scenes from Old Salem, and the Witch Dungeon Museum, known for its live re-enactment of a witch trial.

Those aren't to be confused with the Witch House, the only structure still standing with a connection to the witch trials. It was the home of Judge Jonathan Corwin, a

Above Black Hat Society performance for Halloween, Salem

member of the court that investigated the accused. The name makes it sound creepier than it is, but it offers an interesting peek into 17th-century architecture, as well as some of the beliefs about witchcraft.

At downtown's Essex St Pedestrian Mall, you'll find a cobblestone-and-brick street lined with shops for happy Wiccans, practitioners of the Dark Arts, and tourists wanting a 'Broomstick Parking Only' sign. There are books on the paranormal, shelves full of spells, a mind-boggling assortment of tarot cards, and witch-adorned merchandise by the truckload. Many of the shops even include a curtained-off area where their resident fortune-tellers can read your cards or your palm or your aura.

Salem is also host to a bevy of competing walking tours – lots and lots of them, with names like Spellbound, Hocus Pocus, Black Cat, Sinister Stories and Bewitched. Every night you'll find roving bands of tourists crowding the sidewalk as somber-faced storytellers spin their tales, leading guests into graveyards, past centuries-old inns, and into every dark corner of the town's history.

Salem sports a Halloween-y vibe all year long, but it hits peak frenzy in October during Haunted Happenings, where the event calendar is a nonstop extravaganza of scary movies, haunted houses, séances, costume parties and every other Halloween-related thing that you can think of.

Witch Trial Memorials

It's easy to get caught up in all the spooky charm and witchy mania of Salem. But lest you forget the real reason Salem became Witch City, three memorials have been erected as a reminder of the town's dark history.

Adjoining the Old Burying Point Cemetery is the Salem Witch Trials Memorial, a small lot with stone benches inscribed with the victims' names. No records exist of where the executed were buried, so this serves as the closest thing to a gravesite you'll find.

In adjoining Danvers (formerly Salem Village), the Witchcraft Victim's Memorial pays tribute to 'those innocents who died during the Salem Village witchcraft hysteria of 1692.' It includes quotes from the victims in which they protest their innocence, as well as their names and manner of death.

Most recent is the stone memorial at Proctor's Ledge. For centuries it's been assumed that the hangings took place on Gallows Hill (thus the name). But after poring through mounds of centuries-old documents, historians have determined that the actual hangings most likely took place nearby in what is now some poor unsuspecting Salem resident's backyard. This new memorial, dedicated in 2017, features a stone wall inscribed with the victim's names surrounding an oak sapling – not a broomstick in sight.

To read about:

Voodoo in New Orleans see page 180
Spooky Houses see page 296

Columbia Valley Wine Trail

WASHINGTON / WINE

Over the mountains from foggy Seattle lies the Wild West of US winemaking. It might still be considered cowboy and cowgirl country out here (and there are plenty of cattle ranches and rodeos to prove it), but there's no longer any doubt about its credentials as serious wine country.

Driving east out of the weather-beaten city of Seattle, first-time visitors to Washington State will have no idea what awaits them on the other side of the imposing Cascade Mountains. Within a couple of hours, the verdant green forests and persistent rain give way to the stark desert terrain of the Columbia Valley. It's a barren and unforgiving place that just happens to be one of the USA's most exciting wine regions, and the growing community of winemaking estates here are rightfully proud of the wines that result from their fascinating landscape.

You have to admire the frontier spirit of Columbia Valley's wineries. Viticulture was the last thing that was on the mind of the original settlers in the region, but once they had figured out how to survive, they quickly got to thinking about how to thrive. By the 1980s it was clear that the grape-growing pioneers of the 1970s were on to something, and since then the number of top-quality American Viticultural Areas (AVAs) in Washington State has increased rapidly.

Down in the bottom-right corner of the state is the charming town of Walla Walla, which is full to bursting with winery tasting rooms and places to eat, making it the ideal base when visiting the Columbia Valley. The surrounding vineyards, such as those of the Walla Walla Valley, Red Mountain or the Horse Heaven Hills, are home to world-class wines from some extremely talented producers.

Columbia Crest

When Columbia Crest released its inaugural vintage in 1984, it was a one-wine brand (an off-dry white wine). Nowadays Columbia Crest is easily the largest winery in the state, producing solid varietal wines that are considered to be as consistent as they are great value.

In tandem with its sister property, Chateau Ste Michelle (an excellent place to visit if you're near Seattle), Columbia Crest has spread the message about Washington's wines far and wide from its base in the Horse Heaven Hills AVA, so it's well worth building them into your itinerary. The experience for visitors to the winery and tasting room is second to none, and the setting, overlooking the Columbia River and surrounded by vineyards, is stunning.

Hedges Family Estate

The imposing château at Hedges Family Vineyards is not the only thing at the estate that harks back to the Old World. The family's French heritage also shines through in their elegant, restrained wines and commitment to the land – they are one of the few estates to practice biodynamic farming in the region.

The land in question is Red Mountain, a 1400ft (427m) elevation that was carved out of the landscape a few million years ago by glacial floods. The result is soil that is a blend of clay, loess and granite; ideal conditions for the cultivation of red wine grapes, and thanks to the pioneering work of a select band of true believers, Red Mountain has become one of the most talked about appellations for high-quality wine in the Columbia Valley.

L'Ecole No 41

Founded in 1983, L'Ecole No 41 is the third-oldest winery in Walla Walla and still considered to be one of its very best. The wines never fail to impress, managing to tread the fine line between power and elegance while showcasing Walla Walla's hallmark succulent, dark-berry fruit. Their estate wines can be spectacular in the best vintages.

The name L'Ecole No 41 refers to the location of the winery – a schoolhouse in district number 41 that was built back in 1915 – and the tasting room occupies one of the two classrooms. Appropriate, then, that a visit to L'Ecole No 41 is one of the best ways to learn about the Walla Walla Valley's *terroir.* You can even go on a field trip to the adjacent estate vineyard.

Woodward Canyon

Woodward Canyon has an even longer track record in Walla Walla than L'Ecole No 41 (albeit only by a couple of years). Staff pride themselves on following the 'Woody Way': working hard in the vineyard, never cutting corners or compromising, making balanced wines that age well, and always working sustainably. Clearly there is something to it, as the wines on offer in the beautiful tasting room are as elegant as they are delicious.

Gramercy Cellars

Not so long ago, Gramercy Cellars was little more than an insider's tip (with production at just a few thousand cases per year, that's hardly a surprise), but now it's one of the hottest wineries in the USA. Greg Harrington's wines are light on their feet but packed full of flavor, and reflect what is getting people so excited about the wines in this northwestern corner of the USA.

This is not a winery looking to draw attention to itself, so you won't see any big signage out front. Make an appointment for a tasting; you're assured a warm and knowledgeable welcome.

Charles Smith & K Vintners

All wine regions have their rebellious characters, and Charles Smith certainly fits the bill for Walla Walla – he looks like a rock star, which is no surprise considering he spent years managing rock bands touring across Europe. He returned from the Old World having been bitten by the wine bug and, after a stint as a merchant, decided to teach himself how to make the stuff. Nowadays he makes full-throttle wines with personalities as big as his own, and names like Kung-Fu Girl Riesling or Boom Boom! Syrah. Under his K Vintners label, Smith has created some of the highest-rated (and most expensive) wines in Washington State history, helping to establish the Columbia Valley as a serious wine region and engaging a younger crowd in the process.

Southeastern Washington

Parched, remote and barely served by public transportation, southeastern Washington is the state's loneliest corner and is characterized by the dry volcanic plateaus and denuded lava flows of the inhospitable 'Scablands' region, exposed by the Missoula floods at the end of the last ice age. Tourism – and its attendant attractions – was on a backburner here until the early 1990s, when winegrowers in and around Walla Walla began to recognize the town's potential as a new Sonoma, and wine connoisseurs started arriving from around the globe. For many, the region's fortunes have turned full circle.

A visit to the Charles Smith tasting room in downtown Walla Walla is not a classic wine geek experience: rock music and the converted warehouse setting make for a fun environment. The wines and the winemaker ensure that this is a must-visit on the Walla Walla tasting circuit, so be warned – it can get busy.

To read about:
Willamette Valley Wine see page 156
Farm-to-Table Food see page 194

Sunrises & Sunsets: The State with the Best

MICHIGAN / LANDSCAPES

Pop quiz: which state in mainland USA takes the prize for having both the best sunrises and sunsets? No, it's not California, landlocked on one whole edge. It can't be Hawai'i – although, yes Hawai'i, if you were in the running, you'd win for sure. Listen up, folks: we're talking about Michigan.

Michigan occupies prime real estate, surrounded as it is by four of the five Great Lakes – Superior, Michigan, Huron and Erie. Islands freckle its coast, and surf beaches, colored sandstone-cliffs and trekkable sand dunes woo visitors. But it's the sheer amount of waterfront that wins it top spot in this contest (shh, don't tell Florida). The state, whose motto is 'If you seek a pleasant peninsula, look about you,' consists of two parts split by water: larger Lower Peninsula, shaped like a mitten; and smaller, lightly populated Upper Peninsula, shaped like a slipper. It sports 3288 miles (5292km) of shoreline and more beaches than the Atlantic seaboard. So, which areas have the most spectacular morning and evening vistas?

Mackinac Island

Time-warp back a few centuries to a time when hilltop forts, horse carriages and sublime sunsets prevailed. This small (3.8 sq mile/9.8 sq km) island's location in the straits between Lake Michigan and Lake Huron made it a prized port in the North American fur trade, but the most important date on Mackinac was 1898 – the year cars were banned in order to encourage tourism. Today all travel is by horse or bicycle; even the police use bikes to patrol the town. The crowds of tourists – called Fudgies by the islanders – can be crushing at times, particularly during summer weekends. But when the last ferry leaves in the evening and clears out the day-trippers, Mackinac's real charm emerges. Sundown is the time to grab a glass of whatever you fancy and kick back.

Far left **Right Grand Haven Lighthouse,** Lake Michigan
Left **Lake Superior,** Michigan

Marquette

Lakeside Marquette is the perfect place to stay put for a few days of exploring. It's the Upper Peninsula's largest (and snowiest) town, known as a hot spot for outdoors enthusiasts. Forests, beaches and cliffs provide a playground just moments from downtown: locals ski in winter and hit the trails with their fat-tire bikes in summer. In town, on a peninsula jutting into Lake Superior, the high bluffs of Presque Isle Park make a great place to catch the sunset.

Pictured Rocks National Lakeshore

Stretching along prime real estate on Lake Superior, Pictured Rocks National Lakeshore is a series of wild cliffs and caves where blue and green minerals have streaked the red and yellow sandstone into a kaleidoscope of color. The bluffs feature names like Lovers Leap, Flower Vase and Caves of the Bloody Chiefs. Boat rides and kayak trips along the shore are an excellent way to absorb the dramatic scenery, particularly at dawn and twilight.

Gold Coast

They don't call it the Gold Coast for nothing. Michigan's 300-mile (483km) western shoreline features seemingly endless stretches of beaches, wineries, orchards and B&B-filled towns that boom during the summer – and shiver during the snow-packed winter. All those water views mean one thing: unbeatable golden sunsets.

To read about:
New Mexico Landscapes see page 208
Detroit in Michigan see page 300

Inside the Appalachians

When most people think of US mountains, it's the snowcapped Rockies that pop into their heads. But 1500 miles to the east runs one of the world's oldest mountain chains: the Appalachians. In its heyday its peaks rivaled those of the Alps, but today the range favors vibrant green ridges over rocky cliffs, and its hills harbor a fascinating ecosystem, a distinctive culture and plenty of characterful towns.

THE SOUTH / HIKING & CULTURE

Get Outside: Appalachia's Natural Playground

Those interested in exploring natural wonders won't be left wanting – Appalachia is home to a plethora of ecosystems protected by dozens of state and national parks.

Hikes

The Appalachians stretch all the way from northern Georgia into New Brunswick, and the famous trail that winds along their spine is, at 2190 miles, the longest hiking-only path in the world. Don't let the immensity of the Appalachian Trail put you off, though: these mountains offer plenty of hiking options ranging from easy to difficult, and those willing to dive in will be rewarded with an enormous variety of waterfalls and swimming holes, rock formations, rare flora and wildlife.

National parks such as Great Smoky Mountains National Park and Shenandoah National Park are crisscrossed with well-marked paths and hiking/camping facilities. The 30-mile (48km) Art Loeb trail in North Carolina hugs a series of ridges, offering incredible views from several knobs and balds (grassy mountain summits or crests) along the way. If you're on the hunt for overwhelming greenery, hightail it to Breaks Interstate Park, which straddles the Kentucky and Virginia state lines.

Gorges

Rock climbers will delight in the unique rock formations of Kentucky's Red River Gorge, carved out by thousands of years of wind and water. Experienced folks can test their strength at Georgia's Tallulah Gorge, which offers plenty of sheer rock faces ripe for scaling; for those new to the climbing scene, the via ferrata at Nelson Rocks in West Virginia is a great opportunity to explore the area's rocky landscape with the help of a fixed-anchor cable system.

Views

Do you appreciate sweeping forest views against a clear blue sky, or shifting shadows across a mountain valley? How about green tree lines that turn golden in the sunset? There are plenty of picture-perfect viewpoints scattered across the Appalachian chain, and each one provides its own take on the range stretching before it. Head up to Clingmans Dome in Tennessee, the highest spot in the Great Smoky Mountains, at 6643ft (2025m); it's easily accessible from the road and on a clear day visitors can see nearly 100 miles (160km).

North Carolina has its share of spectacular views, many within the striking Blue

Bioluminescent Fireflies

Perhaps one of the most distinctly magical things about this part of the US are summertime fireflies, which never fail to enrapture audiences with their bioluminescent beauty. While you can see these little bugs blinking away in most parts of the eastern seaboard, the Smokies are the only place where you can watch thousands of them light up in unison. The phenomenon usually takes place in late May or early June, and those interested in attending must enter a lottery to obtain one of the 1800 available passes. To register, visit www.recreation.gov and search for 'Firefly Event.'

Ridge Mountains – famous Max Patch, located in Pisgah National Forest, was cleared as a pasture in the 1800s, and offers 360-degree views of the Blue Ridge and Smokies. If you're passing through Virginia, make the trek to the Hawksbill Mountain summit, the highest point in the Shenandoah Valley, for uninterrupted views of sloping mountain ranges.

It's worth noting that all these views take on a special warm tone in the autumn months – leaf-peeping isn't just for New England.

Watering Holes

Where there are mountains and valleys, there are most assuredly rivers and streams, and the Appalachian region is no exception. Waterways snake down mountainsides and along valley floors, creating plenty of fresh swimming holes, roaring rapids and misty waterfalls. Adventure-seekers had better hold on to their paddles at West Virginia's New River, one of the world's oldest rivers and home to everything from calm pools to Class IV rapids; those with a real hankering for action should hit the nearby Gauley River to experience the wild Class V rapids that make it one of the most intense rafting experiences around.

There are hundreds of Appalachian waterfalls to choose from, ranging from delicate trickles to large walls of water, but perhaps one of the most exceptional is Cumberland Falls, home of the famed moonbow (a rainbow produced by moonlight), a phenomenon that only occurs in a handful of places across the globe.

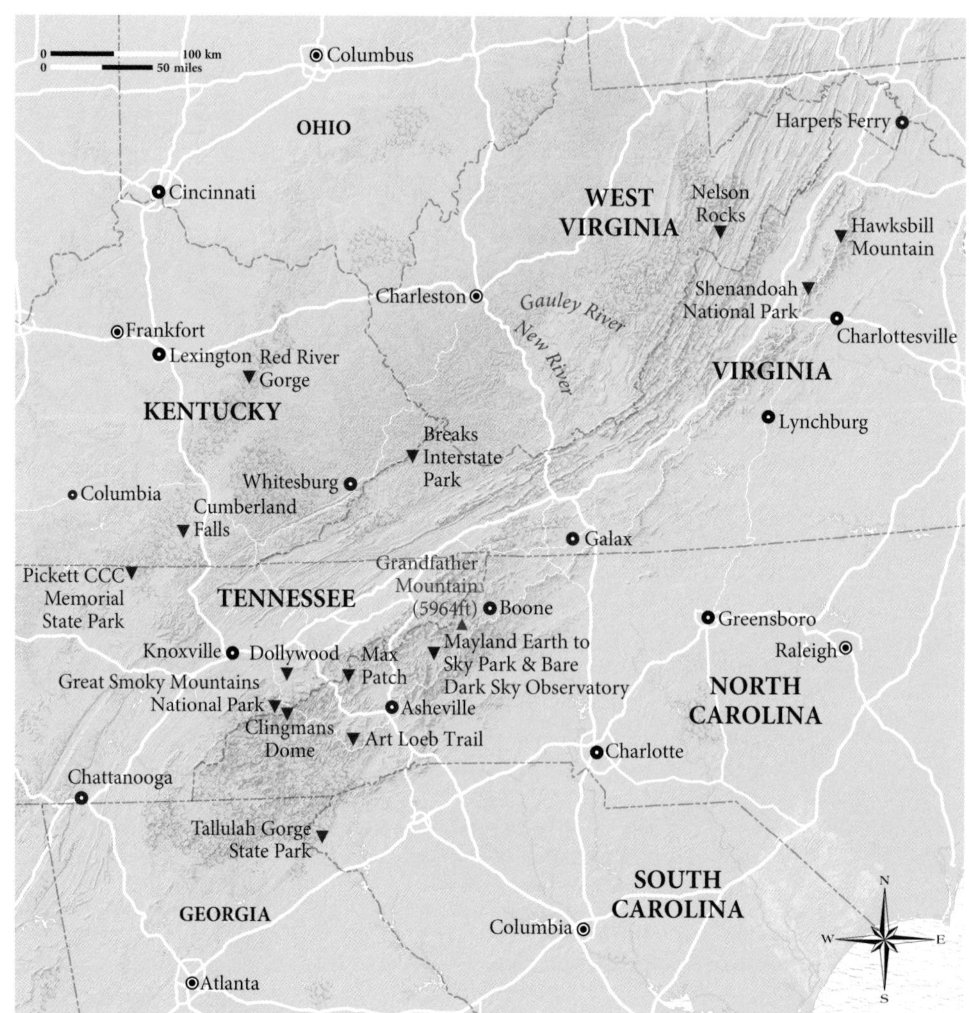

Stargazing

Not all of Appalachia's natural wonders are terrestrial – the area is also home to dark sky parks, a welcome rarity in a country where light usually finds its way into most night skies. If you want to get a closer look at those twinkling celestial bodies, visit Mayland Earth to Sky Park and Observatory and seek out your favorites with their telescopes. Another prime spot for stargazing is Tennessee's Pickett CCC Memorial State Park, but don't stop there – Appalachia harbors more than 20 dark sky parks, plenty to choose from.

More than Mountains: Appalachian Culture

Times haven't always been easy for Appalachia, and cities and towns in the region have seen their fair share of hard knocks. Despite it all, these communities have created a strong cultural tradition that can be felt far beyond the mountains, and today they have become important epicenters of creativity and innovation.

Asheville, North Carolina

Hardly a secret these days, Asheville is widely considered one of Appalachia's most happening cities. While people have long been visiting the area to fulfill all their *Downton Abbey* fantasies at the impressive Biltmore Estate (built by the Vanderbilt family in 1895), in more recent years Asheville has positively blossomed into a cultural haven full of local artists, sustainable and locally run restaurants and, perhaps its biggest cottage industry these days, craft beer. Asheville is home to more than 30 breweries – that's more breweries per capita than any other US city.

Boone, North Carolina

Looking for a laid-back, outdoorsy base for your mountain adventures? Boone's your town. Only a few miles down the road from Asheville, Boone serves as a convenient hub for a number of nearby activities: hike Grandfather Mountain and visit the mile-high swinging bridge, hunt for treasure at the gem mines, or hit the slopes once the winter snow falls.

While its picturesque surroundings are certainly reason enough to pop in, Boone also has the culture factor: it's home to Appalachia State University, so the town has evolved with a little bit of energy behind it. Visit Turchin Center for the Visual Arts, pop into some of the local shops downtown, and hit up local bars and breweries once the sun goes down.

Whitesburg, Kentucky

Whitesburg is a small Kentucky coal town settled at the base of Pine Mountain, and while it may seem fairly subdued to the untrained eye, this place is the heart of an Appalachian art movement. It's where you'll find Appalshop, an arts and education center dedicated to celebrating Appalachia's culture and promoting community programs. The center regularly hosts cultural events including musical performances, local heritage presentations and theater productions.

Chattanooga, Tennessee

Chattanooga entered the public conscious in the 1940s as the subject of the famous 'Chattanooga Choo Choo,' sung by Glen Miller and his orchestra. For decades this was the town's biggest claim to fame, but these days this little riverside city has come alive with creative energy. Expertly combining cool with kitsch, Chattanooga has a little something for everyone: head up to the Bluff View Art District to get a taste of the area's growing art and culinary scenes, or take a stroll along the attractive riverfront. Check out underwater wonders at the Tennessee Aquarium, or head outside of the city limits to find top-notch hiking and rock climbing.

Dollywood

Most Appalachia natives will tell you that Dolly Parton is a national treasure: the legendary singer and actor is somewhat of an institution in these parts due to her immense success and her substantial philanthropy and investment efforts in the region. She's also one of the owners of Dollywood in Pigeon Forge, Tennessee, probably the world's only Appalachian-themed amusement park and resort. Rides and attractions draw on mountain tropes to deliver a big dose of campy charm, and country music lovers will delight in all the Dolly memorabilia and the nods to fellow influential country artists past and present.

Harpers Ferry, West Virginia

Tucked away in the heart of the Shenandoah Valley, at the meeting of the Potomac and Shenandoah Rivers, Harpers Ferry is a well-preserved historic settlement whose important role in US history stretches back to the 18th century. The town served as an industrial center and was the site of the US Armory and Arsenal prior to

Far left & left **Red River Gorge,** Kentucky

Right **Elk River Falls,** Blue Ridge Mountains, North Carolina

the Civil War – in 1859 the arsenal was targeted by an abolitionist raid led by John Brown. Storer College, originally a school for freed slaves, opened immediately after the Civil War, and served as the location for the first meeting of the Niagara Movement led by WEB Du Bois in the early 1900s. To learn more about Harpers Ferry's past, head to the National Historic Park Visitor Center to access the town's museums and historic buildings.

Outdoorsy types, there are plenty of things for you to do, too. The city is situated alongside the Appalachian Trail and serves as a good jumping-off point for exploring the surrounding mountain trails and bike paths.

Galax, Virginia

Galax is a little city with a big voice. This town of 7000 people is one of the best places to discover traditional bluegrass, mountain and country music, thanks to its long musical tradition and the dedication of the local art and music community. Stop in on the second weekend of August for the Old Fiddlers' Convention, the largest event of its kind in the world. If you're passing through any other time of the year, catch a concert at the Blue Ridge Music Center or head down to the historic Rex Theater on Friday nights to sit in on the live bluegrass show, which is broadcast on the radio across the region.

To read about:

Where to Spy a Bear see page 60
Kentucky Bourbon see page 118

Exploring America's Caves

KENTUCKY, CALIFORNIA & NEW MEXICO / NATURE

What lurks beneath the surface of the USA? More than 50,000 caverns, tunnels, otherworldly rock formations, lava flows, prehistoric relics…and plenty of bats. Head deep underground in Kentucky, California and New Mexico to discover three of the country's best dark corners. Mind your head.

Right **Big Room at Carlsbad Caverns National Park,** New Mexico

Mammoth Cave National Park

With stalagmites as tall as trees, cathedral-size chambers and subterranean rivers full of strange, blind cave creatures, visiting Mammoth is like being on another planet.

Descend into an eerie underground world, walking down a damp pathway into a long, dark corridor of rock. Hundreds of feet beneath the earth's surface, rock formations bloom like exotic flowers. There's delicate cave coral; striated 'cave bacon'; long, fluted frozen waterfalls; and walls striped and swirled like taffy.

The longest known cave system in the world, Mammoth has more than 400 miles (644km) of explored passages. It's all due to water drip-drip-dripping its way through the porous limestone for millions of years. Native American remains have been found in the cave, leading archaeologists to believe the first humans entered here about 4000 years ago. According to legend, the cave was rediscovered by settlers at the end of the 18th century, when a hunter chased a wounded bear right up to the cave entrance.

Entrepreneurs soon realized Mammoth was full of saltpeter – which is used to make gunpowder – and began mining during the War of 1812. Later, a doctor bought the cave and turned it into a tuberculosis hospital, believing the cave air would cure his patients. Some died, and the rest left; no one was cured. Noting the great acoustics, locals began holding Christmas singalongs here in 1883; the tradition continues today.

Tourists have been visiting since the 1810s, making this one of the oldest American tourist attractions. Early cave owners used their slaves as tour guides; one such guide, Stephen Bishop, became one of the first people to map the cave and name its features. The limestone hills in the Mammoth region are riddled with caverns; in the early 20th century, local farmers tried to lure tourists heading to Mammoth to their own caves, planting fake signs or claiming Mammoth was closed. The resulting skirmishes became known as 'the Cave Wars.'

Today there are numerous caves to visit in the area, but you can't miss Mammoth itself.

Mammoth's Critters

Even within the depths of Mammoth Cave, life abides. Far below the surface of the earth, creatures such as Kentucky cave shrimp, eyeless cave fish and blind cave beetles are perfectly suited to their subterranean surrounds. Above ground, the limestone hills, hemlock ravines and forest swamps support white-tailed deer, opossums, bobcats, coyote and bats, as well as a plethora of birds and fish. In spring, the valleys and ridges are carpeted in rue, bluebells, wood poppy and larkspur.

Lava Beds National Monument

Perched on a shield volcano, Lava Beds National Monument is a truly remarkable 72-sq-mile (187-sq-km) landscape of geological features – lava flows, craters, cinder cones, spatter cones and amazing lava tubes. Nearly 750 caves have been found in the monument and they average a comfortable 55°F (13°C) no matter what the outside temperature. You can spy Native American petroglyphs throughout the park too.

Above **Common cave cricket,** Mammoth Cave National Park, Kentucky

Lava tubes are formed when the surface of hot, spreading lava hardens upon exposure to cold air. The lava inside is thus insulated and stays molten, flowing away to leave an empty tube of solidified lava. Caves at Lava Beds range in size from the claustrophobic to the grandiose. Many have interesting histories; for example, visitors used to ice skate by lantern light in the bottom of Merrill Cave; and when Ovls Cave was discovered, it was littered with bighorn sheep skulls. Some are easily accessible (beautiful Mushpot Cave, nearest the visitor center), while others are more challenging (Labyrinth, Hercules Leg, Golden Dome and Blue Grotto).

Nearly 400 such tubular caves have been found in the monument, and many more are expected to be discovered. Approximately two dozen are currently open for exploration by visitors, who can borrow flashlights from rangers and rent $5 helmets and kneepads for independent exploration. There's no hand holding, which makes this feel like true exploration. Just make sure to wear good shoes and long sleeves (lava is sharp!), and do not go alone. And check in with the visitor center before exploring, to avoid harming the fragile geological and biological resources in the park.

At the far northeastern end of the monument is Petroglyph Point, with weathered Modoc petroglyphs at the base of a high cliff that are several thousands of years old. Look up for the hundreds of nests in holes high in the cliff face, which provide shelter for birds that sojourn at the wildlife refuges nearby, before climbing to the short trail at the top of the hill for amazing views over the plains and Lower

Above **Stalactites,** Carlsbad Caverns National Park, New Mexico

Other Great Caves

The 'Stalacpipe Organ' at Luray Caverns, in Virginia, is hyped as the largest musical instrument on earth. Meanwhile in Missouri, the family-mobbed Meramec Caverns is as interesting for its Civil War history and hokey charm as for its spectacular stalactites.

Klamath Lake. Also at the north end of the monument is the labyrinthine landscape of Captain Jack's Stronghold, the Modoc Indian's very effective ancient wartime defense area.

Carlsbad Caverns National Park

Hidden beneath the cactus-covered ridges of the Guadalupe Mountains lies a sprawling, subterranean wonderland of 120 known caves, with soaring chambers and otherworldly features.

Elaborately carved by the slow hand of time, the magnificent underground rooms and glittering passageways of Carlsbad Caverns feel like a portal into another realm. It's hard to imagine a more dramatic transition than to leave the desert air behind and step through the cool, utterly silent tunnels, with every twist and turn revealing a wondrous collection of artfully wrought formations.

The magic and mystery of Carlsbad becomes all the more apparent when you realize the extraordinary processes that created these sparkling chambers. It all began some 250 million years ago, when a large but shallow inland sea covered this area, along with a horseshoe-shaped reef that stretched for 400 miles (644km). As the climate changed and the earth evolved, the reef was buried under deposits of salt and gypsum. A few million years ago, uplift caused the ancient reef to rise some 2 miles (3km), creating large cracks and fissures. Over the following millennia, rainwater seeped into the cracks, fresh water mixing with saltwater to create sulfuric acid, its corrosive power slowly shaping the massive underground chambers. The birth of the cave as a magnificent work of nature began about one million years ago, as rainwater, drip by drip, seeped through the layers of the earth, each droplet depositing a tiny mineral load of calcite – thus creating the spectacular array of stalactites, stalagmites, soda straws, helictites, draperies and cave pearls.

Although little early human evidence has been found inside the caves, Native American tribes left their mark in the area, including a 1000-year-old pictograph near the main entrance. Carlsbad's fame, however, really began with Jim White, a 16-year-old cowhand who entered the caves in 1898 – a discovery that would change his life. He became the first to explore the caves and named many of its rooms and major formations (the Big Room, King's Palace, Bottomless Pit, Witch's Finger). He was also the cave's biggest promoter, leading members of a scientific expedition and later serving as the chief ranger of the caves.

It's worth planning a trip around the nightly bat flights, which happen May through October, when hundreds of thousands of Brazilian free-tailed bats roost in the caves. The nightly exodus happens just after dusk; you can watch from an amphitheater built near the cave entrance. Around sunset, rangers give a short presentation describing these fascinating mammals, before the bats take to the Chihuahuan Desert in search of food.

To read about:
Kentucky Bourbon see page 118
New Mexico Landscapes see page 208

Above **Carlsbad Caverns National Park,** New Mexico

Right **Carlsbad Caverns National Park,** New Mexico

Spooky Houses & Multiverses

If home is where the heart is, it might just be the still-beating heart of a dark secret. Descend into the multi-dimensional tale of the Selig family or ponder the mystery at the center of the Winchester House – seek to uncover the mysteries that have perplexed past visitors.

NEW MEXICO & CALIFORNIA / WEIRD & WONDERFUL

Meow Wolf/House of Eternal Return

If you've been hankering for a trip to another dimension but have yet to find a portal, the House of Eternal Return by Meow Wolf could be the place for you. At first glance, the 20,000-sq-ft (1858-sq-meter) Victorian house might look cozy. Flowers hang on the veranda and a warm glow pours from the windows. But a mystery is hidden inside, and visitors have to figure out what happened.

The house was the home of the fictitious Selig family, but they've recently vanished. Visitors must search for clues related to the disappearance of the family: they're encouraged to rifle through papers and books and wander through secret passageways, such as a fireplace that leads to a travel agency or another that empties into an aquarium. As you uncover the family's secrets, a narrative unfolds that leads deeper into fragmented bits of a multiverse, all of which are unique, interactive art installations.

Meow Wolf and the House of Eternal Return is the product of a Santa Fe arts collective (with the assistance of *Game of Thrones* writer George RR Martin, who donated the bowling alley where the installation now sits). The space is large enough that you could spend several hours – or visits – here trying to crack the code to the safe at the top of the stairs, reading every detail of Mom's diary or finding inspiration yourself in the makerspace at the entrance.

Winchester Mystery House

This house is an unsolved mystery with as many twists as a Jason Bourne thriller – but here the plot moves on real-life hidden passageways and doors to nowhere. Built nonstop, 24 hours a day for 38 years, the house has more than 160 rooms and a litany of weird quirks and mysterious designs, including cabinets that lead into rooms, staircases that go up then down and chimneys that don't reach the roof. The house feels haunted, yes, but it's also an exceptional example of late 19th-century architecture, including Tiffany stained-glass windows and finely etched doorknobs.

Sarah Winchester was the solo mastermind behind the house. Heir to the Winchester rifle fortune – 'the gun that won the West' – she allegedly became interested in the occult after the untimely deaths of her child and husband. A medium told her the bad fortune was caused by spirits of those who had been killed by Winchester guns and wanted revenge. She spent the rest of her life trying to outwit the ghosts.

It's impossible not to think of Sarah and her superstitions as you wander the home and property. Each hallway to nowhere or skylight installed in the floor is a chilling reminder of a woman possessed – by what, no one will ever know. Employees have reported creaking floors and smells of chicken soup coming from the kitchens and there have been sightings of people resembling Mrs Winchester's old employees and even Sarah herself. It's impossible to visit without at least one chill running up your spine.

To read about:

Tornado Chasers see page 68
The Spirits of Charleston see page 162

Top left, top right & bottom right **House of Eternal Return,** Santa Fe, New Mexico
Bottom left **Winchester Mystery House,** San Jose, California

TOP LEFT, TOP RIGHT, BOTTOM RIGHT: LINDSEY KENNEDY, COURTESY OF WWW.MEOWWOLF.COM ©

The Mysterious Sailing Rocks of Death Valley

The giant rocks of Racetrack Playa seem, when unobserved, to skid over the lakebed's surface, scoring deep tracks in the earth behind them. Who is moving them? How does it happen? For many, the anticipation of seeing such a rare sight outweighs the fear of tackling the treacherous Racetrack Road and entering this uncanny landscape.

CALIFORNIA / LANDSCAPES

As you slam over the ruts of Racetrack Road in Death Valley National Park, California, a 20-mile (32km) unpaved nightmare in a desert valley flanked by dark mountains, it seems like your bones could rattle right out of your body. With miles of washboard road ahead and empty horizons all around, it's easy to feel vulnerable and alone as you roll towards the Racetrack Playa, a dry lakebed in the northern wilds of the park. Even if you didn't know that Charles Manson and his followers holed up in the southern reaches of Death Valley after the Helter Skelter murders – misfits and malcontents are no strangers here – it's an eerie place.

The first sign you're getting close to your goal is the appearance of Teakettle Junction through the heat haze, a solitary mileage marker typically draped in teakettles. The playa is 6 miles (10km) further ahead. After reaching the south-playa parking area, leave your car and approach on foot.

Boulders dot the parched earth. In their wake, trails are carved into the dirt as though they've been interrupted mid-crawl. How do the rocks move? Some weigh more than 600lb (272kg) pounds. The question bedeviled observers for decades. Aliens? Supernatural forces? Freakish weather?

Scientists finally solved the mystery in 2013. In winter, a thin sheet of ice occasionally covers the playa. As the ice warms, it cracks apart. Winds push these ice patches into rocks that have tumbled from surrounding mountains. The wind-driven ice floes shove the rocks across the slick lakebed. After temperatures rise, the ice vaporizes, leaving the boulders in their new locations.

The boulders dot the southern end of the playa. You can walk among the boulders, and take pictures to puzzle your friends, but don't walk across the playa when it is wet (and don't drive or cycle across it at any time). The park recommends traveling by 4WD, bringing a spare tire and plenty of water, and making sure you have cell-phone coverage. The western border of the park is 230 miles (370km) from LA, and though it will definitely be bumpy, the trip is worth it. Seeing something rare triggers a sense of lightness and wonder. And though the mystery has been solved, the stark beauty of the setting and the rarity of the phenomenon keep the place amazing.

To read about:

The Grand Canyon see page 34
California's Desert in Bloom see page 254

DETROIT

Motor City

In its grand ideas and jarring contradictions, its blight and beauty, Detroit is America. The triumph of the USA's capitalist ideals made Detroit one of the world's leading cities during the auto industry boom of the mid-20th century. Racial and economic inequality and social unrest almost brought it to its knees a generation later. But after a period of bankruptcy and loss, Detroit's comeback has made national headlines and transformed it into one of the most unexpectedly rewarding cities to visit in the USA.

Today, travelers who are willing to venture off the beaten track will find a city of constant surprises and a thriving art scene. After years of redevelopment, downtown Detroit has come alive, boasting a pair of new sports stadiums, a number of night clubs, and Greektown, a walkable district that's home to cozy restaurants, bars and a glittering casino. The neighborhoods surrounding the downtown core offer the kind of sights that could only exist in a city with Detroit's unique history.

The Eastern Market is Detroit's historic public shopping place, with produce, cheese, spice and flower vendors filling the large halls on Saturdays. Even if you don't come when the market is bustling, it's worth a trip for the murals; Eastern Market has become an internationally renowned hot spot for street art. In 2017 alone there were 50 new murals commissioned in the neighborhood.

Nearby, there's more eye-popping public art at the Heidelberg Project – a block-spanning installation consisting of a colorful riot of polka-dotted streets, houses covered in technicolor paint blobs and beautifully bizarre sculptures (including lots of doll heads). It's the brainchild of street artist Tyree Guyton, who spent the past 30 years beautifying his run-down community through this ever-evolving installation. Guyton has designs to dismantle the project and put a cultural village in its place, where he wants to build galleries and art workshop spaces.

One of the city's most rewarding artistic treasures is within the Detroit Institute of Art. There, Diego Rivera's awe-inspiring mural *Detroit Industry* fills an entire room and reflects the city's blue-collar history. When it was unveiled critics called it 'vulgar, blasphemous and un-American' for the evocative nudes and multi-racial workforce, but the immersive work is among Rivera's most impressive murals. It became a National Historic Landmark in 2014. The crowd of faces of Rivera's workers – some determined, some uncertain, others filled with hope and joy – stands as a perfect reflection of the city's past, present and future.

NOTHING
STOPS
DETROIT

GREEKTOWN
CASINO-HOTEL
LEVEL
COLD STONE

MOTOWN: THE SOUND & THE CITY

There's a fierce, unrelenting pulse to Detroit. You can feel it in the echoes of automotive assembly lines that offered the American dream to generations of immigrants, hear it in the soulful rhythms of Motown and experience it in the vibrant, underdog energy of the city's recent rebirth.

DETROIT / MUSIC

If Detroit's turbulent past has left deep scars on the city, they're worn today with energy and elegance. The USA loves a good comeback story, and Detroit is writing a mighty one as it transforms itself from bankruptcy to a center of innovation, culture and art. Murals, markets, greenways, distilleries and inventive chefs have brought the city back from the brink. Through good times and bad, Detroit has always been home to one of the best music cultures in the United States: it's a city that destroyed racial barriers in pop music with Motown, fostered furious punk acts like the MC5, produced game-changing hip-hop visionaries like Eminem and Dilla, and was the birthplace of techno.

Even though the city has an abandoned, otherworldly vibe in some areas, its affordability and wide-open spaces have made it the perfect incubator for creatives who keep moving here in droves. They're converting vacant lots into urban farms and abandoned buildings into cafes and avant-garde museums. They're starting new bands every week. The tricky path to recovery has helped Detroit rewrite the textbook on urban renewal, and while you drive past a checkered mix of abandoned storefronts and glittering renovated theaters, it's hard not to pull for the underdog.

To feel the rhythm of Detroit, you have to understand a little of its history. The city's first streak of fortune arrived in the 1920s, when Henry Ford began churning out cars. He didn't invent the automobile, as many mistakenly believe, but he did perfect assembly-line manufacturing and mass-production techniques. The result was the Model T, the first car for America's middle class.

In an instant, Detroit became the motor capital of the world. General Motors (GM), Chrysler and Ford were all headquartered in or near Detroit – and still are. The 1950s and '60s were the city's heyday, when the population exceeded two million and Motown dominated the airwaves. But racial tensions in the late 1960s and Japanese car competitors in the 1970s shook the city to its core. The city lost two-thirds of

Left & far right **Packard Auto Plant,** Detroit
Right **Derrick May**

Hitsville U.S.A.
Motown...The Best in Bloom
MARVIN GAYE

its population – evident in the abandoned buildings that still mar Detroit's landscape.

Many have become well-known, often-photographed sights. And though some commentators deride the interest in Detroit's decay as 'ruin porn,' others see it as a way to examine and take in the complex history of the city. One of the city's most majestic ruins is the Packard Auto Plant. Renowned architect Albert Kahn designed the 3.5-million-sq-ft factory, and it was a thing of beauty when it opened in 1903. Today, it looks like the set of a zombie movie.

The empty Packard Plant played a vital role in Detroit's music scene. It was a frequent venue in the thriving rave scene of the 1990s, when some of the first techno DJs – Richie Hawtin, Derrick May, Juan Atkins and Kevin Saunderson – threw legendary parties in the big, open spaces and kick-started a global movement. Today, Detroit's Movement Electronic Music Festival carries on the tradition, drawing 40,000 fans every Memorial Day weekend.

But the inexorable connection between Detroit's celebrated exports – cars and music – goes way back. They're famously intertwined in the story of Berry Gordy, founder of Motown records. As an aspiring songwriter, Gordy composed songs while working on a Detroit assembly line; the rhythm of the machines created a beat for songs in his head. With an $800 loan in 1959, Gordy started his first label. By 1961 Gordy had scored his first million-selling single, the Miracle's 'Shop Around.' By the end of that decade, his hot streak was the stuff of legend: 22 number-one pop hits, 48 number-one R&B hits, and the distinction of being the largest black-owned business in the USA.

The Motown Historical Museum is where it went down – a row of modest houses where Berry Gordy launched the label. You can visit humble Studio A and see where stars like the Supremes, the Jackson Five, Stevie Wonder and Marvin Gaye recorded their first hits. A tour takes about 1½ hours, and consists mostly of looking at black-and-white photos and listening to guides' stories. The museum recently announced a $50 million expansion, with new buildings to be added for a vast increase in exhibition space.

Those who want to catch the heirs of Detroit's musical legends have plenty of venues to choose from, and more and more pop up as the city continues its journey toward revitalization. Among them, few are as classy as Cliff Bell's, a venue that will transport you to Detroit's mid-century heyday. After being shuttered in the '80s, this historic jazz venue reopened in 2006. Another classic spot is Baker's Keyboard Lounge, a north Detroit piano bar that's been around since the late 1930s. The list of greats who have taken the stage at Baker's includes Ella Fitzgerald, Louis Armstrong, Miles Davis, Sarah Vaughan and Nat King Cole. Baker's also serves an amazing pork chop with collard greens.

To see the best of Detroit's young acts, go to the Magic Stick, Detroit's most consistent rock club (which – bonus! – has a bowling alley downstairs). The Magic Stick stage has been the home for some of the city's recent musical innovators, including the White Stripes and Sufjan Stevens, and brings in a select roster of touring acts almost every night of the week.

Clockwise from top left **The Supremes,** 1965; **Marvin Gaye,** 1980; **Jackson Five,** 1972; **Stevie Wonder & Peter Noone,** 1966

Five Essential Detroit Albums Beyond Motown

John Lee Hooker's Detroit: Vintage Recordings 1948–1952 Although his day job was at a Ford plant, Hooker's hypnotic blues changed the world.

Dilla: Doughnuts The producer's final release ranks among the best instrumental hip-hop albums of all time.

MC5: Kick out the Jams Bristling with energy, this album shaped the sound of '70s punk.

Techno! The New Dance Sound of Detroit A compilation of dance music from various artists that defines Detroit techno.

Bob Seeger: Night Moves Brimming with emotion and brilliant songs, this was the working-class rocker's triumph.

To read about:
Highway 61 see page 134
Music Festivals see page 212

URBAN FARMING

DETROIT / FOOD & FARMING

The future of farming doesn't look much like you might imagine – no wide-open spaces or big red barns, no tractors tilling the sun-drenched plains. In fact, if you visit farms on the cutting edge today, chances are you'll be in the middle of the city, and there might be no sunlight or soil at all.

Ever since the early 2000s – years before the rest of the country caught onto the trend – Detroit has been on the vanguard of the urban farming movement. The city's rich history of urban agriculture includes victory gardens during WWII and a 1970s program called Farm-A-Lot, which offered free seeds and gardening assistance to residents. In the mid-'90s, the Capuchin Soup Kitchen's Earthworks Urban Farm broke ground on a pioneering 2.5-acre (1-hectare) organic farm to bring quality food to the city's needy. A few years later, Detroit's Garden Resource Program was initiated by a small but dedicated group of urban farmers who oversaw about 80 gardens in the city.

Growing soybeans in the shadow of a skyscraper may seem surreal, but the advantages of urban farming become more apparent each year. Local food production requires less transportation to get food in and out of city centers, which reduces carbon emissions and relieves roadway congestion. Urban farms are a solution for inner-city communities in so-called 'food deserts,' which have limited access to fresh food. Green rooftops and gardens also pump oxygen into the atmosphere and cool the environment, while also reducing the runoff and flooding from heavy rain.

In the early 21st century, Detroit's unique characteristics thrust it to the forefront of the urban farming movement. In the span of 60 years, Detroit went from being the wealthiest city in the United States to a blighted wasteland, with vast tracts of unused land. The city responded with an impressive urban agriculture ordinance that aimed to fill abandoned lots with local food. And it worked. Today, Detroit boasts more than 1500 community gardens, including a square-mile hardwood farm that is the largest of its kind in the nation. Travelers to Detroit will pass large community gardens near many of the city's most popular destinations, places that are celebrated annually with the Detroit Tour of Urban Farms and Gardens, an inspiring annual festival held each August. The event hosts bicycle and bus tours through different areas of Detroit's sprawling landscape, focusing on the most bountiful urban farms and gardens in the city. These include inspiring farms like Keep Detroit Growing, which gives a hand to beginning gardeners and supplies local restaurants and farmers markets, and the now-historic Earthworks Urban Farm.

And while urban farming in Detroit has played a critical role in the city's revival, it's only one example of the broader national movement. Farms in Austin, Texas, produce more than 100,000lb (45,359kg) of fresh food every year. In Minneapolis, a progressive urban agriculture plan led to 250 new community gardens within five years. Los Angeles has seen over 30% more urban gardens pop up within the past decade. New York City – celebrated for inventive greening projects including the High Line – is among the most active urban farming centers of the nation due to places like Brooklyn Grange, a massive endeavor that helps people build their own rooftop farms and promotes sustainable living through food, education and community events.

Many of these farmers use cutting-edge technology to take on the seasonal and climatic challenges that bind traditional crops. The most advanced farms today don't even have to be outdoors; using a technology called aeroponics, crops are grown in vertical stacks of plant beds, without soil, sunlight or water. As a result, these farmers in cities enjoy longer growing seasons and more productive harvests – an encouraging sign for urban communities looking to increase access to fresh food.

To read about:
Saddling Up in Montana see page 138
Willamette Valley Wine see page 156

Index

E

F

G

H

I

J

K

L

M

N

Image Credits

p2 Ignacio Palacios/Getty Images ©
p6 Stewart Leiwakabessy/Getty Images ©
p7 Hero Images/Getty Images ©
p8 Daniel Grill/Getty Images ©
p9 Loop Images/Mike Kirk/Getty Images ©
p10 Darrell Miller/500px ©
p11 Simon Willms/Getty Images ©
p12 Photoshot/Getty Images ©
p13 Tim Mosenfelder/Getty Images ©
p14 Aaron P. Bernstein/Getty Images ©
p16 Marianna Massey/Getty Images ©
p16 photosounds/Shutterstock ©
p17 Cultura Exclusive/Manuel Sulzer/Getty Images ©
p18 Frank Bach/Shutterstock ©
p19 Rudy Balasko/Shutterstock ©
p22 SUNGJIN AHN PHOTOGRAPHY/Getty Images ©
p23 Byba Sepit/Getty Images ©
p24 Stevens Fremont/Getty Images ©
p25 Danita Delimont/Getty Images ©
p26 Atlantide Phototravel/Getty Images ©
p27 Lisa Romerein/Getty Images ©
p28 joe daniel price/Getty Images ©
p29 Doug Lemke/Shutterstock ©
p30 Alexander Spatari/Getty Images ©
p31 tibu/Getty Images ©
p35 Jay Yuan/Shutterstock ©
p36 Sapna Reddy Photography/Getty Images ©
p37 Tomas Rebro/Shutterstock ©
p38 John Cancalosi/Getty Images ©
p40 George Diebold Photography/Getty Images ©
p40 RebeccaAng/Getty Images ©
p41 Sylvain Sonnet/Getty Images ©
p41 Isaac Brekken for Neon Museum ©
p41 Jim Richardson/Getty Images ©
p42 somchaij/Getty Images ©
p43 Checubus/Shutterstock ©
p43 Thomas Janisch#140099/Getty Images ©
p47 njene/Shutterstock ©
p48 Songquan Deng/Shutterstock ©
p49 Buyenlarge/Getty Images ©
p50 ESB Professional/Shutterstock ©
p52 Maremagnum/Getty Images ©
p53 PowerSurge/Getty Images ©
p53 hlphoto/Shutterstock ©
p56 givaga/Shutterstock ©
p56 zamzarina abdullah/Shutterstock ©
p57 Billion Photos/Shutterstock ©
p57 mikeledray/Shutterstock ©
p57 kenary820/Shutterstock ©
p59 Buyenlarge/Getty Images ©
p60 Gleb Tarro/Shutterstock ©
p62 Jan Miko/Shutterstock ©
p63 Gleb Tarro/Shutterstock ©
p64 Greg Jaggears/Getty Images ©
p65 Tony Rowell/Getty Images ©
p65 gmcoop/Getty Images ©
p68 Chris Kridler/Getty Images ©
p71 Underwood Archives/Getty Images ©
p75 Paul Chesley/Getty Images ©
p76 Patrick Leitz/Getty Images ©
p77 Justinreznick/Getty Images ©
p79 Photoshot/Getty Images ©
p79 MIKE NELSON/Getty Images ©
p79 DOSer/Getty Images ©
p81 John Hyde/Getty Images ©
p83 Blaine Harrington III/Getty Images ©
p85 Sean Pavone/Shutterstock ©
p86 Oscity/Shutterstock ©
p88 Timolina/Shutterstock ©
p90 Sean Pavone/Shutterstock ©
p92 deimagine/Getty Images ©
p96 Travelif/Getty Images ©
p96 Photography by Steve Kelley aka mudpig/Getty Images ©
p97 Spondylolithesis/Getty Images ©
p97 Jeff Hunter/Getty Images ©
p99 Car Culture/Getty Images ©
p100 Thomas Barwick/Getty Images ©
p101 John Coletti/Getty Images ©
p101 betto rodrigues/Shutterstock ©
p103 Photos courtesy of The Enthusiast Network ©
p104 Car Culture/Getty Images ©
p105 Pete Ryan/Getty Images ©
p105 Piriya Photography/Getty Images ©
p106 Gary Yeowell/Getty Images ©
p108 Sky Noir Photography by Bill Dickinson/Getty Images ©
p110 Arthur Tilley/Getty Images ©
p111 Bettmann/Getty Images ©
p111 Kurt Hutton/Getty Images ©
p113 Joel Sartore/Getty Images ©
p115 Peter Guttman/Getty Images ©
p116 Joel Bennett/Getty Images ©
p117 Marilyn Angel Wynn/Getty Images ©
p118 a_namenko/Getty Images ©
p119 Richard Cummins/Getty Images ©
p121 Jamie Squire/Getty Images ©
p122 Bloomberg/Getty Images ©
p123 bhofack2/Getty Images ©
p125 The Washington Post/Getty Images ©
p126 SamyStClair/Getty Images ©
p128 Boston Globe/Getty Images ©
p129 The Washington Post/Getty Images ©
p130 Michal Venera/Getty Images ©
p131 Andrey Bayda/Shutterstock ©
p131 astarot/Shutterstock ©
p132 Peter Unger/Getty Images ©
p133 Joseph Shields/Getty Images ©
p133 Jon Lovette/Getty Images ©
p135 f11photo/Shutterstock ©
p137 f11photo/Shutterstock ©
p138 Steffi Pilz / EyeEm./Getty Images ©
p139 Kobby Dagan/Shutterstock ©
p139 The Christian Science Monitor /Getty Images ©
p141 Bill Heinsohn/Getty Images ©
p143 Kushal Bose/Shutterstock ©
p144 stock_photo_world/Shutterstock ©
p146 PiercarloAbate/Shutterstock ©
p147 GSPhotography/Shutterstock ©
p147 GSPhotography/Shutterstock ©
p151 Buyenlarge/Getty Images ©
p152 Gordon Gahan/Getty Images ©
p153 Christina Brunk/Getty Images ©
p154 I love coffee/Shutterstock ©
p156 Zachary C Person/Shutterstock ©
p157 photo by jim fischer./Getty Images ©
p157 Andrea Johnson Photography/
Montinore Estate, Oregon ©
p159 The Eyrie Vineyards ©
p161 tomwachs/Getty Images ©
p162 Andrew Montgomery/Lonely Planet ©
p165 Marko Ristic Serbia/Shutterstock ©
p164 Blend Images - Jon Feingersh/Getty Images ©
p166 NBC/Getty Images ©
p168 Ivan Neru/Shutterstock ©
p169 UniversalImagesGroup/Getty Images ©
p171 vasiliki/Getty Images ©
p172 UniversalImagesGroup/Getty Images ©
p174 Lokibaho/Getty Images ©
p175 Visions of America/Getty Images ©
p177 Boston Globe/Getty Images ©
p177 Mitch Diamond/Getty Images ©
p177 Brandon Bourdages/Shutterstock ©
p177 Christian Mueller/Shutterstock ©
p179 Erika Goldring/Getty Images ©
p180 Krista Rossow/Getty Images ©
p181 Skip Bolen/Getty Images ©
p183 TTstudio/Shutterstock ©
p183 Luciano Mortula/Shutterstock ©
p183 Cultura Exclusive/Henglein and Steets/Getty Images ©
p183 cocozero/Shutterstock ©
p184 Lottie Davies/Lonely Planet ©
p185 Lottie Davies/Lonely Planet ©
p187 Danny Thomas / EyeEm/Getty Images ©
p188 Christian Science Monitor/Getty Images ©
p190 Beverly Logan/Getty Images ©
p194 Bloomberg/Getty Images ©
p196 Magdanatka/Shutterstock ©
p198 PASCAL PAVANI/Getty Images ©
p199 Joshua Resnick/Shutterstock ©
p200 Boston Globe/Getty Images ©
p203 The Artchives/Alamy ©
p205 Giuliano Del Moretto/Shutterstock ©
p206 Chris So/Getty Images ©
p208 Zack Frank/Shutterstock ©
p211 Wolfgang Kaehler/Getty Images ©
p213 Christopher Polk/Getty Images ©
p214 Roger Kisby/Getty Images ©
p215 Baron Wolman/Getty Images ©
p216 Miami Herald/Getty Images ©
p218 Dave Reginek/Getty Images ©
p219 Scott Olson/Getty Images ©
p219 Ethan Miller/Getty Images ©
p220 Science History Images/Alamy ©
p223 Alan Copson/Getty Images ©
p225 Sandy Huffaker/Getty Images ©
p226 Andrew Pielage/Courtesy of the
Frank Lloyd Wright Foundation ©
p227 Foskett Creative/Courtesy of the
Frank Lloyd Wright Foundation ©
p228 Sherman/Getty Images ©
p230 James Caulfield/Courtesy of Frank Lloyd Wright Trust ©
p231 Robert P. Ruschak/courtesy of the
Western Pennsylvania Conservancy ©
p233 Thomas Kelley/Shutterstock
p236 SeanPavonePhoto/Getty Images ©
p237 Underwood Archives/Getty Images ©
p239 Phitha Tanpairoj/Shutterstock ©
p240 John S Lander/Getty Images ©
p241 s_bukley/Shutterstock ©
p242 Julien Hautcoeur/Shutterstock ©
p245 LARISA DUKA/Shutterstock ©
p245 canadastock/Shutterstock ©
p246 Michael Ochs Archives/Getty Images ©
p250 Peter Unger/Getty Images ©
p253 Peter Unger/Getty Images ©
p255 Ron_Thomas/Getty Images ©
p256 Bob Krist/Getty Images ©
p257 Carl D. Walsh/Getty Images ©
p257 Kevin Levesque/Getty Images ©
p260 John Greim/Getty Images ©
p261 Allard Schager/Getty Images ©
p262 Annette Berksan/Texas SandFest ©
p264 Jon Shireman/Getty Images ©
p265 Visions of America/Getty Images ©
p265 Nathan Benn/Getty Images ©
p267 Danita Delimont/Getty Images ©
p267 Jon Shireman/Getty Images ©
p268 Ashley Corbin-Teich/Getty Images ©
p269 Ashley Corbin-Teich/Getty Images ©
p270 ChameleonsEye/Shutterstock ©
p273 JASON REDMOND/Getty Images ©
p274 MPI/Getty Images ©
p276 Boston Globe/Getty Images ©
p277 Pierdelune/Shutterstock ©
p278 Bridget Calip/Shutterstock ©
p280 Inti St Clair/Getty Images ©
p281 Danita Delimont/Getty Images ©
p282 Dean Pennala/Shutterstock ©
p283 Posnov/Getty Images ©
p285 Randy Wells/Getty Images ©
p288 Keith Ladzinski/Getty Images ©
p288 Education Images/Getty Images ©
p289 Jon Reaves/Getty Images ©
p290 Westend61/Getty Images ©
p292 Michael Durham/ Minden Pictures/Getty Images ©
p293 William James Warren/Getty Images ©
p294 James Ronan / EyeEm/Getty Images ©
p295 Danita Delimont/Getty Images ©
p297 Lindsey Kennedy/courtesy of www.meowwolf.com ©
p297 CREATISTA/Shutterstock ©
p299 Copyright Matt Kazmierski/Getty Images ©
p301 f11photo/Shutterstock ©
p301 Photo by Mike Kline (notkalvin)/Getty Images ©
p301 Peeter Viisimaa/Getty Images ©
p302 Peeter Viisimaa/Getty Images ©
p303 Photograph by Geoffrey George/Getty Images ©
p303 VWPics/Alamy ©
p304 Rob Verhorst/Getty Images ©
p304 Michael Ochs Archives/Getty Images ©
p304 Donaldson Collection/Getty Images ©
p304 Michael Ochs Archives/Getty Images ©
p306 James Leynse/Getty Images ©

Front cover images, clockwise from top left:
New York City, Nikada/Getty Images ©
Monument Valley Navajo Tribal Park, Francesco Riccardo Iacomino/500px ©
Jazz musician, Gable Denims/500px ©
Crawfish, Sandra O'Claire/Getty Images ©
San Francisco, Phitha Tanpairoj/Shutterstock ©

Back cover image:
Vermont, Joseph Sohm/Visions of America/Shutterstock ©

Behind the Scenes

Associate Product Director Kirsten Rawlings
Series Designer Campbell McKenzie
Senior Product Editor Kate Chapman
Cartographic Designer Wayne Murphy
Book Designer Katherine Marsh
Product Editor Grace Dobell
Senior Cartographer Diana Von Holdt

Written by Mark Andrew, Amy C Balfour, Sarah Baxter, Andrew Bender, Sara Benson, Alison Bing, Paul Bloomfield, Nate Cavalieri, Garth Cartwright, Lisa Dunford, Bailey Freeman, David Gorvett, Tom Hall, Alexander Howard, Lauren Keith, Leah Koenig, Mariella Krause, Alex Leviton, Emily Matchar, Joe Minihane, Tim Moore, Wayne Murphy, Sarah Maslin Nir, Trisha Ping, Christopher Pitts, Andrea Sachs, Brendan Sainsbury, Simon Sellars, Adam Skolnick, Regis St Louis, Marcel Theroux, Karla Zimmerman, Lonely Planet Travel News (www.lonelyplanet.com/news)

Thanks to Will Allen, Imogen Bannister, Robin Barton, Meri Blazevski, Cheree Broughton, Hannah Cartmel, Barbara Di Castro, Sasha Drew, Evan Godt, Shona Gray, James Hardy, Noirin Hegarty, Liz Heynes, Simon Hoskins, Patricia Kelly, Sandie Kestell, Indra Kilfoyle, Alison Lyall, Neil Manders, Jean-Pierre Masclef, Anne Mason, Fin McCarthy, Jenna Myers, Catherine Naghten, Natalie Nicolson, Darren O'Connell, Lauren O'Connell, Naomi Parker, Piers Pickard, Martine Power, Mazzy Prinsep, Rachel Rawling, Alison Ridgway, Kathryn Rowan, Jessica Ryan, Diana Saengkham, Vicky Smith, Lyahna Spencer, Gabrielle Stefanos, Kate Sullivan, Glenn van-der-Knijff, Tracy Whitmey, Clifton Wilkinson, Amanda Williamson, Juan Winata, Chris Zeiher

Published by Lonely Planet Global Limited
CRN 554153

1st edition – April 2018
ISBN 9781787013322

Printed in China
10 9 8 7 6 5 4 3 2 1

LONELY PLANET OFFICES

Australia
The Malt Store, Level 3, 551 Swanston Street, Carlton, VIC 3053
Phone 03 8379 8000

United Kingdom
240 Blackfriars Road, London SE1 8NW
Phone 020 3771 5100

USA
124 Linden St, Oakland, CA 94607
Phone 510 250 6400

Ireland
Digital Depot, Roe Lane (off Thomas St), Digital Hub, Dublin 8, D08 TCV4

STAY IN TOUCH lonelyplanet.com/contact

Paper in this book is certified against the Forest Stewardship Council™ standards. FSC™ promotes environmentally responsible, socially beneficial and economically viable management of the world's forests.